A Future for N

CW01024621

A Future for Marxism?

Althusser, the Analytical Turn and the Revival of Socialist Theory

Andrew Levine

Pluto Press
LONDON • STERLING, VIRGINIA

First published 2003 by Pluto Press
345 Archway Road, London N6 5AA
and 22883 Quicksilver Drive,
Sterling, VA 20166–2012, USA

www.plutobooks.com

British Library Cataloguing in Publication Data
A catalogue record for this book is available from
the British Library

ISBN 0 7453 1988 2 hardback
ISBN 0 7453 1987 4 paperback

Library of Congress Cataloging in Publication Data
Applied for

10   9   8   7   6   5   4   3   2   1

Designed and produced for Pluto Press by
Chase Publishing Services, Fortescue, Sidmouth EX10 9QG
Typeset from disk by Stanford DTP Services, Towcester
Printed in the European Union by
Antony Rowe, Chippenham and Eastbourne, England

Contents

Preface

Does Marxism have a future? It seems quixotic even to ask this question at a time when it hardly has a present. Everyone these days knows that Marxism is finished; that whatever was right in Marx's thinking was long ago assimilated into the mainstream intellectual culture, and that everything else has been proven wrong beyond a reasonable doubt. Marxism's demise was precipitous. But, by all accounts, it was decisive and irreversible. Therefore, Marx and the *ism* identified with his name are of historical interest only. Anyone who thinks otherwise is blind to the obvious. What follows here challenges this consensus view.

It is instructive to recall that, not long ago, the prevailing wisdom was very different. Well into the 1980s, Marxism was endorsed by some and reviled by others. But no one doubted that it would remain part of the intellectual and political landscape for an indefinite period. There were many 'crises' of Marxism in those days. But its disappearance, on their account, was out of the question. In some quarters, it even seemed that Marxism was being reborn. In addition, a kind of Marxism was still an official ideology in the Soviet Union and China and in their respective spheres of influence. Almost until the moment communism collapsed in Eastern Europe, no one was so prescient as to think that that political reality would change anytime soon. Nor did anyone quite foresee how thoroughly communism would lapse, in substance if not in form, in China. The official Marxism of the communist countries had been an embarrassment to self-identified Marxists in the West for decades before communism's fall. Official Marxism had few defenders, even – indeed, especially – in the lands where it held sway. Still, almost no one questioned the use of the term to designate even that debased form of the genre. As a theoretical and political tradition, Marxism had existed for more than a hundred years. It was, according to the common sense of the time, a mansion with many chambers. Everyone assumed that there was enough of a family resemblance among its varieties, including its Soviet and Chinese versions, to justify calling them all by the same name; and to warrant distinguishing Marxism from rival systems of theory and practice. In this respect, it resembled Christianity. Like the very different branches of that religion, the various Marxisms, for all their diversity, were joined by a common history and, it was thought, by deeper doctrinal affinities as well.

Nowadays, the idea that all self-described Marxisms share a common core seems less secure than it formerly did. And, contrary to what one would have expected only a few decades ago, this sense of where matters stand has had almost nothing to do with a desire on anyone's part to cast one or another offending version of Marxism out of the fold. For self-identified Marxists in the West, the most likely candidates for exclusion would have to have been the reigning doctrines in some or all of the officially Marxist regimes in power. One might therefore have thought that doubts about the soundness of the designation 'Marxist' would have originated with those who wanted to retain the name for their own doctrinal commitments, while renouncing some or all official Marxisms. But this is not what happened. Long before communism fell or lapsed, it was very nearly a consensus view among self-identified Marxists, especially younger ones, that there was no reason to defend, much less extend, Soviet or Chinese communism. Communism in power had brought discredit upon itself and therefore upon Marxism too, insofar as it was understood to be a kind of Marxism. But, for many years after this conviction had become commonplace, Marxism not only survived; it flourished. Then, ironically, as the Soviet Union passed from the scene, Marxism did too. It is a sign of the times that its absence has been so easily accommodated in the intellectual culture; and that even erstwhile Marxists, insofar as they pay it heed, do not seem particularly upset.

It is for future historians to make sense of this strange turn of events. I will only address a small part of the larger story – the part that concerns recent Marxist philosophy and the circumstances in which it existed. From that vantage point, it looks as if, in the end, it was philosophy, more than anything else, that did Marxism in. Almost without realizing what they were doing, some of Marxism's most philosophically adept practitioners effectively – though, for the most part, only implicitly – came to the view that there is nothing distinctive to 'Marxism' at all except, of course, its history. This conclusion, if true, would be of great importance to anyone who would reflect on Marxism's future. For if there is nothing distinctively Marxist, then the question of Marxism's future would amount to nothing more than a question about the future of those movements that took on – and, in a few rare cases, continue to take on – the Marxist name. This is not a question of philosophical moment; increasingly, it does not even appear to be a question of political moment. But, no matter; it is not the right question.

As I will show, the notion that there is nothing distinctively Marxist is wrong. I will argue too that a clear understanding of the respects in which it falls short points the way towards a renewal of socialist theory and practice. It will emerge that the old conventional wisdom was closer to the truth than the new one is; that Marxism or, more precisely, Marxist *theory* is not finished – indeed, that key elements of Marx's thought remain timely and urgent. Does this conviction imply that, eventually, Marxism will revive? Not necessarily. It only implies the absence of a *theoretical* obstacle in the way of such an outcome. Beyond that, no one can say what the future holds. For better or worse, Marxism's future, like its present, depends on circumstances that have little to do with the cogency or viability of the ideas of Marx and his successors. But whatever the future of Marxism will be, it can be said with considerable confidence, even now, that political thinking and political life generally will be much diminished if what is genuinely viable in Marxism, and unique to it, passes permanently into oblivion.

To establish this claim and, more generally, to defend the desirability, if not the inevitability, of a future for Marxism, it will not do just to argue for the conceptual distinctiveness of some of Marx's ideas and for their superiority over rival views. Arguments of this sort are, of course, central to any case for Marxism's future. But to be adequate to the task at hand, theoretical considerations must be grounded historically, and their social and political dimensions taken into account. As readers of Marx should know, and as philosophers ignore at their peril, ideas of political consequence are always historically situated and conditioned by their context. Therefore, to grasp their character, and to speculate on their (possible) role in Marxism's future, it is necessary to deal with a host of historical, social, and political issues too.

This is an enormous and daunting task, and I will only broach certain aspects of it here, even at the risk of providing an unbalanced account. The story I will tell focuses on aspects of recent political history that bear on two significant and revealing *philosophical* currents within recent Marxism, and then on those new departures in Marxist philosophy themselves. The first of these philosophical departures was based on the work of Louis Althusser and his

followers. It was a French phenomenon, with important consequences for Marxists and non-Marxists elsewhere, emphatically
including the English-speaking world. The other, analytical
Marxism, was largely a creature of Anglo-American university
culture. The overall cultural impact of analytical Marxism was slight
in comparison with Althusserian Marxism, even in the universities
in which it briefly flourished. But from a philosophical point of view,
its importance was far greater. At their inception, both of these philosophical ventures claimed to be efforts to recover the core of Marx's
thinking. Ironically, for many of their practitioners, both became
vehicles of exit from Marxism. I will argue that this outcome could
have been different, especially for the analytical Marxists; and I will
show how these strains of Marxist philosophy – analytical Marxism
especially, but also Althusserianism – may yet provide bases for
reviving the Marxist tradition.

*   *   *

The ensuing account falls into two sections. The discussion in Part
I is intended to shed light on the prospects for Marxism's future,
but its principal purpose is to help to explain the context in which
Althusserian and analytical Marxism arose, flourished, and
declined. Part II focuses directly on these philosophical movements
and their legacy.

I begin, in the Introduction to Part I, with some very tentative and
impressionistic reflections on our rapidly changing political
environment. Then, in Chapter 1, I sketch the political and intellectual landscape that emerged in the aftermath of the French
Revolution, situating socialism's place in that larger picture. I also
broach the question of what distinguishes Marxism from other
strains of socialist thought – specifically, its claim to be a 'scientific'
(as opposed to a 'utopian') theory. This contention will figure
prominently in Part II, especially in the chapters on analytical
Marxism. In Chapter 2, I venture some thoughts on the New Left as
it arose, thrived and then collapsed in the period that began in the
mid-1960s and ended in the 1970s. At the time, it appeared that the
New Left represented a new beginning. From today's vantage point,
it looks more like the final Left, the last gasp of an aspiration born
more than two hundred years earlier. Both impressions are false. But
it is only in light of the sudden rise and precipitous fall of this
political moment that the trajectories of Althusserian and analytical

Marxism make sense. In order to convey a sense of the context in which Marxists did philosophy in recent decades, my account of the New Left and of its ancestors meanders across a wide variety of topics. In order to distill what is essential from it, I draw together the principal claims of the story in the Conclusion to Part I. For all their differences, Althusserian and analytical Marxism shared a common enemy. They both rejected what I will call 'historicist Marxism', the Marxism of nearly all Marxists before their appearance on the scene. In the Introduction to Part II, I offer a brief account of this received view. I then go on to consider aspects of Althusserian and analytical Marxism that bear on the question of Marxism's future. Chapter 3 focuses on Althusser's metaphilosophy; Chapter 4 on his notion of an 'epistemological break'. Chapter 5 recounts the trajectory of the analytical Marxist movement; and Chapter 6 describes some crucial and distinctively Marxist positions pertaining to 'scientific socialism' and its implications for political theory. There is much that is of value in both historicist and Althusserian Marxism. Whoever today would set them entirely aside imperils the prospects for Marxism's future. But it is the legacy of analytical Marxism that matters most of all. Wittingly or not, the analytical Marxists, more than their traditional or contemporaneous rivals, 'discovered' – or rediscovered – what remains vital in the Marxist tradition. It is therefore to them, more than the others, that we must turn if we are to continue Marx's work. With this thought in mind, I will conclude with a brief account of where matters now stand, and with some very general speculations on what the future may hold.

The chapters that follow present selective, 'broad brush' accounts of their respective subjects. Each advances views that informed readers may find idiosyncratic, overdrawn, or mistaken. I will, of course, defend the more contentious claims I make. But I will not be able to do so to everyone's satisfaction. This is unavoidable, especially in a short book that ranges over so many topics. It is also not entirely to be regretted. God is in the details. But it is an occupational hazard of academics, especially if they are philosophers by training, to become lost in details. Inasmuch as my aim here is to rebut a tenet of the reigning intellectual and political culture, a protracted attempt to pin down each and every claim would be both tedious and distracting. At this point, what is needed, above all, is a synoptic account dedicated to dislodging the unfounded and debilitating but nevertheless pervasive idea that Marxism's vitality is spent. The *Communist Manifesto* famously proclaimed that in bourgeois society, 'everything solid' eventually 'melts into air'. The view today of those who were on the cutting edge of Marxist theory only a few years ago is that Marxism already has. I will argue that their own best work proves them wrong.

* * *

The story I will recount is one I have lived through. I was involved in New Left politics – albeit only in the United States, and then mainly in New York City, where, for a variety of reasons, including the presence of sectarian Old Left groups of every imaginable description, the experience was somewhat atypical. I became interested in Althusser's work at that time; a period in which he was virtually unknown in the English-speaking world and especially in the United States. My very first publications were on Althusser – in *Radical America* (vol. 3, no. 5, 1969; and vol. 4, no. 6, 1970), then the 'theoretical journal' of the main grouping of radical students in the United States, the Students for a Democratic Society (SDS). Althusser, it seems, ran against the American grain, as SDS understood it; accordingly, the editors of *Radical America* insisted on publishing my papers along with no fewer than five spirited critiques. Undaunted, in 1969, I went to France in the hope of immersing myself in an Althusserian milieu. Unfortunately, 1969 was one of those years when the master was 'indisposed' (for psychiatric reasons that would later become all too clear). Meanwhile, Althusserian circles, like so much else in French intellectual life at the time, proved impenetrable. Nevertheless, I remained a fellow-traveler for most of the next decade, long after the Althusserian 'moment' had passed in France and even in Great Britain. Eventually, my steadfastness lapsed. Then, thanks to some collaborative work I did, beginning in the late 1970s, with Erik Olin Wright, I became directly immersed in the analytical Marxist current. I was never as enthusiastic about analytical Marxism's prospects as most of its leading figures were. But I have remained more committed to the project than most of them have become. To a much diminished degree, the same is true of my present regard for New Left politics and Althusserian Marxism. This may be a sign of the 'foolish consistency' that Ralph Waldo Emerson deemed 'the hobgoblin of little minds'. I hope not. In any case, there is a sense in which what follows is a defense against this charge; an apologia for a New Left, Althusserian and analytical Marxist past. But, of course, that is the least of it. What matters is the future. My contention is that, at this point in history, understanding these political and philosophical phenomena is crucial, perhaps even indispensable, for renewing socialist thought.

*   *   *

A distant ancestor of Chapters 3 and 4, on Althusser, is a paper I published more than twenty years ago called 'Althusser's Marxism' (*Economy and Society*, vol. 10, no. 3, 1981, pp. 243–83). That paper represented, at the time, a 'settling of accounts' with my Althusserian past. Although my view of the importance of Althusser's work is now quite different from what it was then, I find myself, even now, focusing on the same broad themes – Althusser's various accounts of 'philosophical practice', and his useful, but potentially misleading, notion of an 'epistemological break'. Chapter 5, the first of the chapters on analytical Marxism, overlaps substantially with my entry on 'Marxism' in Gerald Gauss and Chandran Kukathas, eds., *Handbook of Political Theory* (Sage, forthcoming) I am grateful to the editors for permission to draw on that material. That chapter and, even more, Chapters 6 and the Conclusion draw on and develop themes I have addressed in many publications over the past several decades, including *The End of the State* (London: Verso, 1987); *Reconstructing Marxism: Essays in Explanation and the Theory of History*, co-authored with Erik Olin Wright and Elliott R. Sober (London: Verso, 1992), *The General Will: Rousseau, Marx, Communism* (Cambridge: Cambridge University Press, 1993); *Rethinking Liberal Equality: From a 'Utopian' Point of View* (Ithaca, N.Y.: Cornell University Press, 1998); and, most recently, the chapter on Marx in *Engaging Political Philosophy: Hobbes to Rawls* (Oxford: Blackwell, 2001). Readers familiar with those writings will find echoes of them here. But my aim in this book, unlike the others, is not to work *in* an analytical Marxist vein. It is to try to make sense of what it all meant, of what it continues to mean, and of what it could mean in the years ahead.

Part I

Introduction to Part I

Marxism's future, like its present, depends, more than anything else, on the ambient political culture in which it exists. At the same time, today's political culture has been shaped, in part, by Marxism's past. I will not attempt to untangle this complex web of causal interactions; it would be an impossible task. But, as a prelude to a more focused account of aspects of Marxism's history that bear on the prospects for Marxism's future, and on the role Althusserian and analytical Marxism might play in it, it will be useful to begin with a few reflections on where we now are and where we seem to be going. Because Marxism is presently in near total eclipse, I will not have much to say about the state of Marxism today. But I will venture some remarks on the larger situation in which its present is implicated. Here, then, are some thoughts on the exhaustion of political imagination in our time; its implications for real-world politics; and on signs that, once again, the world is changing – to an uncertain situation, rife with danger, but with enhanced opportunities for renewing socialist theory and practice. The impressions I will convey pertain most directly to the United States. But they are not, for that reason, misleadingly parochial. It is part of the story of our time that the one remaining superpower is rapidly making the world over in its image.

Needless to say, it is too soon to put the present in anything like a definitive perspective. But the broad outlines of an account are already becoming clear. Thus it is fair to say that, in the last years of the old millennium, political imagination was everywhere in decline and, along with it, the idea that the political institutions of the West could be improved upon fundamentally. This was a massive and sudden development, more remarkable even than Marxism's own precipitous fall. It was also a situation that called for remediation, if for no other reason than that it fed complacency and degraded political life. In the first years of the twenty-first century, the effects of this transformation of the political culture are increasingly felt. Blowback from ill-conceived imperialist ventures and the realities of corporate globabalization are ever more salient; desperation is everywhere on the rise. The world is therefore in for turbulent times ahead. But, as before in human history, the pendulum will surely swing back – provided, of course, that unspeakable catastrophes are averted. Big changes are already under way. Political imagination is stirring. The world seems a more dangerous place than it was just a few years ago. But it is also less complacent. Resistance is increasing and, with it, the possibility that progressive forces will emerge strengthened. This is why the time is ripe to press forward. To seize the moment, though, we must first take stock of the situation at hand.

*   *   *

In the economically developed and liberal democratic West, the exhaustion of political imagination is palpable mainly in retrospect. This is as true for those of us who have lived through the entire sea change as it is for those who have come on board more recently. Until the outbreak of the so-called 'war on terrorism',[1] great events, like wars or revolutions, hardly affected the lives of people in the West. Even the fall of communism and the disaggregation of the Third World had hardly any effect on lived experience. These mutations on the world scene may help to explain the political metamorphoses of recent years. But they have not registered as discontinuities in the lives of most inhabitants of the developed and stable liberal democracies. They resonate, if at all, not with a bang but a whimper, perceived from afar. If, as some claim, history ended with the triumph of Western institutions, one would have to say that it did so discreetly, without calling attention to itself.[2]

The banality of political life in our time is especially evident in the United States, where electoral contests have come to resemble advertising promotions for nearly indistinguishable products, and where everyone knows that, whoever wins elections, more or less the same corporate interests will continue to rule. Remarkably, this fact is accepted with indifference or jaded annoyance, not outrage. Who would have predicted, a quarter century ago, that politics would become so insipid so rapidly, and that people in motion at the time would react by retreating into private life! The generation that came of age politically in the late 1960s and early 1970s, the generation that now controls what used to be called 'the commanding heights' of the state, the economy, and civil society, was thought to have rejected the apathy emblematic of the generation that preceded it.[3] This was what 'the New Left' was supposed to be about. But now, as 'baby boomers' age, apathy reigns in the public arena again, and baby boomers are leading the way.

There are exceptions, of course. There are still unreconstructed leftists from that generation and earlier ones, and hosts of younger militants as well. But thanks to the exhaustion of political imagination, the ever growing numbers of people who are again coming together 'to change life' must not only reinvent the wheel; they must do so in the face of what sometimes seems to be an almost insurmountable inertia. Militants today know, as well as anyone ever did, how to organize and maneuver at a tactical level. They know what to mobilize *against*. But, with political imagination becoming ever more degraded year after year, it is less clear than it has ever been what to mobilize *for*. This uncertainty is increasingly debilitating as new political movements develop and expand.

In much the way that, according to the conventional wisdom, the good side of Marxism has been absorbed into mainstream thinking, while the rest, the 'nonsense' that once seemed important, has been rightfully cast aside, there are 'progressives' today who think that all Left initiatives worth retaining have already taken root in the political culture; and therefore that the Left, or at least the New Left, is the victim, not of a failure of imagination, but of its own success. What they have in mind is the preeminence now accorded in the political sphere to cultural issues, including questions of 'identity' and 'inclusiveness'. There is some truth in this contention. But the victories of the New Left, such as they were, were won at a tremendous price. The causes advanced by the social movements that emerged under the aegis of New Left politics had first to be deradicalized and even depoliticized before they were welcomed into the mainstream. Once there, they have been put to use further depoliticizing the political sphere. In the United States, this process is, by now, so complete that cultural themes, broadly construed, have come to define the terms in which differences register in mainstream politics. Republicans and Democrats part ways, to the degree that they still do, along these lines. It is as if the old axes of political contestation, questions of economic power and ultimately of class struggle, no longer matter. In the electoral arena especially, these issues are seldom in dispute. How could it be otherwise when the same monied interests control both parties!

For the political class or, rather, for those in the academy and the media who rationalize their situation, the reigning idea is not exactly that an 'age of ideology' is over; that the old oppositions have faded in the face of an emerging consensus that integrates formerly contending parties. That was the view of some former leftists decades ago.[4] They evidently felt a need to defend their turn away from radical politics. It seems that no comparable need is felt by former activists of the New Left. The view today is just that radicalism lost, and that on the whole, it was a good thing that it did – because Western, liberal institutions beat all rivals on all counts, and because the economic system that has matured under their auspices has provided a degree of prosperity that would have been unthinkable had a more radical vision prevailed. This is why many erstwhile New Leftists, when they think about it at all, look back on their youthful enthusiasms with a certain nostalgia for the idealism of the time, but without regret for a political venture that went awry.

One clear consequence of the exhaustion of political imagination over the past quarter century has been a sharp shift of the political mainstream to the right. In this regard too, the American case is exemplary. Not long ago, in the United States, liberalism was the order of the day. The political settlements of the Roosevelt and Truman eras were firmly in place. Lyndon Johnson's Great Society even promised a renaissance of New Deal liberalism, one that would at last address problems of institutional racism and other consequences of slavery and white America's near annihilation of indigenous peoples. The Great Society became a casualty of the Vietnam War. But, at the time and for a few years thereafter, it seemed that American liberalism, still in command, was becoming more like European social democracy in its post-World War II phase. The difference was just that the American version lacked the historical connection to socialism that was part of social democracy's heritage. Not unrelatedly, American liberals also had weaker ties to the labor movement than their social democratic or laborite counterparts. Therefore, their politics was, on the whole, more business friendly than theirs and their self-representations were generally less visionary than was commonplace in European social democratic parties or in the British Labour Party. Even so, the general drift of American liberalism and therefore of mainstream politics in the United States was of a piece with social democracy elsewhere. The idea that affirmative state programs should play a predominant role in insuring economic well-being and in rectifying social problems seemed well entrenched and beyond serious dispute.

It was only at the fringes of the political culture that anyone thought otherwise. In the United States, there had long existed a dedicated minority intent on dismantling the New Deal. In 1964, with the nomination of Barry Goldwater for president, they seized control of the Republican Party. But after the resounding defeat of Goldwater's presidential bid, liberal dominance appeared more secure than it had ever been. The economic and social policies that were in place before the Roosevelt presidency, the old neoliberal regime the Goldwaterites favored, appeared to have fallen irreversibly into 'the ashbin of history', much as Marxism seems to have done today.

How things have changed! Today the ideas of that defeated fringe are even more hegemonic than New Deal and Great Society liberalism formerly were. And the dismantling of the vestiges of that earlier orthodoxy, and of bolder social democratic initiatives in countries with more vibrant political traditions, has been carried out with zest and efficacy by political leaders drawn from the generation that produced the New Left. Goldwater's politics has succeeded on a world scale beyond the imaginings of its most ardent proponents decades ago. It has taken over the political common sense of our time – to such an extent that it even informs the thinking of those who still call themselves liberals or, more often, proponents of a 'Third Way'. It is of some interest to observe that many of the principal exponents of these ostensibly new political orientations, the real undoers of liberalism and social democracy, cut their teeth politically on the fringes of the New Left and even, in a few conspicuous European cases, at its core.

Since the account I will give of Marxism's future focuses mainly on philosophical departures within Marxism and on related developments in political theory, it bears notice too that a largely unacknowledged but equally remarkable transformation is evident from the professional vantage point of academic political philosophy. The change there has been more complex than in the larger political culture, and considerably more equivocal. On the one hand, in the past quarter century, political philosophy, especially in the English-speaking world, has insulated itself with great success from the real world of politics. In fact, for reasons peculiar to its own internal dynamic, it has proceeded on a somewhat different course from the prevailing political culture. But, viewed in retrospect, no matter how apolitical and even contrary-minded mainstream political philosophy has become, it too reflects the zeitgeist. A profound diminution of political imagination is evident even in this domain. But because it has divorced itself so effectively from ongoing political affairs, because its trajectory has been, to some degree, internally generated, and because it remains connected to earlier, more vibrant, moments in the history of political thought, academic political philosophy today provides conceptual resources indispensable for those militants, already in motion, whose need for a revival of political imagination has become acute.

*   *   *

Perhaps the most telling indicator of the nature of politics in our time has been the virtual disappearance of an organized Left. I will use *Left* and *Right*, as I have to this point, to describe the political orientations these terms have designated, loosely but unmistakably, since that moment in revolutionary France, more than two centuries ago, when the more radical delegates to the National Assembly seated themselves to the left of the presiding officer. It is fortuitous that this usage stuck because it introduces a useful ambiguity into descriptions of political orientations. It is ambiguous because *left* and *right* are relational concepts; *left* is defined in contrast to *right*, and vice versa. Strictly speaking, therefore, these terms have no fixed meaning. Political parties and social movements that everyone understands to be on the Left have their own left and right wings, as do movements and parties of the Right. Here, however, except when otherwise indicated, I will use these terms to designate positions on an idealized political spectrum. Until recently, these notions were inscribed in the 'collective consciousness' of nearly everyone who thought about political affairs. In recent years, however, along with the exhaustion of political imagination and largely in consequence of it, the idea has been floated that the longstanding division between Left and Right has somehow become obsolete. I would venture that this thought is itself an effect of the rightward drift of mainstream politics. In what follows, I will, in any case, assume that claims for the irrelevancy of the notions of Left and Right are without merit. The problem today is not that Left and Right no longer have any meaning. It is that there is hardly any Left left.

It is also commonplace to use the term *Center* in reference to this idealized political spectrum. This usage can be misleading, however, because, in politics, the Center is not exactly a 'midpoint' between the Left and the Right. As a rough approximation, though, and in accordance with conventional understandings, it is fair to think of the Center that way, at least for now. In speaking of the virtual disappearance of the Left, then, I mean that those political formations that traditionally comprised the Left no longer stand on the left end of that idealized spectrum – that they have moved to the center or even the right, even when, as is often the case, they acknowledge a continuous historical connection with their pasts. To cite a pale example, the Democratic Party in the United States has been understood, at least since the Roosevelt era, to be, if not exactly a party of the Left, then the closest approximation of one that mainstream political life in the United States provided. But, on the idealized Left–Right spectrum that defines political orientations, the Democratic Party, whatever it may once have been, nowadays is, at most, a party of the Center or Center-Right, with a small and increasingly marginalized left wing. Much the same is true of political parties in other countries that, more plainly than the Democratic Party, genuinely did once belong to the Left.

*   *   *

It is instructive to use a medical analogy to describe the situation we are in. In dealing with illnesses, it is customary, first, to identify symptoms, then to diagnose a disease, and only at that point, finally, to look for an explanation that can facilitate a cure. So far, I have called attention to a few important symptoms. In real medical contexts, it is often possible to abbreviate this step or to eliminate it altogether because it is seldom necessary to establish that a patient is ill. But with political imagination depleted, our sensibilities have become, as it were, so run down that it is difficult to see that there is a problem at all, much less a debilitating condition from which public life suffers. It is as if having lived for a long time with a chronic ailment, we have come to think that this is the way that life must be, and no longer notice our distress. Hence the need to establish that the political culture is sick. This is the first step towards arriving at a diagnosis and ultimately an explanation illuminating enough to suggest a remedy. To continue this analogy, good diagnoses reveal how disparate symptoms hang together, how they indicate the presence of a single underlying disease. In this respect, the condition that afflicts our political life runs true to form. Just as a well-defined disease can have many distinct and overlapping causes, a whole panoply of factors have no doubt joined together, each in its own way, to bring about the current state of affairs. But what is crucial is the common thread that runs through the symptoms. This is what suggests a common diagnosis and therefore a single disease; one that may indeed be amenable to a cure.

That thread, I submit, is a loss of faith in progress or, more precisely, in a better world that differs in kind, not just degree, from our own. It was an idea of progress sufficiently broad to encompass a notion of radical, not just incremental, change that motivated the political orientation of the historical Left – especially, but not only, its socialist wing. Without such an idea in the background or, better still, at the forefront of political thought, the Left, if it survives at all, can only devolve into a motley of good causes, bereft of any guiding vision or indeed of any unifying principle whatsoever. We will find that, for no compelling reason, a defensible rational intuition, sustaining that notion of progress, has been set aside – apparently in consequence of perceived flaws in efforts to give it theoretical expression. But there was never any need to take such a step. Quite the contrary. Socialist theory, or at least the version of it that emerges in those new departures in Marxist philosophy that appear, from today's vantage point, to have sealed Marxism's fate, provides ample resources for vindicating faith in the possibility of a genuinely better – and fundamentally different – social, political and economic order.

Nevertheless, it is likely that observers looking back on this period will conclude that a loss of faith in progress was a conspicuous feature of the spirit of the time, perhaps the most conspicuous feature. It is a theme played out repeatedly in the work of culture critics, literary scholars, and public intellectuals. So-called postmodernists, especially, are quick to advance the idea that there are no 'master narratives' in human history and therefore no defensible notions of human progress. I will not take on this murky but still fashionable *fin de siècle* form of 'discourse' here – partly because I think that the trouble required to make postmodernist claims clear enough to engage polemically is not worth the effort, and partly because it is unnecessary. The idea that historical narratives and therefore notions of qualitative progress are neither true nor false, but only better or worse for some social groups, is best refuted by showing how sense can be made of the ideas postmodernists reject. This form of indirect rebuttal will be a recurrent, albeit tacit, theme throughout the chapters that follow.

But it is not only, or even mainly, postmodernists who have come to the conclusion that there are no ways of organizing basic social, political and economic institutions that are both better and radically different from liberal democratic and capitalist ways. For want of imagination, this view of the human prospect has come to be assumed by almost everyone. From this imaginative deficit, it follows, if not quite with logical necessity then very nearly so, that the idea of a qualitatively better way of organizing human affairs is an illusion in the Freudian sense, an expression of a wish generated by an (unconscious) desire, irrespective of its relation to reality.[5] The next step is to conclude that it is wise to forbear from attempting to realize alternative social visions and even from seriously entertaining the thought that they might constitute feasible human possibilities. So long as the present condition is bearable, why even think of changing it fundamentally, if there is no reason to believe that *any* contemplated structural transformation can change the human prospect for the better? On this view, the very idea of radical change is utopian; and utopian thinking, the argument goes, is a great and constant danger. It was responsible, in part, for the crimes perpetrated in the name and for the sake of communism. The utopian temptation must therefore be exorcized. In the present historical period, this position has become the consensus view among academics and public intellectuals. This is why our distinctively contemporary political ailment could be described as a fear – rationalized by a few, presumed by the vast majority – of utopian thinking. Facetiously but correctly, it might be called *utopiaphobia*, the irrational fear of contemplating radically different and ostensibly better ways of organizing human affairs. No doubt, there is good reason to be wary of utopian thinking in some, perhaps even most, circumstances. But not in all, and not now. A realistic utopianism is a remedy, perhaps the only one available, for the exhaustion of political imagination in our time. And if, as many believe, history is approaching another of its infrequent watersheds – whether because the one remaining superpower will sooner or later overestimate its ability to control events, to the detriment of global political stability; or because capitalism itself is entering into a debilitating structural crisis; or for any of a panoply of other reasons, separately or in conjunction – what was utopian yesterday may not be so tomorrow.

* * *

Before faith in progress lapsed, the Left had a unified project. To focus just on Marxism – the most important and influential case, and the one that will occupy our attention here – it was always assumed that there was an integral link between its vision of a radically better way to organize human affairs and its account of how to get from where we now are to that desired end. According to the Marxist account, the agent of fundamental social change in this historical epoch, the bearer of new and better social relations, was the proletariat, the principal part of 'the wretched of the earth' Thus support for the 'utopian' vision Marx advanced implied support for a theory of social agency which implied support, in turn, for the proletariat and, by extension, for other downtrodden groups. That vision and its corresponding theory of history and social change are therefore partisan to their core. In its theory as well as its practice, Marxism sided with the wretched of the earth against their oppressors.

But without anything like the unifying vision that motivated the Marxist project, all that remains, for those who are similarly intent on fighting oppression, is their identification with the interests of subordinate groups. This has become the position assumed by the successors of the historical Left. But nothing any longer underwrites the generosity of spirit they continue to evince. Struggles against corporate domination, environmental degradation, and racial and sexual oppression go on. If anything, the pace and intensity of these struggles is increasing. But even heroic efforts to combat these scourges are bound to remain diffuse, reactive and, in most cases, ineffectual, if they are not grounded in a rationally compelling theory and practice. Otherwise, good will alone is left. This is estimable, but it is not enough. Thus the longstanding and honorable determination 'to build a new world on the ashes of the old', a world that fully incorporates the wretched of the earth on principles of liberty, equality and fraternity, has given way to a diffuse dedication to side with those who were formerly held to be the builders of that new order, but who are now thought of only as victims of a basically unchangeable regime. How could it be otherwise when it is taken for granted that it is folly to want to change the system itself fundamentally for the better!

Utopiaphobia not only diminishes Left politics; it is also self-defeating. It leads to the permanent stagnation of those genuinely progressive impulses that refuse to die because they are continually reborn by the experience of daily life. It is one thing, after all, to be a self-conscious maker of history, and something else to be a victim of a system that is, at root, beyond fundamental repair. Thus progressive forces are caught in a vicious circle in which a sense of permanent and unalterable victimhood spawns the conviction that the system is unchangeable, and vice versa. It is therefore no surprise that the prospect of fundamental change has dropped away even from the thinking of those generous and well-intentioned souls for whom nearly everyone who is not healthy, wealthy, white, heterosexual and male – in other words, the vast majority of the world's population – is an object of concern. Without a vision of a better end in view, the most one can reasonably demand on their behalf – and, more importantly, the most they can reasonably demand for themselves – is indemnification for their condition and inclusion into the regime that has generated it. The consequence is plain. What was once a struggle in and over social, political and economic institutions has devolved into a well-meaning but futile promotion of an inauthentic, coerced civility that threatens no entrenched economic interests and that 'enlightened' establishments are therefore all too happy to accommodate.

If this situation is ever to be rectified, it is crucial that the long march on which Marx embarked be resumed. I submit that Althusserian and especially analytical Marxism pointed the way forward; and that continuing what they began is a way to breathe new life into that democratic and secular notion of progress that animated the historical Left, and that supplied the generosity and dedication of its various constituencies with unity and purpose. Perhaps, if circumstances change and interest in Marxism revives, they can serve as a basis for a new Marxist renaissance. There is no sounder basis at hand. But if, in consequence of its historical associations, 'Marxist' remains a category in disrepute, these recent departures in Marxist philosophy, 'translated' into another idiom, can still serve as points of departure for renewing socialist theory. The pages that follow elaborate on these contentions and their implications.

1 After the Revolution

For nearly two hundred years, the French Revolution was held by everyone, Left and Right, to have been an event of epochal political significance. In some quarters, this consensus has lately given way to a different view, according to which the social and political transformations that began in 1789 and continued through different phases until the end of the Napoleonic period were part of a larger process of state building that would have proceeded on roughly the same course, at far less human cost, and with a generally better outcome, had the Revolution not taken place at all.[1] It is likely, as a new generation of historians breaks away from the orthodoxy of the present generation, that the pendulum will eventually swing back to the earlier assessment of the Revolution's importance. No doubt a political climate friendlier to radicalism would also hasten a revival of the traditional view. But, even as political contestation becomes livelier, it is still commonplace, in this period of diminished political imagination, for historians and others to deflate the importance of 1789 and its aftermath.

However, even the most ardent deflator of the traditional view would have to concede that the French Revolution was an event of epochal significance for political *theory*. If we use the term *ideology* in its most general and uncontroversial sense, to designate a more or less coherent system of social, political and perhaps also economic ideas, it is plain that the three principal ideologies of the past two centuries – conservatism, liberalism and socialism – would not have developed as they did and, in the case of socialism, might not even have developed at all, but for that revolutionary event. Conservatism, or rather the strain of it that arose early in the nineteenth century, was a reaction against ways of thinking and acting that, in the early stages of the revolutionary process, propelled the Revolution along an increasingly radical course. Liberalism, as it evolved almost contemporaneously, was a self-conscious effort to incorporate the Revolution's ostensible achievements, while providing institutional guarantees against its excesses. Socialism sought to complete the revolutionary project by transforming a mainly political revolution into a social revolution, a thoroughgoing transformation not only of the political sphere, but of social and economic life as well.

Conservatism has roots extending back at least to the beginnings of the Christian era. In its pre-nineteenth-century form and in some contemporary versions too, it rests on the idea that human beings are incapable of doing well for themselves through the free expression of their own natures; incapable even of maintaining order in the absence of powerful *political* (that is, coercive) authority relations, and the complementary constraints of family life and the Church or of other, functionally equivalent, institutions. These constraints save human beings from themselves or, as Christians might say, from their own sinful natures. Thus one might say that this form of conservative ideology takes Sin seriously. Even when it is expressly secular – as it was, for example, in Thomas Hobbes's account of sovereignty[2] – some analogue of the doctrine of Original Sin plays a crucial role in its account of human nature and the human condition.

In its original form, the idea was that Fallen Man is so utterly insufficient that the free expression of human nature must be suppressed lest it wreak devastating effects. For St. Augustine, the first great exponent of this view, society would degenerate into disorder without a powerful coercive authority in place. The resulting chaos would then disrupt the execution of Providential design, which requires peace so that, in preparation for the Final Judgment, the (visible) Church can expand throughout the entire world, as it must if it is to fulfill its mission by administering the sacraments to the elect of all nations.[3] For Hobbes, more than a thousand years later, Original Sin gave way to an account of human psychology impelled by the materialist metaphysics he endorsed. It was Hobbes's view that, were individuals to act on their natural dispositions, the result would be a war of all against all, a condition radically opposed to these individuals' (not God's) interests. Therefore, insofar as individuals are (means-ends) rational, they are obliged, to the degree necessary to insure order, to make themselves unfree to act in accord with their natures. This they do by concocting a sovereign, an overwhelming power, who establishes order by issuing enforceable commands. Thus, from Augustine to Hobbes, the idea was the same: order is the paramount political objective, but human beings cannot attain it without the imposition of *unnatural* constraints. Left on its own, human nature, tainted by Sin or its secular equivalent, leads to disorder of the worst kind.

Order must therefore be imposed. This is a role Augustine ascribed to God. God establishes political institutions, means of coercion, as one of several punishments for Original Sin. Thus He imposes earthly sanctions on those who would act in accord with their (sinful) natures or, more precisely, on those who would do so in defiance of the commands of the authorities who rule them. Ironically, in so doing, God also supplies a (partial) remedy for the consequences of Sin. For out of repression comes order – not, to be sure, the peace of the Heavenly City, but 'the peace of Babylon', a perpetual truce in the war of all against all, sufficient for the visible Church to complete its mission. This is why total and unquestioning submission to existing authorities is required. Those authorities, whomever they might be and whatever their faith (or lack of it), are the executors of Providential design.

A similar thought led Hobbes to maintain that individuals are rationally compelled to agree among themselves to enforce the commands of one of their number against each other. In so doing, they invest that fortunate individual, thereafter the sovereign, with absolute authority over themselves. Then, to the extent that they fear the sovereign they have contrived, they will not, except on pain of irrationality, act on desires that conflict with his commands. In these conditions, the war of all against all gives way to the order the sovereign's might establishes – again, an armed truce, but the only kind of order within human reach. No matter how oppressive the sovereign's rule may be, no matter how susceptible the existing order may be to improvement, it is still better by far, given individuals' interests, than its sole feasible alternative, a devastating war of all against all.

The Hobbesian account makes particularly apparent how it is human nature that puts order in jeopardy, and therefore why human nature must be repressed for order to exist. But institutional arrangements that go against the free expression of human nature are, for that reason, fragile. A wise politics will take this fact into account. This is why one must take care to insure that 'that which is Caesar's' is indeed 'rendered unto Caesar', as Jesus taught and as Augustine insisted. This is why one must combat rebellion against existing authorities by any means necessary, as Hobbes maintained. This thought led Hobbes to oppose radicalism of any kind. Because the institutions human beings concoct to hold back the war of all against all are prone to becoming engulfed by forces that, at best, are only barely held in check, it is inordinately risky to disrupt the structures and practices in place. Of course, it is neither necessary nor possible to remain forever frozen in time; changing circumstances will not permit it. But Augustinian–Hobbesian conservatism suggests proceeding *gradually* and with the utmost caution. This counsel becomes increasingly urgent the more far-reaching and therefore potentially unsettling proposed changes might be.

It is this defining conservative commitment to gradualism that Edmund Burke and Alexis de Tocqueville and others seized upon after the Revolution in France.[4] Their conservatism was indifferent to Original Sin or its secular analogue. It was based instead on a view of the nature of governance. Their idea, in short, was that governing more nearly resembles cooking or carpentry than it does geometry; that it is an activity in which a reservoir of accumulated wisdom and good sense, built up over generations and materialized in techniques, implements and traditions, matters more than rational insight or deductive acuity.[5] These post-Revolutionary conservatives faulted the more radical French revolutionaries for being moved by a rationalist spirit. The revolutionary's aim, the conservatives discerned, was to replace the old regime with a more rational alternative, concocted from the ground up on new, ostensibly more solid, bases. These revolutionaries were therefore political analogues of philosophical rationalists like René Descartes who sought to overthrow existing knowledge claims in order to start over from the beginning on sound, rationally compelling foundations. But whatever the merits of rationalism in philosophy, it is, in the view of these conservatives, out of place in politics. To their way of thinking, political actors ought to be moved by respect for extant traditions and governing styles, and the cumulative wisdom they embody; not by putative 'first principles'. Post-Revolutionary conservatism was therefore less worried about the eruption of a war of all against all than about the imposition of unwise and therefore harmful forms of governance. This is why its proponents were, on the whole, less ill-disposed towards change than were conservatives who take Sin seriously. Burke, for example, pleaded in favor of the American Revolution, which he saw as a justifiable war of independence; and Tocqueville, some half century after independence was achieved, was an ardent exponent and defender of American democracy.[6] Perhaps they would both have defended the French Revolution too, had the revolutionaries moderated their radical impulses and contented themselves with installing a constitutional monarchy in place of the old and obsolete absolutist autocracy. But the French revolutionaries were extreme in their repudiation not only of outmoded political institutions, but of the fundamental structure of the Old Regime itself. They wanted 'to build a new world on the ashes of the old'. This these conservatives could not abide.

*   *   *

Liberalism too has roots that antedate the French Revolution. As a coherent political ideology, it appeared in the aftermath of the wars of religion that convulsed early modern Europe. As the various sides fought to exhaustion, liberalism emerged as a doctrine of tolerance – at first of rival religious persuasions, ultimately of any and all competing conceptions of the good life. Thus liberalism was, from the start, a theory of *limited* sovereignty, a political philosophy organized around the claim that there are principled limitations to the rightful use of public coercive force. The imposition of religious orthodoxies transgresses these limitations. So too do other efforts to enforce or proscribe particular, contentious conceptions of the good. For the first liberals, (most) state interferences with market exchanges were similarly proscribed. These liberals stood for virtually unlimited rights to accumulate property privately, and for individuals' rights to do as they please with the property they hold. They were divided, however, on what may be privately owned. Nearly all external things were, of course, candidates for private acquisition and market exchange. For many years, there was an ongoing, though often muted, debate about slavery, about whether and under what conditions other persons could be owned. The first liberals were ardent defenders of self-ownership, however, at least for free persons: they maintained that free men – and, sometimes in theory but never in practice, women – are the absolute owners of their own bodies and powers. They were therefore proponents of labor markets and, by extension, of market arrangements generally – not just in the economic sphere, but in the larger society as well. From its inception, then, liberalism has been doctrinally committed to the idea that individuals ought to be free to do as they please, provided only that they not inflict *harms* on others. Then and only then may states rightfully interfere with individuals' lives and behaviors. In articulating and joining together these components of early liberal theory, John Locke is an exemplary figure. Locke was a defender of religious toleration, a proponent of market arrangements and of the right to accumulate property privately and without limitation, a believer in self-ownership, a defender of patriarchy (at least in practice) and, on slavery, like many other 'enlightened' thinkers of the time, an apologist of sorts.[7]

The liberalism of the past two centuries has remained faithful to its original commitment to tolerance and, more generally, to state neutrality with respect to competing conceptions of the good, even as its enthusiasm for private property and market exchange has waned outside so-called libertarian circles. Liberals of all stripes have, of course, also repudiated slavery and, more recently, patriarchy. But it was only after the Revolution in France that liberal political philosophy developed into a full-fledged ideology, friendly to many of the causes the French revolutionaries advanced, but hostile to the theory and practice of revolution itself. Liberalism became a doctrine of permanent reform, of change – sometimes substantial, more usually incremental – imposed from above. Post-Revolutionary liberalism was, nevertheless, a progressive ideology, organized around the notion of progress implicit in contemporaneous understandings of the very Revolution that liberals (ambivalently) disavowed. But, unlike the revolutionaries in France, post-Revolutionary liberals were dedicated to changing the world from the top down, within the framework of existing legal and institutional norms. For them, the agent of change ought always to be elites in place; never insurrectionary masses. Their aim was to engineer improvements – in accord with a design that was more or less worked out, but in a piecemeal way; not by taking on the existing system in its totality.

In principle, though, this liberalism is antirevolutionary only where liberalism is already established. Where it is not, a post-Revolutionary liberal might well be moved to take up revolutionary positions or, at least, to sympathize with those who do. Before the French Revolution, liberalism was largely a Dutch, English and French phenomenon. In the immediate aftermath of that Revolution, it was mainly a creature of the English-speaking world. After the Revolution had run its course, liberalism became influential in France again and throughout other parts of the world too, especially where English or French (or, later, American) influence reigned. In these places, liberalism was antirevolutionary. But where existing political arrangements were illiberal, and where there were no available institutional means for advancing liberal prospects, then, as even a pre-Revolutionary liberal like Locke maintained, and as the founders of the American republic agreed, a right – and, in some cases, even a duty – of revolution is triggered. Throughout the nineteenth century and into the twentieth, therefore, liberalism was a revolutionary ideology in much of the world, even as it was an antirevolutionary ideology in those fortunate countries where it was most entrenched.

It is therefore fair to say that liberalism is more continuous with socialism than was assumed when these ideologies arose, and than is still commonly supposed. Its affinities extend beyond ultimate objectives, even into the realm of means for achieving them. It is also fair to say that, after the Revolution, liberalism became an ideology of the Left, albeit of the Left's right wing. Ever since it came into being, liberalism has been for liberty. Since the Revolution, it has been for equality and fraternity too, though its purchase on these values may not always be recognizably continuous with revolutionary and later socialist understandings. Liberalism's connection to equality and fraternity will be revisited in Chapter 5, in connection with the trajectory of analytical Marxism. It will emerge that, with respect to valuational commitments, liberalism and socialism are more alike than most people have recognized over the many years that these ostensibly rival doctrines have coexisted. But, again, this claim holds only for post-Revolutionary liberalism. The pre-Revolutionary liberalism that libertarians have revived – a liberalism that worships private property and markets and that upholds liberty in the economic sphere to the detriment of equality and fraternity – is a different matter. In nearly all imaginable circumstances, it is an ideology of the Right.

*   *   *

From its inception, the socialist idea was to carry forward the revolutionary commitment to liberty, equality and fraternity to the point of full realization. Thus even more than conservatism or liberalism, with their roots in pre-Revolutionary political theories and practices, socialism developed in consequence of the French Revolution or, more precisely, in consequence of its failure fully to realize the objectives for which it was waged. Socialists embraced the revolutionary project wholeheartedly. If they faulted the events begun in 1789, it was only for their insufficiency, for what they did not achieve. They had little quarrel with what the Revolution actually did in its most radical phases. The socialist idea, then, was not to retain continuity with the Old Regime, as conservatives wanted, nor to contain the Revolution that overthrew it, in the way that liberals proposed, but to advance it – to its next, perhaps its final, stage.

Very early on, in both England and France, this objective was joined to the struggles of the nascent working-class movement. Thus Marx, writing in the early 1840s, at a moment when the German proletariat scarcely existed, predicted a full-fledged social revolution in Germany in consequence of the proletariat's revolutionary interests and its 'radical chains'.[8] Almost from the beginning, then, the socialist project focused on the economic sphere. The idea, as it developed in the years preceding the revolutionary upheavals of 1848 and even more so in the decades that followed, was to carry the liberals' commitment to equality beyond the political arena into the economy and, from there, into all spheres of social life.

The Old Regime was a hodgepodge of status relations and therefore of political inequalities. Instead of citizenship for all who comprised the nation, there was, outside the monarchy itself, a hierarchically structured nobility, a clergy, also structured hierarchically, with a variety of public powers, and a mass of 'commoners' with hardly any rights at all. The French Revolution ended this situation definitively, establishing a norm of political equality, equal citizenship, that is now espoused everywhere, even if, too often, it remains more honored in theory than in practice. Thus it is now universally believed that citizens ought to stand equally before the law, that their votes ought to count equally in elections, and, in general, that they ought to enjoy the same rights and liberties as all other citizens. Liberals endorse this egalitarian vision unequivocally, at least in theory.[9] Socialists embrace it too – faulting only its partiality, its commitment to equality in just one sphere of human life.

The French Revolution also established a norm of equal opportunity, of careers open to talents. Equality of opportunity has become an essentially contested notion in our political culture, an idea that everyone accepts in principle, even as they struggle over what it involves. For some, equal opportunity collapses into political equality; it exists whenever there are no legal or customary impediments based on status inequalities that affect individuals differentially in competitions for scarce resources or offices. At the other extreme, equality of opportunity is thought to exist only if outcomes (for specified groups and/or individuals) are equal or nearly so; in other words, only if corrections are made for all the extralegal and extracustomary impediments that exist in real world competitions. This interpretation evidently exceeds what all but the most radical of the French revolutionaries had in mind. It was only in the aftermath of the Revolution that significant numbers of people began to envision a world in which everyone's holdings are in some meaningful sense the same.[10] But the liberal tent is sufficiently broad to accommodate these extremely disparate understandings of equal opportunity and any number of intermediate positions as well. Socialists too support equality of opportunity, though, for them, the importance of this ideal pales in comparison with other, deeper egalitarian commitments. Characteristically, therefore, socialists emphasize equal opportunity less than liberals do. But, to the degree that it is a concern of theirs, socialists side with those liberals whose purchase on equal opportunity leads them to want to compensate for all or nearly all those factors that diminish the prospect of arriving at genuinely equal outcomes.

More than liberals, socialists have also advocated material equality or, at least, equality of income and wealth.[11] However, the strain of socialist ideology of concern here, Marxism, has always evinced a certain ambivalence towards material equality. Of the three objectives the French revolutionaries proclaimed – liberty, equality and fraternity – it is, significantly, the latter that has most fired Marxists' imagination. It is this objective too that is most saliently missing in today's depleted political culture.

* * *

One of the dangers in grouping together Soviet or Chinese Marxism with the Marxism of Marx and his close followers bears special notice because it touches on an issue that is of particular relevance to the prospects for transforming the larger political culture in a progressive direction. This has to do with *democracy,* the rule of the *demos* – government of, by and for the people. Whether or not the French Revolution was the watershed event it was once universally thought to be, it is plain that it registered, as nothing else has, what is perhaps the most unmistakable and irreversible political fact of the modern era – the entry of the *demos,* the popular masses, into the political arena. Even the officially antidemocratic, fascist regimes that blighted the political landscape of the mid-twentieth century implicitly acknowledged this fact. Their defenders represented the fascist state as an instrument for executing the peoples' will. What the fascists denied was not the desirability of investing power in the people. Their claim instead was that the legislative and judicial institutions of liberal democratic states implement that ideal in a factitious and ultimately debilitating way. In any case, with the worldwide defeat of fascism after World War II, support for democracy – for the word, that is, if not for the reality – has become universal. Thus, throughout the years of their coexistence, defenders of both liberal democracy and communism claimed the title 'democratic' for themselves.

For much of the latter part of the twentieth century, then, *democracy,* like equality of opportunity, was an essentially contested notion, an idea all sides endorsed, even as they advanced radically divergent views about what it implies. But, in contrast to equality of opportunity, none of the received understandings of democracy hold up well under scrutiny. It goes without saying that the *peoples' democracies* of Eastern Europe and Asia were hardly democratic on any plausible construal of what democracy is. They were regimes ruled by elites drawn from their respective Communist Parties. Moreover, in the peoples' democracies of Eastern Europe, even these ruling elites were dominated by their counterparts in the Soviet Union. Liberal democracies fare better in comparison. But we should not exaggerate their virtues. With respect to liberal values, liberal democracies do well. But with respect to democracy, they fall short. In recent decades, real democracy – government of, by and for the people – has been everywhere honored, but nowhere truly observed.

* * *

Paradoxically, the leading ideologies of the post-Revolutionary period have each, in their own way, contributed to this unhappy state of affairs.

Socialism and democracy are inextricably joined, at least in most Marxist and non-Marxist strains of socialist thinking. But from the time that the Russian Revolution devolved into Soviet Communism, this linkage has largely disappeared from view. To the extent that the idea of a more authentic, democratic socialism remained alive throughout the Cold War period and in the decades immediately preceding it, democratic aspirations survived within the larger socialist movement. But, thanks to the enormous authority, both political and moral, exercised by those who came to power in the aftermath of the first successful workers' revolution, the idea that the *demos* ought directly to rule themselves effectively dropped out of the socialist creed. The workers' state became a state in which a self-appointed vanguard party of the working class controlled the levers of power, governing ostensibly on the workers' and therefore the people's behalf. The only vanguard parties actually to rule were, of course, the Communist Parties. They were uncontrolled by and unaccountable to the citizens they governed. They were also notoriously undemocratic in their internal organization. With only a few minor exceptions, so were their excluded and marginalized rivals for Bolshevik legitimacy. In consequence, a politics reminiscent of the emergency government of Robespierre and the Committee of Public Safety, based on dictatorship and rule by terror, replaced the idea of government of, by and for the people in practice and even in theory. Marxist and other strains of socialist theory suggest very different institutional arrangements. But, in consequence of the reality and authority of the Soviet model, democracy came to be, at most, only a peripheral concern for most socialists, Marxist or not. Too often, it was an ideal actively sinned against.

In contrast to socialism, with its roots in the social movements that installed the democratic idea permanently everywhere, conservatism is in principle at odds with democracy, even if it is not strictly opposed. This is true of both its post- and pre-Revolutionary variants. For post-Revolutionary conservatives, governing well is an art, no more susceptible to being well exercised by the entire population than any other complex and difficult-to-acquire skill. Governance is therefore best left in the hands of those who are born to rule – literally, for proponents of hereditary aristocracy, or, more commonly, as the democratic ethos spread, figuratively. However, in deference to the *demos,* even conservatives came to want to hold ruling elites accountable, through periodic elections or by other means, to the citizens they govern. But the people must not govern themselves. The antidemocratic bias of Augustinian–Hobbesian conservatism is even more pronounced. Because conservatives of this type are wary of anything that puts order in jeopardy, and because they know that democracy politicizes and that politicization can be destabilizing, they have every reason to be ill disposed to the idea of the people in power. For them, unlike others on the right wing of the Right – including the fascists, who were, after all, revolutionaries themselves – politicization is always dangerous. It threatens to reignite the war of all against all.

From a contemporary vantage point, the ideology that has mattered most in the post-Revolutionary period is, of course, liberalism; and liberalism and democracy are often confounded. But, in fact, the two ideals are, at best, in tension with one another. The reason why is clear: there is no principled connection between empowering the people, the *demos,* on the one hand, and, on the other, respecting individuals' rights or otherwise protecting individuals' lives and behaviors from public coercive force. The first liberals were acutely aware of this situation. In their view, the property-holding few, whose right to accumulate property they sought to immunize against state interference, had everything to fear from the tyranny of an empowered propertyless majority. It is easy to lose sight of the problem these liberals confronted because, since the middle of the nineteenth century, liberalism effectively superseded democracy in the minds of democrats friendly to liberalism; in other words, in the minds of democrats generally. Liberal democracy was the result. But liberal democracy is not what its name implies. It is not a political system that somehow combines the rule of the *demos* with limited government. It is more nearly a regime in which periodic elections, rendered all but innocuous by the party system and other institutional arrangements, legitimate reforming projects undertaken by liberal elites. In both theory and practice, liberal democracy served to attenuate democratic impulses in a world in which the presence of the *demos* in the political arena had become an ineluctable fact of life. To be sure, even as anemic a concession to rule of, by, and for the people as this one turned out to be is nothing to despise. Because of it, ruling elites in liberal democracies are accountable to popular constituencies to a degree that they are not in other political systems.[12] But liberal democracy is still, at most, only a feeble approximation of real democracy. It would be more apt to think of it as a form of benevolent despotism or, more precisely, as a despotism in which benevolence is promoted through the institutionalization of democratic forms.

In the triumphalist fervor surrounding the end of the Cold War, it may seem odd to oppose real democracy to liberal democracy. The collapse of communism and its immediate consequence, American hegemony, is registered in the popular imagination as a victory for democratic forces. But this common sense view is wrong. Its widespread acceptance is just one more unhappy consequence of the decline of political imagination in the past several decades, since the demise of the New Left, and of the not unrelated trajectory of socialism in the period from the Russian Revolution through the end of communism to the present moment. Today, even in those few, not entirely marginalized quarters where the epithets 'socialist' or 'social democratic' are not rejected outright, the only remaining component left of the Left is liberal – indeed, liberal democratic. Thus, *democracy* is almost everywhere understood in a liberal democratic way. This is an unfortunate state of affairs. But it is also eminently contestable, as we will go on to see [13]

*   *   *

Marx and Engels and their successors called themselves 'scientific socialists', deeming their predecessors and rivals in the socialist movement 'utopian socialists'. This designation was polemical. Even if they were not utopiaphobic, as so many academics and public intellectuals are today, 'utopian' still had a bad connotation for nineteenth-century socialists. 'Scientific' also had a polemical aspect; it was and is a term of approbation. But there is also a substantive theoretical difference indicated by these characterizations. Utopian socialists rest their faith in humanity's future on the appeal of a vision of ideal social, political and economic arrangements. Scientific socialists do not. For them, the possibility and perhaps even the inevitability of socialism is underwritten by a rationally compelling theory of history.

It is unfortunate that the term 'scientific socialism' has fallen into disuse. It is preferable to 'Marxism'. Its diminishing role in the socialist's lexicon began in the 1870s and 1880s, when 'Marxism' ceased to be just one tendency among others within the larger socialist movement, becoming instead a comprehensive body of doctrine, a full-fledged *ism,* to which most socialists adhered and against which all the others defined their positions. I have, to this point, used 'Marxism' in the way that has become commonplace, and I will continue to do so, except where there is a point to be made by focusing just on that aspect of it that 'scientific socialism' captures. 'Marxism' is so entrenched in the political vocabulary of everyone everywhere that there is no hope of dislodging it, and no point in trying. Moreover, as standardly understood, 'Marxism' includes what Marx and Engels meant by 'scientific socialism'. It is worth recalling that, during Marxism's so-called Golden Age, the period from the founding of the Second International in 1889 until the outbreak of world war in 1914, the terms were often used interchangeably. [14]

Even so, the redescription of scientific socialism as Marxism is inapt. It suggests the idea, taken up by later generations of Marxists, communist and otherwise, that Marx's theory of history and society is a closed system in which all truths or, at least all truths bearing on social, political and economic life, reside. Thus it supports a view of Marx's work that smacks more of religion than of science. Perhaps this was why Marx maintained that he was not a Marxist.[15] It is telling, though, that Marx and especially Engels insisted with equal fervor on the distinction between utopian and scientific socialism. They were right to do so, inasmuch as there is a genuine difference, of fundamental importance to socialist theory and practice, between these types of socialist ideology. For a long time, scientific socialism had the upper hand. Now, the very idea is almost everywhere either rejected or ignored. But this reversal of fortune is unwarranted, as we will see. We will also find that the near extinction of socialist thought today is, in part, a consequence of the triumph of utopian over scientific socialism.

I will argue in Chapters 5 and 6 for the cogency of the idea of a scientific socialism. I will maintain that it was Marx's signal contribution to social and political theory to discover this idea and to offer persuasive reasons in its defense. I will argue too that it is only insofar as socialism is scientific that it is theoretically distinctive and therefore unassimilable into other, more mainstream ways of thinking. Now that scientific socialism has fallen into disrepute, those who still identify with the socialist tradition are, almost without exception, utopian socialists, if they are socialists at all.[16] For them, therefore, the way is open to becoming absorbed into the mainstream. It is easy to see why. Utopian socialists defend socialism on normative grounds. But the normative commitments of socialists are hardly different from those of the majority of nonsocialists, including liberals. Therefore, if socialism is utopian in Marx's and Engels's sense, the debate between socialism and liberalism can only be a debate about strategies for achieving commonly recognized aims. There is no dispute about these aims themselves, nor could there be, because there is nothing about which the contending parties disagree. In consequence, the collapse of socialism into liberalism becomes possible. In Chapter 5, I will show how the realization of this possibility became nearly inevitable.

*   *   *

Because the terms 'utopian' and 'scientific' admit of many different understandings, it is easy to get the distinction wrong, especially inasmuch as rhetorical excesses have muddied the waters considerably. Some clarification is therefore in order.

When Marx and his cothinkers took aim at the *utopianism* of their rivals, what they opposed was not exactly what people have understood by the term from the time that Sir Thomas More coined it in 1516 [17] The utopianism they scorned is therefore not the specter feared by the utopiaphobes who dominate our political culture. In Marx's and Engels's view, utopian socialism was not an impractica- ble and therefore dangerous idea. Quite the contrary. The founders of scientific socialism endorsed what the utopian socialists favored. Their own understanding of socialism, they insisted, owed a great debt to the utopian socialists.[18] For Marx and Engels, utopian socialism is utopian only because it is grounded in a normative ideal rather than a theory of history. Otherwise, it is of a piece with scientific socialism. Socialism, utopian *and* scientific, is based on the conviction that there exists a coherent – and feasible – vision of ideal social arrangements, true to the values the French Revolution advanced – liberty, equality and fraternity – that capitalist societies cannot realize, but that socialist societies can. But the utopian socialists then went on to hold that their principal – indeed, their only – task was to educate others to this fact by promulgating a socialist vision and perhaps also by living it, to the extent that they were able. They maintained that, in consequence, a sufficiently large portion of humankind would eventually embrace the socialist vision too and, in this enlightened state, make the world conform to it. Scientific socialists had other ideas about political practice; ideas grounded purportedly in 'the laws of motion' of capitalist society. Marx's and Engels's case against utopian socialism therefore had to do with how to defend the idea of socialism, and with how to attain it. There was no dispute about what socialism is or about its feasibility.

By the time utopian and then scientific socialism emerged as mature political ideologies in the early and middle nineteenth century, it was clear to everyone that what was at stake when socialists contended against proponents of *other* ideologies, rather than against each other, were *economic* structures, ways of organizing the production and distribution of material things. It was nearly as universally accepted that the relevant economic structures, capitalism and socialism, differed mainly in the forms of property relations they support. Under capitalism, most external things are privately owned. Under socialism, they are owned collectively or 'socially'. What private ownership is was well understood. This is not surprising – liberals and others had promoted private property for more than a century before socialism emerged as a distinct political ideology. What social ownership is was obscure at the time that socialism first appeared, and remains so to this day. Presumably, *state* ownership is a form of social ownership. But it would be a mistake, one to which socialists have often succumbed, to suppose that it is the only form. What other forms there might be is, however, unsettled. This is a very serious shortcoming of socialist theory. But it is one that, until now, the socialist movement has been able to live with – and then, recently, to all but die with. Thus utopian socialists believed that social ownership, in one or another form, was indispensable for realizing the normative ideal(s) they advanced. Scientific socialists defended social ownership in a different way, as we will see. But even as they were equally vague about what it was that they had in mind, they were equally determined that the objective, however understood, is feasible.

In their case for socializing private property, scientific socialists appealed to a theory of history and society that is 'scientific' in a sense of that term that is commonplace today, and that was widely accepted in the nineteenth century. Very generally, explanations count as scientific if they identify causal processes of the sort that have engaged investigators in the natural sciences since the great scientific revolution of the seventeenth century. Medieval science, with its Aristotelian roots, accorded pride of place to *teleological causes;* to the *ends* or *goals* of natural phenomena. Modern scientific explanations instead invoke what medieval philosophers, using Aristotle's terminology, called *efficient causes.* Premodern scientific explanations of natural phenomena were, typically, teleological; they sought to discern what phenomena *mean* or *signify* by identifying their *telos*, their end or goal. It was a tenet of modern science, however, that nature has no *telos*; that it *signifies* nothing, that it just is. Nevertheless, nature is intelligible because it has a causal structure that can be discovered, at least in principle. To explain a phenomenon on this view, is to identify its real causal determinations, its efficient causes. This is what Marx did with respect to property relations, their histories and futures, and their extraeconomic consequences.

*　*　*

For Marxists before Althusser and analytical Marxism, and for those who never assimilated the implications of these new departures in Marxist thought, scientific socialism somehow coexisted with the idea that history can only be made sense of teleologically; a notion they derived from Hegel. In fact, however, scientific socialism is best understood in *contrast* to Hegel's account of history's structure and direction. Hegel's philosophy of history was indeed the main *philosophical* source of Marx's theory of history. But, as Althusser would insist and as the analytical Marxists would implicitly demonstrate, their relation was not a simple one, and was certainly not the one that was commonly supposed.

Hegel's thinking was both teleological and secular. But teleological philosophies of history like Hegel's are all, in a way, theodicies, justifications of God's ways or, in Hegel's own case, of the ways of a secular equivalent of God. It is instructive, therefore, to look back to the first great teleological philosophy of history, St. Augustine's, for a prototype of the kind of theory scientific socialism emerged out of and eventually came to oppose.[19]

Augustine sought to make sense of human history – or, at least, of that part of it through which the Roman Empire was passing in his time – retrospectively, from the standpoint of history's *telos,* a vantage point that he, like Hegel, thought he could assume because it was already nearly at hand. Augustine's telling of the story of human history or, rather, of the swathe of it that mattered for his theodicy, implied an account of history's structure and direction. Augustine therefore 'explained' history itself, in addition to proffering explanations for particular historical events. The key structuring moments in his account of human history came from theology. They include the Creation, the Fall, the Resurrection, and the (impending) Final Judgment. Thus it was from the standpoint of the Final Judgment, the literal end of human history as well as its *telos*, that Augustine attempted to make sense of what had come before. Hegel's philosophy of history recounts a very different story, that of the career of the Idea of Freedom. But the thought that history as such can be explained by telling a story from the vantage point of its end, and the corresponding thought that what it is to make sense of human history is to discern its real structure and direction, were Augustinian.[20]

Vantage points are, of course, relative to the particular positions individuals assume. But for philosophers of history of the Augustinian–Hegelian type, the narrative that explains human history is nevertheless *objectively* true. The idea is not that the perspective assumed somehow replicates a godlike 'view from nowhere', relative to no particular position. Objectivity of that sort is unattainable in principle in a narrative account. Rather, it is objective in the sense that it is relative to no theoretically *arbitrary* perspective. Augustine's and Hegel's idea, which they each tried to defend in their own ways, was that there exists a definitive (albeit particular) vantage point from which the true story of history can be told, the vantage point of history's end. From that position, the story that unfolds renders the past intelligible in a way that makes the real structure and direction of history apparent. But because this perspective represents only one point of view, it excludes everything that falls outside its horizon. Thus it excludes nearly everything that happened in the past – not just for pragmatic reasons, because there is not time to recount it all, but because most of what happened is irrelevant from the perspective from which the story of history unfolds. There are entire peoples whose pasts therefore fall outside the scope of human history. Had Augustine been aware of the existence of civilizations beyond the ken of the Roman empire – in China, say, or in sub-Saharan Africa – he would have had to conclude that the Chinese and the Africans were peoples without histories because their pasts play no role in the *true* story of humanity's march towards the Final Judgment. Since Hegel had knowledge of the earth and its inhabitants that Augustine did not, and since geographical separation mattered less in the early nineteenth century than it did in the fifth, Hegel's view of the world was more cosmopolitan. Still his story of the career of the Idea of Freedom excludes nearly everything that happened in humanity's past – and everything that ever happened outside the Eurasian landmass. For Hegel too, many of the world's inhabitants belong to peoples without histories.

The idea that history itself has an explanation is foreign to mainstream historiography. History, as it is commonly practiced, is a nontheoretical discipline. It proceeds on the assumption that anything that has already happened can count as an historical *explanandum*, an object of explanation; and that virtually any way of making sense of an historical explanandum counts as an historical explanation. But even if every historical event, no matter how it is identified, can in principle be explained, it still makes no sense, in the mainstream view, to maintain that history itself can be explained. Not even a trivial explanation, produced by joining all particular explanations together, is possible because, in order to concoct such a conjunction in a way that would explain history in its entirety, there would have to be a theoretically defensible way to divide the past into discrete, mutually exclusive parts; and that is impossible in the absence of a theory that constrains what counts as an historical explanandum. Philosophies of history of the Augustinian–Hegelian type therefore stand apart from contemporary understandings of history. In his analyses of revolutionary episodes of contemporaneous European (especially French) history, Marx proved himself an historian of the first rank, according to the usual understanding of what historical writing involves. Even so, he never abandoned the idea of a theory of history. In fact, he systematically integrated the historical explanations he advanced into his own account of history's structure and direction. To do so, however, he had first to transform the Augustinian–Hegelian idea of what a theory of history is – in a way that accorded with understandings of causality and explanation commonplace in modern scientific practice.

*   *   *

It is this aspect of Marx's work, filtered through the lenses of Althusserian and analytical Marxist philosophy, that I focus on in Part II. At this point, a few general indications will help to set the stage.

Marx was, at first, one of a number of fledgling German intellectuals known as the Young (or sometimes Left) Hegelians.[21] As such, he was committed, in the main, to Hegel's philosophy of history. However, by the mid-1840s, Marx was already at odds with aspects of Young Hegelian thought. Eventually, he broke away altogether from Hegel's teleological account of history's structure and direction. The first intimations, in his work, of a nonteleological alternative to a philosophy of history of the Hegelian type are evident in *The German Ideology* (1845). It was this moment in Marx's intellectual development that Althusser would later describe as an 'epistemological break'. In *The German Ideology*, Marx and Engels set out an account of history's real *natural-kind* divisions, identifying structural discontinuities within human history that have, in their view, genuine theoretical significance. Natural-kind divisions contrast with convenient classifications. Classifications that do not represent theoretically meaningful natural kinds include, for example, in the theory of evolution, the Age of Mammals or the Age of Dinosaurs. These classifications represent investigators' interests, not real differences underwritten by theoretically grounded principles of evolutionary theory. In contrast, *the capitalist mode of production* and the various precapitalist economic structures identified in *The German Ideology* and elsewhere – the feudal mode of production, for example, or the ancient and Asiatic modes – purport to represent fundamental differences internal to human history as such, real (as opposed to convenient) structural divides.

Marx's theory of history or *historical materialism,* as it has come to be known, aims to account for history's structure and direction by identifying a real causal process internal to human history; an *endogenous* process that supplies history with a determinate trajectory from one *mode of production* or *economic structure* to another. The Althusserians grasped the general nature of this project. The analytical Marxists invented themselves, and breathed new life into the idea of scientific socialism, by doing what the Althusserians only proclaimed – identifying and developing Marx's theory. I have more to say about what the analytical Marxists did in Chapters 5 and 6. There is, however, one consequence of their work that bears mention now.

The analytical Marxists, unlike Marx and Engels and unlike Althusser, were never interested in differentiating their views from those of other socialists – or, for that matter, from nonsocialists. Long before their identification with Marxism waned, even as they still defended orthodox Marxist positions, they were friendly to moral philosophy. They were therefore always disinclined to adopt Marx's rhetorical opposition to 'utopian socialism' or to suggest, in any other way, that normative considerations have no place in the struggle for socialism. But, in truth, there never was any compelling theoretical reason for Marx and the others to reject normative discourse as such. For them, opposition to utopian socialism, when it wasn't a blind reflex, was a polemical move undertaken for political reasons. The analytical Marxists operated in different circumstances and in a different way. Political exigencies hardly impinged on their thinking, and they harbored no sectarian intentions. They therefore never suggested that scientific socialism should somehow excise normative theory, or that the case for a socialist future should depend entirely on the identification of inexorable historical forces.

But they were nevertheless scientific socialists. As became clear thanks to their work, one could be a scientific socialist without disparaging normative theory in the way that Marx and the Marxists had. It is enough to claim that the prospects for socialism do not rest on normative considerations *alone*; or, what comes to the same thing, that there are reasons, grounded in a rationally compelling account of history's structure and direction, for thinking socialism possible and even necessary. In short, what is essential to the theory and practice of scientific socialism is historical materialism. As we will see, it is this theory – and what follows from it – that makes Marxism distinctive, and also distinct from liberal or other conceptual frameworks. Historical materialism, the foundational theory of scientific socialism, is the core upon which any future Marxism must build.

2 The Last Left

The 'New Left' emerged suddenly in the late 1950s and early 1960s. It then flourished briefly before sputtering into oblivion, sometimes violently, during the 1970s.[1] By the onset of the Reagan–Thatcher era, it was almost entirely defunct. At the time, the New Left seemed to augur a new wave, a fresh start in the socialist tradition. Around 1968, there were even people, reasonable people, who thought that it might in the immediate future actually make the slogan 'power to the people' real. More sober New Leftists were confident that, at the very least, it would inaugurate a process of intensified struggle, of uncertain duration, but with excellent prospects for success. Today, the nearly unanimous view is that the New Left was anything but a *beginning*; that it was more nearly a last gasp of Left enthusiasm. The New Left has come to look like the last Left. But appearances are deceiving. The New Left was not what its proponents believed. But neither does its demise have quite the implications that are generally supposed.

To speculate thoughtfully on Marxism's future and on the role that Althusserian and analytical Marxist philosophy might play in it, it will be instructive to reflect on this phenomenon – with a view to understanding its place in the history of the Left and of socialism. The New Left generated very little theory of philosophical interest. The one partial exception was the work of Herbert Marcuse, aspects of which I will consider towards the end of this chapter. But Marcuse's views have not held up well, and neither has the work of any other political or social theorist directly associated with New Left politics. On the whole, the New Left was a social and political phenomenon, aspects of which are of philosophical interest. It was not a philosophical phenomenon in its own right. But it affected Marxist philosophy in significant ways.

The New Left was largely a work of people of comparatively privileged backgrounds, from the generation born in the wake of World War II, entering adulthood in the last days of the postwar capitalist expansion – in the midst of worldwide national liberation struggles and at a moment when the Soviet Union was no longer a pole of attraction for intellectuals or workers. These factors, more than any conceptual breakthroughs made by New Left thinkers, help to explain the respects in which New Left thinking was *new*. It was a response to a situation that was unprecedented for socialist movements, a situation in which the working class no longer appeared to be an engine of fundamental social transformation. This fact, more than anything else, shaped New Left ventures into social and political theory – not always explicitly, but nevertheless unmistakably.

The fact that it was comprised, for the most part, of well-off young people also helps to explain why the New Left was so remarkably radical and visionary, especially in comparison with other contemporaneous and near contemporaneous Left tendencies. Because they were less encumbered by material necessities, New Left activists were freer to dream than those born into less fortunate circumstances. And dream they did! A quarter century later, in a world depleted of political imagination, it is staggering to recall how radical the New Left's vision was.

But it is also sobering to reflect on the predicament the New Left faced. Socialists generally, and Marxists in particular, whether or not they were of working-class origin themselves, had, from the beginning, identified with the labor movement – not just in solidarity with 'the wretched of the earth', but because they saw the industrial proletariat as the agent of the changes they sought to bring about. At the time the New Left emerged, this idea was still pervasive throughout the Left. It was assumed in the Marxist philosophy of the time, and there was hardly a New Left thinker who denied it outright. But, by the 1960s, the idea that the working class, or any segment of it, had either the interest or the capacity to install new social relations had come to seem increasingly untenable. This fact on the ground registered in mainstream thinking. The Left, however, had yet to come to terms with it. The New Left, intentionally or not, assumed this burden. Its struggle with it is part of its legacy – not just to the political culture generally but, as we will see, to Althusserianism, which came into being and then faltered in tandem with the New Left, and to analytical Marxism, which arose and flourished in the wake of its decline.

*   *   *

It will be well to recall, at the outset, some of the shared assumptions of the political culture at the time of the New Left's rise, decline and fall. For most of the twentieth century, there has existed a pervasive, largely unquestioned, view of what is feasible in the way of social, political and economic arrangements. This understanding was assumed throughout the New Left – but with one key modification to be identified and discussed presently. This modification underlies some of the more enduring legacies of New Left politics. But it was, at the time, more a wrinkle than a fissure in the consensus view.

The universally accepted idea was that there are two, and only two, forms that modern, industrialized societies can take, two economic, political and social regimes. In one, most productive assets are privately owned; in the other, they are the property of the state. In one, markets allocate most economic resources, though state fiscal and monetary policies affect market outcomes, and states protect, regulate, and sometimes even create the markets they superintend. In regimes of this kind, markets also largely determine levels of economic well-being, though states typically redistribute market-generated distributions to some extent – by supplying public goods and by enacting welfare state measures (insofar as they are distinct from public goods) that provide protections against the uncertainties of life in market societies with private property. With markets (largely) organizing the economic order, outcomes at the societal level emerge as unintended consequences of individuals' voluntary choices. States do affect incentive structures that, in turn, affect what individuals choose. In this way, they engineer outcomes indirectly. But there is very little deliberate control from the top. In contrast, where state property is the rule, the state plans economic life from the top down, implementing its policies directly. States also largely determine levels of economic well-being by controlling wages and prices and by directly providing or extensively subsidizing what, in the rival system, individuals and their families would mainly obtain through markets – housing, transport, education, health care and even basic foodstuffs.

In the more industrialized regions of the world throughout the past century, but especially after World War II, when fascism suffered an historic defeat, market systems with private property have been associated with (procedurally) democratic political structures. In regimes of this kind, political authority is vested in legislative and executive institutions, filled by periodic, competitive elections. State property regimes, on the other hand, are run by single party states, with strong party structures. They may hold periodic elections, but these elections are not genuinely competitive. More generally, there is very little *institutionalized* public accountability. Similarly, throughout the past century, but especially after World War II, private property regimes have been joined with constitutional systems of governance, superintended by independent judiciaries that protect individuals from certain kinds of state (and also non-state) interferences with their lives and behaviors.[2] The range and extent of these protections in single party states is less developed and more precarious – to a degree that permits, even if it does not strictly license, the institutionalization of terror as a mechanism for social control. Private property regimes and their accompanying political structures typically foster the development of non-state institutions that partially regulate and organize public life, a *civil society*. The rival societal form is generally hostile to independent partial associations, encouraging instead a more direct and unmediated relation between the individual and the state. In social orders of this kind, political structures tend to overwhelm non-state forms of social organization and control. In the alternative system, political structures are limited, not just in law, but also because a robust civil society, outside the political regime, stands between the individual and the state. These regimes differ as well in countless, more particular ways. But these very general contrasts suffice to indicate what, for many decades, nearly everyone believed.

We should resist the temptation to call the forms of societal organization I have identified by their own *theoretical* self-descriptions – *(capitalist) liberal democracy* and *communism*. These designations are misleading on many counts. For one thing, as work in an analytical Marxist vein established, the philosophies that ostensibly undergird these models of society are not nearly as opposed as is generally believed, and are, in any case, much less opposed than the two models they supposedly motivate. For another, neither of these forms of societal organization is all that consonant with the visions of ideal economic, social and political arrangements advanced within the philosophical traditions with which they are identified. This claim plainly holds for communism, but it is true as well of liberal democracy. It is also plain that the urge to find liberal, democratic and Marxist roots for actually or formerly existing economic, political and social arrangements had more to do with the needs of political elites to legitimate their own power than with any guiding philosophical visions. We therefore risk going astray if we accede to the commonplace view that it was two political ideologies, liberal democracy and communism, that were in contention. We risk falling into an even more insidious error if we conclude that, by 1989, liberal democracy defeated the rival view.

To make sense of the common sense view, it is crucial to keep in mind the bipolar Cold War order that emerged after World War II. This system served the interests of elites on both sides of the so-called Iron Curtain. In retrospect, it seems that it worked to the advantage of many nonelite sectors too, at least in comparison with what has come to succeed it. But the Cold War system was dangerous and unstable. As one ought to have expected, though no one did, the communist side eventually ceased to maintain its role – in part because important segments of its ruling stratum lost interest in keeping *their* regime afloat. Perhaps some day it will become clear why they gave up the ghost when and how they did. No doubt, the thought that they could make themselves better off by adopting the economic arrangements of the other side played some role. In any case, the expectations of many in the former communist elite that they would do better without communism have been largely fulfilled. Along with a few others who pulled themselves up out of the masses through entrepreneurship or racketeering or both, many of them have enriched themselves egregiously. Meanwhile, nearly everyone else is, in most respects, worse off than they were, except, of course, that they are able to dream that someday they too will become obscenely rich. But however the end of communism is explained, it is plain that the Cold War order that dominated world politics between 1945 and 1989 powerfully reinforced the common sense view that had preceded it for many decades – the idea that there are two and only two ways to organize modern, industrial societies. Now that the international system is dominated by only one of the two erstwhile superpowers, common sense has followed in tow. So thoroughgoing has this transformation been, that the remaining superpower, the United States, has already, to some considerable degree, succeeded in imposing its favored neoliberal world order on its former rival. Hence the new political assumption of our time, the idea that the American way is the only feasible and desirable way imaginable.

The pre-1989 consensus view emerged and changed under specific geopolitical conditions. This is why, in describing contemporary understandings of what is on the historical agenda, it is appropriate to refer to the models I sketched by names that recall the states that dominated the world political system during the Cold War period. I will therefore call these systems the *American* and *Soviet models*, respectively. Unlike 'liberal democracy' and 'communism', these terms are unambiguously nonphilosophical. This is appropriate, inasmuch as neither system came close to exemplifying the ideals intended by their philosophical self-representations. These terms are also deliberately narrow in their focus. One could imagine a wider variety of institutional arrangements consistent with the general features of the now defunct Soviet model than actually existed during the Soviet period. The countries where this model reigned could have been more liberal and democratic than they were. Had there been more institutional variation, it might now be appropriate to talk of a communist model, and of the Soviet model as only one form of it. But for reasons having mainly to do with the power and prestige of the ruling elite of the Soviet state, all communist countries, including those that freed themselves from Soviet domination, gravitated toward the Soviet model. It was in this form, therefore, that communism took hold of the political imagination of years past, and it is this alternative that has passed from the scene.

One might think, even so, that 'liberal democracy' would be an appropriate name for the model that survived the Cold War's end, inasmuch as there were a variety of institutional patterns in place in the states that comprised the so-called 'free world'. This was a plausible view several decades ago. Then, the United States was an outlier – with two entrenched probusiness political parties, a first-past-the-post electoral system that impedes democratic impulses to an exceptional degree, welfare programs that were feeble in comparison with those of other developed countries, and a labor movement without a political party of its own. For these reasons, among others, its governing institutions have always been unusually subservient to business interests. But for many years now, and especially since the end of the Cold War, alternatives to the American model, especially Left alternatives, have been on the wane everywhere. Thus the model that won out is now almost as constricted in its realizations as the model that was defeated. Accordingly, throughout the developed world, the welfare state is everywhere under attack and business interests are everywhere in ascendance. Without exception, political parties of the Left have, with varying degrees of enthusiasm, gone over to the American form of liberal democracy. In this instance, as in so many others, the victors rewrite history in their own image, impressing their own understandings on the collective consciousness. Thus the meanings of liberal democracy and the American model have come to coincide. However, to think clearly about where we now are and where it is still possible to go, it is well to resist this elision. What liberal democracy means in philosophical contexts should not be confounded with the debased understanding of what is historically possible that pervades the political common sense of the post-communist world.

Needless to say, the Right, the Center and what remains of the Left still contend along any of a number of familiar and important axes. But because they do so within the framework of a shared assumption, that the societal order now in place nearly everywhere cannot be improved upon fundamentally, their differences increasingly pale. Political contestation continues; parties still compete, elections are held as they always were. But to the detriment of the vast majority, electoral competitions are *about* less and less, and political life is profoundly diminished. Of course, local factors, differing from place to place, contribute to this state of affairs. In the United States, where electoral campaigns depend slavishly on monied interests, the situation is worse than elsewhere. But everywhere the absence of an alternative has become a fact of political life. The idea that none exists has followed ineluctably in its wake.

No one can say what would have happened had the Bolshevik Revolution failed and the Soviet model not come into existence in the way that it did. But in the world that formed in the aftermath of the Bolsheviks' victory, this model became a point of reference for the political Left everywhere in the world. Of at least equal importance, its specter, the specter of communism, frightened the ruling classes of the West enough to cause them, when forced by indigenous social movements, to make concessions that improved life enormously for the vast majority of their domestic populations. If only for this reason, the existence of even a deeply flawed alternative to the American model – joined however tenuously, to the socialist tradition – was a godsend. Its demise is hardly the unequivocal blessing it is nowadays thought to be.

*   *   *

The New Left never dissented from the pre-1989 consensus. But the take on this consensus advanced in some of its most conspicuous quarters was something of an innovation. The idea emerged that there was, if not exactly a third way, then a variation of the second way, of the Soviet model, that merited esteem and perhaps even imitation. Outside of small, sectarian groups, this second-and-a-half way, as it were, was seldom expressly acknowledged, let alone developed theoretically. But a vague conception of it nevertheless exercised a certain fascination. This new idea was drawn from contemporary images of Chinese communism and of national liberation movements in Vietnam, Cuba and elsewhere. It was an incoherent notion at its root, inasmuch as the regimes that inspired it were so unlike one another as to make the prospect of categorizing them together unthinkable. Nevertheless, it struck a chord. As many older Leftists insisted at the time, the New Left's departure from the norm owed more to ignorance than to insight; specifically, ignorance of the nature of Third World liberation struggles and of the Chinese Cultural Revolution. But it is clear, in retrospect, that, paradoxically, this ignorance was a blessing for the vitality of political imagination.[3] It also made it easier than it had been for older Left political formations to join quotidian political practice to a radical political vision; and, more generally, as in the case of the student movements for civil rights and against the war in Vietnam, to be radical.

There was a deeply ironical aspect to this state of affairs. The reality of the Soviet model – of a live alternative that seemed at least to negate, if not necessarily to improve upon, features of the American model that leftists opposed – created a space for the New Left's political vision. But it was the (partly) willful disregard of that model that made the radicalism of the New Left possible. For insofar as New Leftists looked to the real world of politics for inspiration, it was not to the conservative and bureaucratized Soviet Union that they turned (even if, as in Italy or France, a significant minority of them were still nominally communists). It was to the Third World and to China or, rather, to a certain (largely fanciful) idea of these then little known parts of the world.

New Left 'third worldism' was highly selective. One reason it was is that the idea of a Third World, though pervasive, was never very clear. It is still not possible to say exactly what the Third World was supposed to be. For some, it was the 'nonaligned' world, the countries that were not entirely integrated into either the American or Soviet systems through overt military alliances or treaties.[4] More commonly, the Third World was just the underdeveloped world. But 'underdevelopment' was and is a contested notion; and it is far from clear that it can serve to construct a category into which all putatively Third World countries fit. The problem is that the countries that everyone agreed comprise the Third World are too unalike with respect to levels and types of development.[5] What sense does it make to group a comparatively rich country like

Argentina, with its substantial middle class and highly educated citizenry, with a desperately poor country like Haiti, where, apart from a tiny elite, nearly everyone who is not part of the urban sub-proletariat is a subsistence farmer? Yet, according to the then standard view, both were part of the Third World; they were therefore categorized together.

Nevertheless, the idea of a Third World loomed large in the minds of many on the New Left, and in the Third World itself. It functioned as a geopolitical analogue to the pre-Revolutionary Third Estate, the vast majority of the French 'nation' who, lacking the rights or privileges of the first two estates, the aristocracy and the clergy, and suffering under the burdens of endemic poverty and oppression, nevertheless asserted themselves on the world stage in a revolutionary rupture with the Old Regime. By doing away with the privileges of the first two estates (along with many of their privileged members!), the Revolution turned the Third Estate into the nation. It was imagined, by some, that another revolution would soon take place on a global level; and that, in consequence, 'the international working class would become the human race', as proclaimed in the *Internationale,* the anthem of the entire revolutionary Left. It was in this sense too that, in New Left thinking, the Third World intruded into the First; as when, for example, the civil rights movement became transformed, in some peoples' minds, into a struggle for black liberation.

It was clear, though, even at the time, that the Third World seldom lived up to expectations, except perhaps in unsustainable heroic moments during anticolonial or national liberation struggles. There was hardly any thought, in Third World precincts, of moving beyond the forms of life achieved in the First or Second Worlds, and there were no sustained attempts at doing so. Instead, industrialization or, rather, *development* – catching up with the first two worlds – was and continues to be the normative principle undergirding forms of societal organization in Third World countries. For a variety of reasons, both historical and political, most of the countries of the Third World did remain at least partly outside either the American or Soviet ambit, especially with respect to military entanglements. In part for this reason, but also because their histories and circumstances were so different, these countries developed social orders that were neither quite American nor quite Soviet in form. But even in the Third World, the American and Soviet models functioned as regulative ideals, imperfectly realized but still dominating views about possible developmental trajectories.

Thus, the conventional wisdom was still that there were essentially two paths to follow. Either developing countries might join the world system of states that follow the American model – attracting foreign investments in agricultural and extractive industries and, then, with improvements in communications and transport, sometimes in manufacturing too (relying on the United States and other First World countries to supply a market for their goods). Or they might pursue a strategy of rapid, autochthonous growth through central planning and related economic policies derived from the Soviet experience after 1917. Until well into the 1970s, the latter model was favored, especially in Africa and parts of Asia, where, for historical reasons, American influence was comparatively weak. The reason why was not always that Soviet influence was strong. It was because it was believed that the Soviet Union had industrialized at an astonishing pace, and because the leaders of newly independent nations wanted to keep both the United States and their former colonial masters at bay. For this latter purpose, it was useful to have a Soviet card to play. Openness towards the Soviet Union – and imitation of its developmental model – often followed. But with the decline of the Soviet Union and then with its demise, the Soviet strategy for economic development fell into disrepute. Then, just as the idea that there is no alternative to American institutions has come to predominate elsewhere, the developmental model favored by the United States nowadays reigns even in those parts of the formerly insurgent Third World that the New Left most admired.

What mattered to New Left militants, however, was not development per se, though they had no quarrel with that objective. What drew the New Left to the Third World was the thought of the people in struggle – for their own liberation. Vietnam was the paradigm. It was widely believed that the potential for other Vietnams (for 'two, three, many', as Che Guavara famously said) existed throughout the Third World and, by extension, among ostensible Third World peoples in the First World. It was this prospect that fired the imagination.

In retrospect, though, just as it was never clear what the Third World was, it was never clear what 'liberation' meant either. But the nature of its appeal was plain. It was the vague but compelling notion that enthused the revolutionary movements of the seventeenth through the twentieth centuries. It had two components – the one democratic, the other 'rationalist' (in the sense sketched in Chapter 1). The democratic idea was that the people themselves should take their own affairs in hand, that they should shake off the domination of their former masters and rule themselves. The rationalist idea was to build a new and better, more rational, world on the ashes of the old. For (revolution-friendly) socialists, these aspirations were intimately joined; within the (anti-revolutionary) liberal tradition, they were severed. Liberals, including those who were also genuine democrats, were ill disposed towards those who wanted to overthrow and reconstruct 'Old Regimes'. Thus many New Leftists came to think of liberalism as an obstacle to liberation. This perception was enhanced by the fact that the Vietnam War, which soon became the principal focus of New Left attention, especially (but not only) in the United States, was initiated and waged, at first, by political leaders of an impeccably liberal stamp, and that it was facilitated and sustained by the most liberal sector of civil society – the institution with which, as it happened, most New Left militants were intimately involved, the university.

In the seventeenth-century English revolutions, where the Church, the Crown and the landed aristocracy were the targets, these aspirations, following ancient demotic precedents, took on a puritanical form. In one way or another, puritanical asceticism and seriousness marked all subsequent revolutionary ventures. Contrary to what is widely believed, the New Left was no exception. In the 1960s and 1970s, imperialism and racism were the targets – not clerical, aristocratic, or royalist domination. But the zealotry of the Puritans, Jacobins and Bolsheviks survived, even in this middle-class environment, nurtured in the liberal democratic West. The Vietnamese waging armed struggle against American domination were the model; the idea, according to a slogan of the time, was 'to live like them'.

But, of course, this is not the side of the New Left that is etched in the popular imagination. Today, the New Left is thought to have been a fountain of reckless and willful self-indulgence. In part, this perception exists because the New Left and the so-called 'counter-culture' are often confounded in historical memory. But there was a sense in which New Left puritanism genuinely did meld with licence in personal behavior. In the minds of some militants, this paradoxical combination of attitudes rose to the level of principle. It was not just a question of attacking the regime by shocking 'bourgeois' sensibilities. Rather, the idea was that the liberation of desire went hand in hand with more traditional emancipatory projects, and therefore with political styles inherited from earlier periods.[6]

* * *

In retrospect, perhaps it was not a bad thing that the virtues of the Vietnamese and others struggling for national liberation were exaggerated. Partly in consequence of this mistaken perception, a palpable wariness of imperialist ventures has become a permanent legacy of New Left politics. In the United States, there were sustained attempts to overcome 'the Vietnam syndrome' even before the presidencies of Reagan and the first Bush. These efforts accelerated during the Clinton era, and they have become emblematic of the foreign policy and military establishments under George W. Bush. But, even in the present political climate, it is hard to mobilize support at home for imperialist ventures. For Americans today to support or at least not oppose the use of military power abroad, it is not only necessary that U.S. troops incur few, if any, casualties; more importantly, it is imperative that the targets be easily and successfully demonized. What the Vietnam War taught the political class and the military in the United States is not that they cannot win Vietnam Wars, much less that it is wrong to try. The lesson they have taken to heart is that they cannot have Vietnamese for enemies. The New Left romanticized the Vietnamese. But not even today's media, with all its means for manufacturing consent, could have made the Vietnamese look like worthy targets of what used to be called 'humanitarian interventions', and now goes by the name of 'the war on terror'. Another permanent advance seems to have registered with respect to racism – to its appearance certainly, but also to its reality – particularly when it is directed against peoples in whom the white New Left took a special interest (for both anti-imperialist and antiracist reasons): persons of African, Asian and Latin American descent in North America and Europe, and indigenous populations in the Americas and Australasia.

Even so, it must be said that, to some degree, New Left third worldism was based on an illusion, in much the way that the religious zeal that motivated the original Puritans was. As remarked (in the Introduction), an 'illusion', in Freud's sense of the term, is a belief elicited and maintained by unconscious desires, irrespective of evidential support. It was in this sense that, in *The Future of an*

Illusion, Freud argued that theism is an illusion, one that is excep-
tionally difficult to dislodge because of the depth and tenacity of the
psychological processes that sustain it. A delusion, on the other
hand, is a belief held, perhaps for similar reasons, but in flagrant
opposition to the truth. In these terms, the New Left's glorification
of national liberation struggles was more illusional than delusional.
Or, rather, it had illusional elements – for there genuinely were
aspects of the Vietnamese struggle that were known and that were
worthy of unequivocal esteem. But what matters more than the
merits or shortcomings of peoples struggling against imperial
domination is the fact that the faith New Leftists vested in the
Vietnamese and others in struggle was grounded on an analysis of
the dynamics of capitalist economies drawn from Marxist sources.
The New Left was an anti-imperialist movement. As sectors of it
matured, this aspect of its politics became increasingly salient. Thus
it spawned significant, clearheaded solidarity movements that
continue to this day. Any sound anti-imperialist politics must be
grounded, ultimately, in an overall political vision and strategy; not
on an assessment, justified or not, of the virtues of the victims of the
system. New Left politics encouraged the development of such an
outlook. At its best, it achieved it to some degree. But, even so, the
enthusiasm national liberation struggles elicited in New Left
militants – in all of them, some of the time; and in some of them,
the vast majority, all of the time – was largely, though not entirely,
an expression of a wish.

*   *   *

Cuba inspired many New Leftists, especially in the United States,
where, almost immediately after its revolution, it was demonized in
the mainstream culture, thereby assuming the mantle of the enemy's
enemy. It therefore became incumbent on New Leftists to defend it.
It is significant too that the Cuban Revolution was at high tide in
just the period when the New Left was coming of age. Many took
notice of how the Cubans emphasized moral, not material,
incentives for work. And many were impressed by the degree to
which internationalism became a fact of life in revolutionary Cuba
– not just in theory, but also in practice; and not just in Latin
America, but in Africa as well. However Cuba was a nearby and tiny
island nation. Thus it could hardly be a model, in the way that the
Soviet Union once was, nor could it serve as a tabula rasa onto which

(unconscious) desires could be projected. It was too well known. Even the most naive New Leftists realized that, however admirable the Cuban Revolution might be, it hardly presented an alternative to the Soviet model. The anti-imperialist New Left supported it, but seldom identified with it wholeheartedly.

China, on the other hand, was a significant pole of attraction. Anti-imperialist purity attached to Western perceptions of China in this period; a condition that undoubtedly explains much of its appeal. In this instance, ignorance was indispensable; China took on almost mythic proportions because it was unknown. No doubt, self-deception was unavoidable in this case. For the entire life span of the New Left, China was all but cut off from the rest of the world. It was therefore easy to maintain illusions about it – to imagine a country comprising almost a quarter of the world's population, single-mindedly taking its own affairs in hand, and resolutely building a new and better world on the ashes of the old.

It was also significant, especially in countries like France or Italy with important Communist Parties, that being pro-Chinese was a way not to be a communist, without being anticommunist. A more authentically Leninist way was to become a Trotskyist. But the Trotskyists had no country. Nevertheless, Trotskyism was a pole of attraction for some of the most politically committed New Left militants. By its nature, though, Trotskyism appealed mainly to those with a taste for doctrinal disputation. Thus the Marxist movement in those days resembled Western Christianity in the early modern period. There was the Church that had the best or, at least, the most obvious claim on apostolic succession, the Church of Rome. But then there were rival Churches that claimed legitimacy for themselves in the same way, depicting the Pope as the Antichrist. In the English-speaking world, the Church of England was the best known example, though by no means the only one. Finally, there were the rival Protestant sects that effectively denied the idea of apostolic succession, claiming legitimacy for their own theologies on biblical grounds. The official Communist Parties were like the Roman Catholics, and the Maoists like the Church of England. They each claimed to be the legitimate successors of the regime installed by the Bolshevik Revolution. The Trotskyists, on the other hand, based their claims for legitimacy on the fact that, more than any of the others, they were faithful to classical Marxism and Leninism. But having no one Church, they were inclined to fragment into countless denominations. Thus they were the true Protestants of middle- and late twentieth century Marxism. It is therefore surprising that the Trotskyists were, for the most part, marginal to New Left politics. It seems that, despite their vaunted raucousness, New Leftists tended to be 'High Church'. But the former Church universal, the Soviet Union, was thoroughly associated with old Lefts of various kinds. By the mid-1960s, it was also known by everyone who was not a communist, and by some who were, to be in an advanced stage of decrepitude. Many New Leftists therefore felt they had nowhere but China to turn to for inspiration. They fell into Maoism, or rather into a Maoism of their own imagination, *faute de mieux*.

There was, however, more to New Left flirtations with Maoism than wishful thinking. At an ideological level, the Chinese really did pose a partial exception to the Cold War consensus view. China, or at least the China of its own self-representations, challenged the Soviet model, while remaining steadfast in its opposition to anything that smacked of its American rival. According to their own account, the Chinese put 'politics in command'; in other words, they subordinated the task of economic development to the larger project of revolutionizing life. In its fine points, this thought was lost on most of those New Left militants who, in the late 1960s and early 1970s, identified, in one or another way, with the Great Proletarian Cultural Revolution. For the vast majority, the idea was only that the Chinese somehow made cultural practices political; a thought that coincided with the notion that 'the personal is political'. But there was at least the germ of a new idea in perceptions of Maoism, for those who had eyes to see it. Althusser was one who did. It was a signal achievement of the New Left that he was not alone.

We now know, however, that the China the New Left admired, and that Althusser and others turned to in developing their own ideas, existed mainly in the minds of its defenders; that the Chinese never really implemented a new organizational principle for industrializing or industrialized societies. Instead, Mao and his cothinkers developed an innovative strategy for seizing power in agrarian societies with large peasant populations. Revolutionary movements throughout the Third World adapted elements of this strategy. So too did a few political groupings in the nonrevolutionary West – in countries where the peasantry was either vanishing, long gone or, as in the United States, where it had never existed at all. For the most part, the consequences of Maoism in Asia were tragic; one need only recall the fate of Cambodia under the Khmer Rouge. In the West, Maoism was never more than a marginal phenomenon. But because the fascination with China was mostly illusory – because it rested on beliefs sustained by desires, not on evidence – and because the applicability of these illusions to real-world conditions in the West was so implausible, none of it struck very deep. It was the perceived radicalism of the Chinese, not the institutions the Chinese concocted, that moved China's supporters. In practice, therefore, being pro-Chinese seldom meant more than being defiant and uncompromising. Thus the vast majority of students who carried the Little Red Book in those days or who had posters of Chairman Mao on their walls cannot be said to have identified with China in the way that important segments of the Left had once identified with the Soviet Union. When communist China's nature stood revealed, the Maoist allegiances that so many professed dropped away, abruptly and (very nearly) painlessly. Today, the Maoist challenge to the conventional wisdom of the Cold War period is virtually without resonance. This is all the more true now that China combines a Stalinist political structure with a passion for markets, private property, and foreign investments. The desuetude into which Maoism has fallen is unfortunate, inasmuch as the Chinese variant of the second model, the idea if not the reality, has merit – a fact that Althusser, for one, was able to exploit, as we will see. But, like so much else in our political culture, its passing has become a fact of political life.

*   *   *

According to the conventional wisdom, the New Left is joined inextricably with 'the Sixties', which is joined, in turn, with the 'counterculture' and therefore, for the high minded, with the rejection of consumer society and managerial liberalism, and for others, the vast majority, with sex, drugs and rock and roll. Of course, it is the former connection that bears most pertinently on Marxism. But these associations melded together, even at the time; and until this morass of historical memory is sorted out, it is impossible to reflect constructively on the place of the New Left in the history of the Left generally, or to come to terms with the thought that the New Left might indeed be the last Left. There is just enough that is sound in the conventional wisdom that sifting through it would be a major undertaking. It should suffice, though, to advance some general observations, the soundness of which, though seldom recognized, should be obvious, once stated.

First, as regards 'the Sixties', it is relevant to note that, at least in the United States, for the first part of the decade, a right-wing movement of the young – a New Right, as it were – was perhaps as influential in shaping political life, even among youth, as the burgeoning New Left was. Thus one of the most astute political journalists of the time, Murray Kempton, wrote contemporaneously: 'We must assume that the conservative revival is *the* youth movement of the '60s'.[7] It was not until the Vietnam War intensified and its impact became clear, around 1965, that the majority of politicized youth mobilized unequivocally around causes associated historically with the Left.[8] It should also be recalled that what we now think of as 'the Sixties' was as much a phenomenon of the (early) 1970s as of the decade from which it takes its name. For political theory, especially of a Marxist stamp, the 1970s was, by far, the more important decade.

In any case, 'the Sixties' has come to designate the so-called counterculture, and it is a mistake to identify the counterculture with the New Left. It is true that when New Left militants succeeded in mobilizing students and other young people, it was because their politics struck a chord that resonated throughout the segment of their generation that was, in some degree, in cultural revolt. But only a small portion of that larger mass was seriously politicized, let alone committed to the New Left in an organizational way. The counterculture, such as it was, seldom manifested itself politically; it concerned mores and values instead. Moreover, it never ran very deep. Even its sex, drugs and rock and roll were absorbed, in short order, into mainstream consumer society and rendered innocuous. Still, at the time, the counterculture seemed to mark a break from the past. Many, though hardly all, New Leftists identified with it – at least as much as others in their generational cohort did. For a while too, the mass of students and young people were content to let the New Left be its political expression. Thus New Left militants were able to coopt countercultural themes and put them to use in mobilizing large numbers of people who were not otherwise politically engaged. In a sense, then, the New Left made itself the political vanguard of a larger cultural and generational phenomenon. But despite this overlap, and despite what many believed then and now, the New Left and the counterculture always remained distinct. The counterculture was never really a political movement, much less a 'subversive' force associated with the historical Left.

There were, however, influential thinkers associated with the New Left who thought otherwise. As noted, the best known and most influential was Herbert Marcuse.[9] Marcuse seemed to believe that the counterculture revived the prospect of social revolution in the West; that, for the first time since the opportunities opened up by World War I and the Bolshevik Revolution had passed, it put revolution back on the agenda. To be sure, he never quite articulated this view explicitly, nor did he defend it directly; in his published writings especially, it was more intimated than argued for. But, for a time, those who heard Marcuse speak, and those who read his work looking for what they wanted to find, did conclude that he thought that countercultural youth had become an agent of fundamental social change. Again, it is not clear whether Marcuse really believed this. The pessimism of a lifetime led in the shadow of the failure of the Germans and other Central and Eastern Europeans to continue what the Russians began after World War I, and then the experience of fascism, militated against faith in the revolutionary prospect. Perhaps this is why Marcuse never fully explained or defended the view often ascribed to him, and why he never espoused it expressly. But it is a position towards which his thinking gravitated. Two related rationales for subscribing to it can be imputed to him and to those who drew on his work.

The first rested on a tacit acceptance of prevailing views of the nature of modern economies. By the mid-1960s, everyone, as Richard Nixon would later say, was a Keynesian. Despite his reputation as the godfather of a generation in revolt, Marcuse was no exception. His view of the way the world worked was roughly of a piece with the left wing of the Keynesian consensus. He thought, following Keynes, that modern industrial economies suffer from excess productive capacity. Thanks to economic development, the potential supply of most of the things people are prepared to buy exceeds the demand for those things – not in the sense that no one needs or wants more, but in the sense that, given existing budget constraints, consumers are unable to purchase all that can be produced. Thus there is a chronic problem: capitalism requires investments in new productive capacities, but productive capacity is already too large to absorb additional investments. However, without outlets for investment, the economy will fall into a depression and remain fixed there, with all the attendant human costs and political risks. The Keynesian solution was to boost effective demand through public spending.[10]

Orthodox Keynesians would do so through state fiscal policies, especially public works financed, if need be, by deficit spending. Keynes himself was keen on public investment in housing, especially council flats for workers. In the United States, in part because of the prosperity brought on by the expansion of military production during World War II, and in part because it was politically unfeasible for the state to compete openly with private capital, so-called 'military Keynesianism' came to be the reigning view – seldom described in those terms (except by its critics), but relentlessly practiced. Military spending boosted effective demand by turning the state into a purchaser of weapons and other goods and services necessary for sustaining a large military force. As critics pointed out at the time, military Keynesianism is dangerous inasmuch as whoever has the means for war is tempted to put those means to use; it threatens the peace. It is also wasteful in the sense that it spends public monies on items that will never be used (unless war breaks out), and in ways that are generally less effective for advancing prosperity than other forms of public expenditure. Building bridges or roads – or council flats – improves an economy's infrastructure; it enhances business activity generally. Buying weapons is a much less efficient means to that end. Nevertheless, according to the common sense of the time, accepted on both the Left and the Right, even military Keynesianism was effective for keeping the specter of depression at bay. It therefore fulfilled a functional requirement of the economic system in a way made necessary by the political context in which it operated. Like others on the Left, Marcuse was a critic of military spending. But he imagined it was inevitable, so long as the system remained unchanged.

Perhaps this is why Marcuse's main targets were non-state means for boosting effective demand. He was especially opposed to the ways that businesses inculcate unnecessary and ultimately irrational needs for consumer goods. Implicitly, therefore, he joined that strain of contemporaneous social criticism that took aim at modern advertising, along with other means for stirring up 'false' or unnecessary wants – for example, by building planned obsolescence into consumer goods.[11] These plaints struck a chord with rebellious young militants born into an increasingly ubiquitous consumer culture. Marcuse invoked this sensibility in the august but obscure idiom of the Frankfurt School. Thus he brought the prestige of classical German philosophy – indeed, of Marxist philosophy – to bear in behalf of what was, at the time, a not uncommon critique of the inauthenticity of life in consumer society.

It is not surprising, therefore, that, for a while, hippies, along with less extreme members of their generational cohort, could seem to be in revolt against consumer society, especially when many of them said that they were. It is not far-fetched either to suppose that this revolt posed a challenge to the prevailing order. The call was to 'drop out'. But what there was to drop out from was the imperative of relentless consumption, the ostensible motor of economic development in late capitalist societies. Thus the counterculture seemed to be a cog in the wheel of the economic structure. Ironically, of course, consumer society – and even advertising – came to absorb this challenge, and to turn it to its own advantage. The counterculture was quickly coopted into the consumer society. As this became increasingly clear, those who would continue the Marcusean project could only become even more conspicuously outrageous, as a few hardy souls attempted. The vast majority effectively joined the enemy by collapsing into its fold.

But there was more than consumerism to drop out of. There was managerial society itself. The constituency from which both the counterculture and the New Left drew was, for the most part, privileged and young. It was therefore comprised, in part, of persons in training to assume elite positions in society. For large numbers of such individuals to drop out of that (preordained) future was worrisome to existing elites. If the process went too far, it could pose a challenge to the regime's ability to reproduce itself. Dropping out could therefore be construed, as it was at the time, as a 'great refusal', a rejection of the pillars of the existing order. It was not uncommon to invest it with portentous significance, as Marcuse and those who thought like him did.

The other side of the coin was of far greater moment to the future of Marxism. It was the idea, also consistent with mainstream thinking, that the working class, the agent of radical social transformation in traditional socialist theory, had become 'integrated' into the existing order. Partly thanks to victories won by the labor movement, and partly due to changes in the nature of work itself, it had *dropped in* – inserting itself into the existing order, thereby gaining a stake in its perpetuation. That the working class in the West was not revolutionary was beyond dispute. For all but the most doctrinaire, it was no longer even, strictly speaking, a proletariat, a class with 'nothing to lose but its chains'. As remarked, this stubborn fact posed a challenge to the socialist project, and especially to Marxism. It rendered the notion that the agent of social change must be in civil society but not of it – that, like the bourgeoisie in the French Revolution, it must take control at a political level of a society it already effectively constitutes – increasingly untenable. In these circumstances, the move that Marcuse and others made was a last desperate attempt at finding a revolutionary agent in Western societies. If the existing order no longer produced its own 'gravediggers' in the way that Marx thought it did, then its gravediggers must be willed into being. Otherwise, an indefinite capitalist future awaits – a future of totalitarian repression, if all goes badly, or of 'the American dream' turned nightmare, if all goes better; of barbarism or inauthenticity and pervasive alienation.

This Marcusean argument is of a piece with the New Left's third worldism. Third World liberation struggles were supposed to be peasant revolutions writ large. And just as, in Maoist strategic thought, the countryside, the peasants, would surround and eventually conquer the urban centers, the Third World would surround the First, bringing the revolution 'back home'. Therefore, even without a revolutionary proletariat, revolution was not off the agenda in the West. But to make it a live prospect, the impetus would have to come from *outside*; from agents at its peripheries (including perhaps Third World communities within the metropolitan centers). It was never quite clear just how Third World insurgents were to become agents of revolutionary change in the West. Perhaps their role was only to create conditions in which the working class would come to resist integration and resume its former, historic role. In any case, what Marcuse and his cothinkers maintained was that, in addition to Third World insurgents, there was yet another force positively affecting the prospects for revolution. That force was not comprised of individuals or groups involuntarily excluded from the benefits of the system in place. It was made up, instead, of privileged individuals, mostly young, who excluded themselves; not just in the traditional way of intellectuals or other revolutionaries of bourgeois origin, by siding with their class enemies, but by 'dropping out' altogether. In short, just as the working class was becoming increasingly integrated into the existing order, its functional equivalent was taking shape within the ranks of those who benefitted from its exploitation. A remarkable irony of history was unfolding.

For the most part, though, all this was beside the point for the masses of students and others whom the New Left mobilized. It was not exactly that the majority didn't care about political strategies or visions of a better world, or that they were indifferent to the choice between a socialist alternative to barbarism, on the one hand, and a nominally free but alienated existence, on the other. It was rather that, for the vast majority, these were remote and therefore secondary concerns. Most of the people who were active politically in that period, especially in the United States, were set in motion by the war in Vietnam. Their opposition to the war and to policies and institutions connected with it was a consequence of their awareness of the rank immorality of what the U.S. government and military were doing in Southeast Asia. Political analyses of any kind, Marcusean or otherwise, therefore had less to do with their radicalization than most theoretically minded activists, at the time, supposed. But the analyses Marcuse and the others provided were consistent with the majority's perceptions, and the majority, in turn, did not object to the arguments of their more theoretically minded comrades. Thus it came to pass, for a short time, that the view just sketched – or some vague approximation of it – gripped a sizeable oppositional force, that it spoke to their lived experience, as Marx said radical theory must if it is to be effective at all.[12] But then, as opposition to the Vietnam War was taken up by persons of all ages and social strata, the antiwar movement drifted away from – or, rather, left behind – the cultural base with which it is still associated in the popular imagination. In short order, the so-called counter-culture lost even the semblance of being, in any way, subversive. The moment in which political theory and 'cultural revolution' coalesced passed. Shortly thereafter, the New Left itself effectively disappeared.

*   *   *

The ideas that registered along the way were of small moment in their own right. Even Marcuse's work seems, in retrospect, an exercise in wishful thinking. But Marcuse's analysis brought to the fore a fact that could hardly be denied by the time he set it out, and that is impossible to deny today. That fact is that the agent of social change in the Marxist scheme, the proletariat, has gone missing; that if there ever was a class with 'radical chains', as Marx had put it, a class in society but not of it, whose emancipation was tantamount to the emancipation of all of humankind, it now no longer exists.

The New Left, by its nature and composition, attested to this reality. To be sure, it had 'workerist' components. But it had few real ties to the working class, even in countries, like Italy or France, where the majority of workers were much less integrated than in the United States, and where the working class had political parties of its own.

The episodes in Marxist philosophy that emerged during or after the period of the New Left's rise and fall reflect this reality in telling ways. They represent efforts to maintain a Marxist theoretical framework in a world without a proletariat. This is not *ipso facto* an incoherent project. But neither is it an undertaking guaranteed to succeed. But the future of Marxism depends on its success. So too does an answer to the question posed at the outset: whether the New Left was in fact the last Left, an exuberant but doomed expression of a long-standing, glorious, partially successful, but now defunct endeavor, or whether it was just the most recent node in a long and still unfolding chain, leading, as its proponents have always hoped, to the full-fledged emancipation of the human race.

In Part II, I argue that the problem of an absent proletariat is not as intractable as may appear. More precisely, I argue that the analytical Marxists' defense of scientific socialism suggests ways in which some of Marxism's core theoretical insights – and the political program they underwrite – can survive even the disappearance of the class in whose interests Marxists invested their hopes for a communist future. The New Left was the first Left to encounter this problem head on. It grappled with it valiantly and ultimately foundered on it. But its possible successors need not meet a similar fate.

*   *   *

Why does the New Left matter for philosophy? To begin to answer this question, it will help to connect these reflections on its trajectory with some of the points registered in the Introduction and Chapter 1. It is especially instructive to do so at this point, before turning to Althusserian and analytical Marxist philosophy, because these new philosophical departures only make sense in light of what made the New Left new. In relation to the various old Lefts that preceded its emergence, two features stand out. There was, first of all, its romanticism, epitomized by its glorification of Third World liberation struggles and its sympathies with a certain idea of Chinese communism. And, then, there was its effort to adapt Marxism to a world without a genuine proletariat. New Left romanticism was succeeded, inevitably, by disillusionment. Partly in consequence, Marxism, or rather the versions of it that New Leftists embraced, beat a hasty retreat back into the academy – only to become transformed into something entirely different or else to fall into a nearly total eclipse. This is why, in recent years, the ambient culture of university life, much more than the exigencies of involvements with social movements or political parties, has conditioned Marxism's fate. But the academicization of Marxism occurred against the background of the ineluctable fact, already evident in New Left politics and in the philosophies it helped to shape, that the world had taken a turn that neither Marx nor any of his close followers ever imagined – that, confounding all expectations, the proletariat had melted away. A proper appreciation of this state of affairs is indispensable for understanding the character of Althusserian and analytical Marxism, and for speculating on Marxism's future and the role the legacy of these philosophical ventures might play in it.

The task Marxist philosophy assumed in the last half of the twentieth century was to discover the authentic core of Marxist theory, and then to reconstruct Marxism on that basis. This is not unequivocally what Marxist philosophers of earlier periods understood their own task to be. Many of them, including the most radical among them, thought that their project was to express the 'world view' of a class with 'radical chains' – in other words, to produce a *proletarian* philosophy. But it was clear by the time the New Left emerged, for reasons that have nothing to do with philosophy and everything to do with the ways the world has changed, that this was not – or not any longer – a plausible objective. If Marxists were to lead socialism to triumph, they would have to articulate a new role for Marxist theory. In effect, and without quite realizing it, this was what Althusser and the analytical Marxists did. By their own lights – and in the eyes of the larger intellectual culture – they failed in this endeavor. Wittingly or not, however, they laid foundations upon which others might succeed.

Conclusion to Part I

It will be helpful to draw together the main strands of the story so far. In broad outline, the main points are these:

1. Throughout the modern period, but especially after the French Revolution, there has existed a political Left, wedded to an idea of progress that is, at root, democratic and egalitarian. Its goals, expressed in the language of the revolutionary traditions from which it sprang, are liberty, equality and fraternity (or community); and its fundamental commitment is to democracy – to government of, by and for the people. Fortunately, for the vast majority of the world's inhabitants, the Left has helped to shape the politics of the past two centuries. In the past quarter century, however, it has been in plain retreat. This state of affairs works to the detriment of political life everywhere. There are many signs of revival. But the way forward is less clear than it used to seem. Left constituencies nowadays know what they are *against*; they are much less sure of what they are *for*.

2. Since the beginning of the nineteenth century, the Left has been composed of liberal and socialist wings. The liberal wing took on its distinctive political orientation in reaction to the radicalness of the French Revolution. In contrast, the socialist wing faulted the French Revolution only for the respects in which it was incomplete or, in other words, insufficiently radical.

3. Liberal politics is essentially reformist. It aims at correcting problems arising in existing social and political structures by imposing solutions from above. Thus, it tends to be gradualist and ill disposed to fundamental structural transformations. Despite its roots, it is therefore susceptible to making common cause with forms of conservatism that also took shape in reaction to the French Revolution. This possibility has been realized more often than not. This is why, despite its affinities with socialism, liberalism has frequently served as a political philosophy of the Center or Center-Right, not the Left – especially in twentieth-century liberal democracies.

4. While socialism can be reformist too, its guiding principle is to transform society as a whole. Socialists aim to construct a new world order based on rationally compelling principles. In this sense, they are rationalists in politics.

5. The rationalism implicit in socialist politics derives, in part, from its prorevolutionary orientation. Revolutionaries aim to overthrow existing structures in order to reconstruct society on rationally defensible foundations. Historically, then, socialism was revolutionary because it was rationalist, and rationalist because it was revolutionary. Marxism, which came to be the overwhelmingly dominant strain of socialist ideology, epitomizes this mutually reinforcing combination of positions.

6. Marxists, from the beginning advanced two related claims: that human history is moved along by processes that make a socialist (and eventually communist) future possible; and that, in the current historical period, the proletariat, a class in civil society but not of it, is the agent of socialist transformation. The latter contention, but not the former, has been made untenable by events that no 'classical' Marxist foresaw, but that no one nowadays can deny. In consequence, it has become unclear how much, if anything, that is fundamental and distinctive in the Marxist or larger socialist tradition can be retained; in other words, how much of 'classical' Marxism can survive the absence of a genuine proletariat.

7. The New Left effectively acquiesced to the fact of the proletariat's absence, but without relinquishing the revolutionary impulse emblematic of the socialist tradition, and without giving up other socialist goals either. It therefore sought to find new agents of revolutionary transformation – in Third World liberation struggles, in (some) communist societies (especially China), and in the so-called counterculture. But its efforts were based, mostly, on wishful thinking, and were ultimately in vain.

And, finally,

8. It is an open question what the future of Marxism – and also of socialism and of the Left generally – will be. Was the New Left the last Left or did it represent a step forward towards the full installation of liberty, equality and fraternity? This question cannot now be answered with finality. But a purchase on it can be obtained by reflecting on the New Left's rise and fall, and on the ways it affected Marxist philosophy.

*   *   *

I will go on to argue that some findings of Althusserian and especially analytical Marxist philosophy – particularly those that undergird the idea of a scientific socialism or that follow from it – make it possible to retrieve and develop distinctively Marxist ideas, even in a world without a 'classical' proletariat. This may not suffice to assure a future for Marxism. That prospect depends on historical and sociological factors that defy reckoning. But the socialist project – whether or not it is pursued under a Marxist banner in the years ahead – will suffer considerable, perhaps even irreversible, harm should the lessons of Althusser and the analytical Marxists become unlearned or lost.

New Left militants were attracted, perhaps too much, to the romantic–revolutionary side of the socialist tradition. Correspondingly, they were inclined to minimize its rationalist side. It was therefore comparatively easy, for those who had passed through the New Left crucible and whose faith in the revolutionary prospect lapsed, to jettison the entire socialist idea. This outcome, an effect of the recent and, one hopes, temporary exhaustion of political imagination, is politically disastrous, for reasons that become increasingly apparent day by day. It is also unnecessary. For it is possible, without illusions, to reappropriate and build on Marxism's determination to forge a rational social order. Unwittingly, Althusserian Marxism points the way. So too, more trenchantly, does analytical Marxism. This is not the lesson most of the erstwhile practitioners of these nearly defunct philosophical departures came to endorse. But it is implicit in what they accomplished.

Part II

Introduction to Part II: Historicist Marxism

Despite their differences, Althusserian and analytical Marxism shared a common enemy – historicism. Marxist philosophy had always been, to some degree, historicist. This is not surprising inasmuch as Hegel's philosophy was one of Marxism's sources; and Hegel, more than anyone, brought historicist thinking into its own. To oppose historicism, from within a Marxist ambit, was therefore to set off on a new course. It was also, one might suppose, to oppose Hegelian elements in Marxist thought. This supposition is not mistaken. But it is misleading. As we will see, the philosophical bearing of Hegel's work, particularly in Althusser's philosophy, is more complicated than first appears. We will find too that Hegelian philosophy shares certain affinities with the thinking of analytical Marxists. It is therefore better to say that what Althusserian and analytical Marxism opposed was not exactly Hegelianism as such, but historicism, a way of thinking that Hegelian philosophy underwrote and encouraged.

To say precisely what historicism is would be a daunting task, partly because the idea resists clear formulation, and partly because there are so many versions of the doctrine – in the larger intellectual culture and in Marxist circles as well. To examine the various, not always compatible, rationales that motivate these strains of thinking would amplify the difficulty manyfold. But there is no need to take on this burden here, inasmuch as the reason for venturing into this matter at all is only to provide a context for the discussions that follow. For this purpose, it will suffice to sketch, in broad outline, what historicist Marxism is – emphasizing large historical and philosophical themes, not fine-grained philosophical positions. Questions pertaining to how historicist Marxism might be defended or attacked will be broached only insofar as they are pertinent to conveying a sense of what it was that Althusserian and analytical Marxists were *against*.

Because both Althusserian and analytical Marxism represented themselves, initially, as efforts to defend Marxist orthodoxy, and because that orthodoxy was steeped in historicist thinking, practitioners of these philosophical tendencies were loathe to acknowledge their common enemy expressly. It was not that they were disingenuous. Rather, given the ambivalence towards traditional Marxism that was such a palpable feature of each of these new departures in Marxist thought, a clear conception of what they each opposed never quite emerged. It should also be said that the idea that historicism itself was the enemy, rather than particular features of earlier strains of Marxist philosophy, never quite registered unambiguously either to Althusser or to the analytical Marxists. Thus one looks in vain for direct attacks on historicism in writings emanating from these quarters. But even if neither philosophical movement was antihistoricist in a consistent and thoroughgoing way, they were both, in their own ways, hostile to the dialectical method Hegel had developed. It was mainly in this context that they opposed the core intuition motivating historicists – the idea that what is the case and/or what can be known has an irreducible historical dimension.

*   *   *

The historicism Marxists endorsed was a creature of Hegelian philosophy, as it developed during and after Hegel's lifetime. Historicism did, of course, have antecedents in the centuries preceding Hegel's express development of the idea. It would not be far-fetched to say, for example, that those Protestant theologians who sought to ground the legitimacy of their faith – and their Church – on the vicissitudes of ecclesiastical history anticipated the historicist's principal idea. They claimed, in effect, that ecclesiastical legitimacy was relative to a Church's place in human (or sacred) history. Thus they introduced a certain notion of historical relativity, congenial to historicist thinking. But this was, at best, a pale approximation of what was to come. It was Hegel whose work had a seminal effect not just on theorists who identified with it, but also on those who opposed his views, and set their course by their opposition to them.

Throughout the nineteenth century and well into the twentieth, the Hegelians' main opponents were, of course, the *positivists*. By the time Marxism emerged on the scene, understandings of Hegelianism were shaped, in large part, by this rivalry. Positivism too had roots that antedate its official origins in nineteenth-century, anti-Hegelian thought. Thus early modern philosophers, like Descartes and Locke, who set out to discover a 'method' suitable for apprehending the nature of the real, anticipated the core positivist conviction that science alone yields genuine knowledge. Positivism was anticipated, even more clearly, in the efforts of Enlightenment *philosophes* to establish civil order on secular bases, sometimes in express opposition to the historical justifications advanced by ecclesiastical authorities. Still, on the whole, it is fair to say that neither historicist nor positivist views about history came to fruition before Hegel succeeded in formulating a genuinely historicist philosophy; and Auguste Comte, who gave positivism its name, reacted against it.

It is possible, in retrospect, to identify a number of features that all historicist positions of Hegelian provenance have in common. But it is not always possible to describe these positions without using metaphors or resorting to vague explications. The problem is not only that the idea is obscure. It is also that Hegel and his successors were frequently unclear as to whether their core convictions pertain to reality as such or only to human beings' way(s) of apprehending the real. The question, in short, is whether historicity, relativity to location in historical time, is a property of entities themselves, or of knowledge of them, or both. For Hegel, there was ultimately no difference. At the end of their developmental trajectories, the ontological and epistemological aspects of historicity converge. Because all there is is Mind or Spirit (*Geist)* becoming conscious of itself, the Real just is the Rational. But for historicist Marxists, the question cannot be answered this way. Marxists are, by their own account, 'materialists', not idealists. What materialism is is also contentious. But however that venerable metaphysical doctrine is construed, it always bears the implication that the object of knowledge, that which is known, is in principle independent of knowledge of it; that, *pace* Hegel and other idealists, the real is mind-independent. Therefore the question is posed: Is Marxist historicism a claim about the structure of (material) reality; or is it a claim about knowledge of the real? Or is it somehow both together? It is natural to suppose, following Hegel's lead, that it is the latter. But then Marxist historicists would have to join ontological and epistemo-logical questions together as Hegel did, but without reverting back to Hegel's idealism. This is an unlikely task; one that, not surpris-ingly, Marxist philosophers seldom addressed directly, and never succeeded in executing. Thus there is no clear, unequivocal answer to this question.

I have little more to say here about how, if at all, a genuinely historicist Marxism can be made cogent. It is not necessary to do so because, in order to convey a sense of what historicist Marxism is, there is no need to have an unproblematic version of it at hand. It is enough to list and briefly comment on some general features of Hegelian thinking that historicists, including putatively materialist ones, endorse. At the risk of misrepresenting some of these positions, I portray the items on this list as claims about *explanation*. This is the most cogent and least controversial way to represent Hegelian historicism (and also positivism). But, where it is appropriate, as it is with respect to the first of the features identified, I also indicate how these views suggest – and, in some cases, follow from – ontological positions, claims about the nature of the real. I also point out how positivism takes issue with Hegelianism's, and therefore historicism's, principal contentions.

*   *   *

It suffices to identify just a few areas of dispute:
    A. *Holism*. For Hegelians and therefore for historicists whose views derive from Hegel, to explain anything it is necessary somehow to invoke everything – because everything is related to everything else in a way that explanations must acknowledge. Adequate explanations therefore make reference not only to parts but also to wholes – by employing categories that imply the reality of the interconnectedness of all things. So understood, holism follows from the ontological claim that, in the final analysis, all is One – that everything that exists *expresses* a fundamental, underlying unity. Hegelian historicists therefore take issue, at least implicitly, with the Aristotelian idea, assumed by positivists, that the world consists of discrete parts, 'natural kind' divisions, that are each explainable in their own right, without reference to larger wholes. Positivism dispenses with any notion of the whole or, as historicist Marxists usually say, the *totality*. For positivists, a theory of X, where X is a natural kind division of the real, can be adequate and complete without in any way taking Y into account, where Y is distinct from X. For historicists, on the other hand, explanations must deploy a notion of totality, if they are to succeed. A theory of X that does not connect X to everything else, including Y – if only by revealing X's connection to an underlying unity that somehow encompasses both X and Y – can never be adequate or complete.
    There is another sense of 'holism' that should not be confused with the holism of the historicists. I have in mind claims that are advanced within particular sciences and in philosophical theories of

various kinds that expressly or implicitly accept the division of the whole into discrete natural kinds. Holism, in this sense, is the view that, for particular explanatory purposes, it is best (or perhaps even necessary) not to decompose particular wholes into their constituent parts. It was in this sense, for example, that Quine famously maintained that there is no simple correspondence between words and objects. To understand the connections between them, it is necessary, he argued, to look to links between entire theories or even conceptual schemes, on the one hand, and sensory experiences, on the other.[1] This sort of holism is compatible with the denial of the metaphysical notion that, ultimately, all is One. One can therefore be a holist in this sense without also being a holist in the historicist's sense. But even this nonhistoricist form of holism is incompatible with extreme positivist views, according to which there is – or must be – a one-to-one correspondence between words and objects or between facts, however identified, and the real.

B. *Antiscientism*. Ever since Plato (or Socrates) first advanced the idea that knowledge is 'justified, true belief', it has been the accepted view that knowledge claims require justification. Knowledge can be *about* many things, but the idea motivating the historicist's antiscientism can be made apparent by focusing just on existence claims. In the modern view, existence claims can be justified in only two ways. One can follow the model established in mathematics and logic, grounding claims for the existence of entities on rationally compelling, formal demonstrations. Or, one can follow the strategy employed in modern (postmedieval) science, where the idea, very generally, is that existence claims are established or not depending on the degree of evidential support that can be mustered in their behalf. For the positivist, there are no other ways of knowing; scientific knowledge is the only kind of knowledge there is. This is what *scientism* maintains: it claims that science (including mathematics), and science alone, affords knowledge of the real. Hegelianism, though friendly to science and therefore not antiscientific, is anti*scientistic*. With its roots in (post-Kantian) German Romanticism, it claims that aspects of experience beyond the ken of modern science and mathematics are knowable. For some thinkers within this tradition, the world of affect and immediate experience lies within the scope of human knowledge, even if it is impenetrable to science. On their view, poets, composers and artists are as much seekers after Truth as scientists are. For others of a more philosophical bent, the idea is that knowledge of the real is attainable, even in the face of Kant's investigations of the conditions for the possibility of (theoretical) knowledge. According to Kant, knowledge of the real, as opposed to the apparent, is impossible in principle because human beings' cognitive capacities, applied to sensory experience, cannot gain a purchase on it. Knowledge of the real therefore falls outside the scope of any possible science (including mathematics). But knowledge of the Real is precisely what Hegel's dialectical method supposedly makes possible. It provides access to what science is incapable in principle of apprehending: knowledge not of the merely apparent, but of what Kant called 'things-in-themselves'. Thus Hegelian historicists believe that there are extrascientific, distinctively philosophical ways of knowing. If they are materialists, as Marxists are, they may also believe that there are extrascientific ways of knowing mind-independent things; and that these extrascientific cognitive practices, even if they deviate from the notions of justification implicit in formal demonstrations or empirical inquiries, take precedence over standard ways of knowing. This, apparently, is what some historicist Marxists had in mind when they insisted that social and economic theory should somehow be dialectical.

C. *The fact–value distinction.* Hegelian historicists are disinclined to abide by Hume's insistence that what is the case and how human beings evaluate what is the case, their 'value judgments', are independent of one another from a logical point of view; and therefore that an *is* can never imply an *ought*.[2] Positivists, on the other hand, agree with Hume. In their view, facts and values exist in realms apart, even if, in consequence of human nature or social conditioning or both, the sensibilities of many or all human beings converge. Where there is convergence, many or all people will evaluate situations the same way. But then agreement will be a consequence of contingent circumstances, not of any intrinsic connection between facts and values. This is what historicists deny, especially if they follow Hegel's lead, as historicist Marxists do. Assuming that, despite their materialism, Marxists are somehow able to make sense of Hegel's claim that the Real is the Rational, then whoever becomes conscious of what Reason requires – and of the way(s) that the actual or apparent falls short of the ideal – is rationally compelled to seek to transform the actual, to make it become what it already potentially is, and therefore ought to be. Thus historicist Marxists are committed to the idea that reason requires rational agents to move history along. This is part of the meaning of the famous *Eleventh Thesis on Feuerbach* – that 'the philosophers have only understood the world, while the point is to change it'. What it is 'to understand the world' is 'to change it', to make it what it potentially is.[3] This outlook is particularly evident in the thinking of those historicists, including historicist Marxists, who advert to the idea of teleological causality (see Chapter 1). Insofar as processes are identified by their *ends* (their *telos*), then whatever fully is, whatever is entirely self-realized, is what ought to be. Reason therefore compels agents to advance history to the point that all teleologically given destinies are realized; or, what comes to the same thing, to make the actual rational, thereby undoing the difference between the apparent and the real.[4]

Hegelianism and positivism differ along other dimensions as well. Positivists are committed to the idea that the best way to explain some (or all) phenomena is to go, as it were, from the simple to the complex – to build up from 'elementary' forms, adding complexities from the ground up. Historicists are inclined to explain from the top down, to apply totalizing categories to particular instances, revealing the general in the particular. In the extreme, an historicist might attempt to explain an event by showing how it expresses the spirit of the time, the zeitgeist; in other words, how it expresses what ostensibly different but contemporaneous events express. This difference resonates in historicist Marxism; the explanations provided there too generally have a top-down character. But the fact is that the Marxist philosophy Althusserian and analytical Marxists encountered seldom descended to the level of particular explanations. Accounts of social or economic phenomena, including those produced by Marx himself or by social scientists working in a Marxist vein, were invoked more often to illustrate claims about the nature of Marxism than as matters to ponder in their own right. Marxist philosophy was given over to programmatic theorizing; not to the execution of theoretical programs. It hovered above the finer-grained differences one finds in historical or sociological writing, and in economic analysis, Marxist or otherwise.

The problem, in short, is that Hegel's intellectual style, taken up by thinkers less gifted than the master, too easily degenerates into obscurantism – encouraging a philosophical practice in which metaphors of dubious heuristic relevance and plays on words take the place of arguments, and in which theoretical posturing stands in for theory construction and adjudication. The same is true for historicist Marxism which, by its own account, was just Hegelianism stood on materialist feet. More than any particular doctrinal commitments, this stylistic characteristic defined Marxist philosophy as it existed at the time of the New Left's appearance on the scene. It was, partly, in reaction to it that the Althusserians, more than a little disingenuously, represented their own positions as 'scientific' and 'rigorous'. And it was because the rules of the game being played within the Marxist fold were so patently deficient, compared to the much more rigorous standards of the academy, that some hardy souls, academic refugees from the New Left, forged analytical Marxism.

These philosophical developments amounted to genuine breaks with Marxism's historicist past. But they were not only reactions to the grand theoretical posturing and intellectual sloppiness that had come to pervade Marxist philosophy. They were also accommodations to a world without a proletariat or its functional equivalent – without agents with interests and capacities sufficient for constructing a socialist and then communist order. Even in the face of this stubborn fact, New Left politics had sustained and deepened the revolutionary idea. But to no avail – an agent of social change with genuinely universal human interests, in society but not of it, could not be willed into being. Such was the world Althusser and the analytical Marxists confronted.

*   *   *

On the surface at least, Althusser never acknowledged this problem – except, indirectly, in his struggles with historicist Marxism. Indeed, he was even more inclined than his historicist contemporaries to represent his philosophy as proletarian. But it will become evident that he did 'protest too much'. Althusser's alternative to historicist Marxism – implicit in his later metaphilosophy and in his earlier claim for an 'epistemological break' in Marx's thinking – amounted to a repudiation of the old rivalry between Hegelians and positivists, not an endorsement of one or the other view. This fact was lost on Althusser's critics who were quick to observe that his work smacked of positivism, a fact they regarded as a taint. It will emerge, however, that Althusser's rejection of historicism was positivist only in an oblique and unilluminating sense; and that, wittingly or not, he set Marxist philosophy on a different track – one that was neither Hegelian nor positivist, as these terms had come to be understood, but that incorporated some of the rational intuitions of both.

A similar claim could be made, with even greater force, for the analytical Marxists. But, despite their efforts to rehabilitate the idea of scientific socialism, the analytical Marxists, from the beginning, never quite connected with the ongoing 'conversation' in which Althusser, for all his novelty, was still immersed. They therefore cannot be said, like Althusser, to have subtly changed the terms of the debate that engaged Marxists of preceding generations. They rejected it outright. Seen through the old prism, they too courted the charge of positivism. But, in their case, it would have been transparently anachronistic even to raise this as an issue. No one did. It was not just because their Marxism was academic. Of greater importance was the fact that their efforts to recover the core of Marxist theory were remote from the already venerable quarrel between Hegelians and positivists. When the analytical Marxists set out to reconstruct and defend Marxist positions they saw themselves, correctly, making a fresh start.

Thus, for different reasons, the lack of a genuine proletariat was never Topic A for either Althusser or the analytical Marxists. But, ironically and without quite realizing what they were doing, they each, in their own way, addressed this challenge. It would be an exaggeration to say that they triumphed over it. As we know, the absence of a revolutionary agent, in conjunction with countless other circumstances, led to Marxism's precipitous decline. These facts on the ground eventually helped to quash even these new ventures in Marxist philosophy. But, in the end, the greater irony may be that the unfocused and incomplete efforts of Althusser and the analytical Marxists to reconcile Marxism to its real-world situation may someday be seen to have aided the socialist cause in a way that historicist Marxism never could. Their work led to discoveries, connected to Marx's thinking but at some remove from the main currents of historicist Marxism, that future socialists can appropriate and put to use. Unlikely as it may seem to contemporary observers, the achievements of these recently defunct departures in Marxist philosophy auger well for a renewal of socialist theory, and perhaps even for Marxism itself.

3 Althusser and Philosophy

In the decade of the 1970s, no Marxist writer attracted as much attention – in France, where his celebrity began nearly a decade earlier, in the English-speaking world, and throughout Europe, Latin America and parts of Asia – as Louis Althusser. The reactions of historicist Marxists were, on the whole, negative. For them, Althusser represented most of what was objectionable in Marxism's, and communism's, past. But for many others, especially those who came of age intellectually in the 1960s and who were unencumbered by traditional Marxist ways of thinking, Althusser's work was a pole of attraction. His most influential writings were products of the French intellectual and political scene during the period that immediately preceded the rise of the New Left. But it was during the time of the New Left's ascendance and decline that his ideas became widely known outside of France. *For Marx,* Althusser's best known book, was not translated into English until 1969, four years after its publication in France and nearly a decade after the appearance of some of the essays collected together in it. *Reading Capital* was published in English in 1970, five years after its French publication.[1] It was around that time, therefore, that Althusserianism emerged as a major presence in the intellectual world of the English-speaking Left. Thus its impact was felt at a time when the heady optimism of the late 1960s was receding, but before the New Left's demise, and in a period in which Marxism still enjoyed considerable prestige.

Althusser was prone to couch constructive and largely defensible positions in provocative formulations – intended, it almost seems, less to enlighten than to entice or outrage practitioners of historicist Marxism, as well as devotees of that antihistoricist but still resolutely obscurantist and peculiarly French contemporaneous phenomenon, structuralism. Althusser assumed this guise with great virtuosity. His style was ironic and elegant; and his writing, though limpid, was often difficult to decode. But it is eminently feasible, in retrospect, to penetrate through to the core of Althusser's thought, and therefore to judge his contribution to Marxist theory, and to the larger socialist tradition, for what it is. Despite the ways his writings were taken at the time and despite how he is remembered, Althusser was, first of all, if not quite a philosopher of science, then a philosopher who advocated positions that converge with important currents in the philosophy of science today. The enduring importance of his work, his contribution to the (possible) future of Marxism, lies in the way he joined these positions to Marxist themes.

It is indicative of the difficulties facing Althusser's readers that, having distinguished Marxism from Hegelianism in no uncertain terms in *For Marx* and *Reading Capital*, Althusser proceeded, in his later writings, to enlist Hegel as a proto-Marxist, declaring in terms intentionally reminiscent of a celebrated aphorism of Lenin's, that a century after the publication of Hegel's *Logic*, '... no one has understood Hegel because it is impossible to understand Hegel without having thoroughly studied and understood *Capital*'.[2] To uncover Althusser's contribution to Marxist thought, it will be instructive to focus, in this chapter and the next, on the twists and turns of the Hegel–Marx relationship or rather on the ways in which it is depicted in Althusser's writings. This question speaks not only to the connection(s) between historicist and Althusserian Marxism, but also to the issue of Althusser's (largely implicit) philosophy of science.

Althusser's thought ranged widely. Many topics taken up in his writings will be addressed here only indirectly, if at all. I will have something to say about Althusser's general political orientation, but I will not discuss his express political views, except insofar as they affected his account of Marxist theory. Accordingly, I will only briefly note his (plainly inadequate) notion of 'the Stalinist deviation', and I will be brief with his (few and unenthusiastic) pronouncements on 'the events' of May 1968, and on French Communist Party policies before or after the momentous Twenty-Second Party Congress in 1976. Neither will I have much to say about Althusser's discussion of ideology and 'the ideological state apparatus'. I will not say anything at all about Althusser's views on art or psychoanalysis, or his work on Machiavelli, Montesquieu, and Rousseau. Finally, I will pass over the remarkable, almost surrealistic, 'confessional' writings Althusser produced towards the end of his life, in which he attempted to make sense of the 'temporary insanity' that led him, on November 16, 1980, to strangle his wife of many years – an act for which he avoided criminal prosecution but not confinement in mental institutions.[3] The focus here and in the following chapter, instead, will be on some of the main theses of *For Marx* and *Reading Capital,* as expanded and 'corrected' in Althusser's later work.[4] Althusser's arguments were often wanting, and so were his ways of formulating his views. But those views themselves are often insightful. To take over a metaphor of Althusser's, itself taken over from Marx, my aim will be to uncover the 'rational kernel' of Althusserian Marxism, and to cast aside its outer, polemical shell.

Althusser's views on philosophy, his metaphilosophy, serve as a guiding thread to the entire corpus of his writings. I will therefore focus first on this topic, and on the ways Althusser represented his own 'theoretical practice'. Doing so will prepare the way for investigating Althusser's best-known and most important contention – the claim that, within Marx's intellectual trajectory, there occurred an 'epistemological break' with prescientific ways of thinking about human history and that, as a result, Marx launched a new science, the science of history, and a new practice of science. It is this notion that underwrote Althusser's declared understanding of his own philosophical project.

Althusser identified emphatically with the materialist tradition in philosophy. Not unrelatedly, he claimed that the epistemological break gave rise to a 'materialist dialectic', by which he meant a new method for apprehending the real. What Althusser had to say about this method was sadly wanting. But his way of motivating the idea is of continuing importance. In making a case for it, Althusser showed, contrary to his express intention, that the very idea of a dialectical method is untenable. In this respect, he anticipated what would become a standard assumption of the analytical Marxists. Thus, in opposing the historicists' conviction that Marxism is distinguished by its adherence to the Hegelian dialectic, Althusserian and analytical Marxism stand together, even if the Althusserians never quite realized exactly where they stood. In the end, Althusser's greatest contribution to the future of Marxism may lie in the way he fostered a sense of the untenability of the received view – from *within* a conceptual space that historicist Marxists could identify as their own. Althusser engaged the historicist tradition on its own terms in a way that the analytical Marxists never did – despite their greater philosophical acuity and despite their initial dedication to reconstructing and defending Marx's views.

*   *   *

Althusser insisted repeatedly that even his most abstruse writings be taken as 'political interventions in the field of theory'. This is good advice. To understand *For Marx* and *Reading Capital,* it is useful to bear in mind contemporaneous debates within the French Communist Party, to which Althusser adhered throughout his adult life, and the vicissitudes of the Left generally, especially the communist Left, during the time these books were composed. This was the period of partial and tentative de-Stalinization in the Soviet bloc, the split between China and the Soviet Union, and the reemergence of *gauchisme* – that is, of significant political formations to the left of the Communist Parties. On the surface, Althusser's work seems removed from all of this. He was a philosopher, writing from the summit of the French university system. His express concerns, beyond those that pertained to philosophy itself, had to do with the epistemological break and the positions that follow from it – on the Marx–Hegel relation and the connections between the thought of the young Marx and the Marx of *Capital*, on Marx's alleged anti-historicism and 'antihumanism', and on what Althusser called 'structural causality'. In his later writings, where the epistemological break partly faded from view, Althusser also advanced the idea of a 'process without a subject'. Arguably, all of these claims, except perhaps the one having to do with structural causality, can be made plausible once the 'rational kernel' buried in Althusser's formulations is extracted. But they are also, at the same time, components of an extended political argument. Althusser did theory and politics together in a way that makes it always difficult and sometimes impossible to separate the one from the other. In the days when Althusser's views were of intense interest to a still flourishing intellectual Left, his critics understood this. There was hardly an objection to Althusser's work that was not, in one way or another, politically motivated.

In his later writings, Althusser expressly defended the fusion of politics and theory. In *Lenin and Philosophy*, he maintained that all philosophy is 'partisan'; that it is always 'a practice of political intervention carried out in theoretical form'. Whether or not this metaphilosophical claim is true in general, it does describe Althusser himself and those Marxists with whom he was most concerned. The Young Hegelians, including Marx in his Young Hegelian period, were explicitly engaged in a revolutionary project. Marx continued this commitment, in different ways, throughout the rest of his life. He was a revolutionary mainly, though not exclusively, 'in the field of theory'. So too were the *gauchistes* of the 1920s, the early Lukács and Karl Korsch, the unacknowledged adversaries of many of Althusser's theoretical departures. Most important of all, a political line was readily apparent in the thought of Althusser's immediate opponents, the 'Marxist humanists' who exercised considerable influence in the

French intellectual scene generally, and in the French Communist Party, at the time the essays comprising *For Marx* and *Reading Capital* were composed. It may be mistaken to say that philosophy in general is always partisan. But Marxist philosophy, as it existed up to Althusser's time, certainly was.

Part of the reason for Althusser's prominence in French intellectual life in the 1960s, and a decade later among francophile English-speaking academics, was his leading role in the then fashionable 'structuralist' turn in 'the human sciences' in France. It is therefore striking that Althusser represented his views in a very different idiom. Instead of engaging the work of his contemporaries or addressing their express concerns, he wrapped himself in the mantle of Marxist–Leninist orthodoxy – taking up an orthodox vocabulary and defending ostensibly orthodox positions, even while investing them with manifestly unorthodox content.[5] He did so for reasons that can only be described as political. To appropriate the vocabulary and positions of the Leninist tradition, in the time and place that Althusser did, was to register opposition to the direction taken by the communist movement in France and elsewhere in the 1960s and 1970s. Althusser's Leninism defined his politics, as did his continuing affiliation with official communism. Even at the height of his celebrity in the 1960s, but especially after the 1976 Twenty-Second Party Congress, Althusser was a pariah within the Party – prominently displayed, but isolated and without influence. Still, he never broke from the French Communist Party organizationally, even as he faulted its increasingly evident repudiation of its Leninist past. By criticizing it while remaining within it, Althusser evinced an attitude, not uncommon in Catholic countries, of opposition to the Church hierarchy (or, in this case, the Party leadership), joined with a steadfast conviction that 'outside the Church (or Party) there is no salvation'. This orientation marked Althusser's political interventions in the field of theory.

It is fair to say that, for Althusser, defending the positions of Lenin and Marx was a way of intervening into the then ongoing process of de-Stalinization. Despite his declarations of fidelity to the communist movement, and despite the ways his opponents depicted him, Althusser's call to return to Marx and Lenin amounted to a repudiation of communism's Stalinist legacy. It set his views against the 'dogmatic' (and crude) version of Marxism–Leninism that had immobilized communist theory and practice for so long, and that continued to resonate in the French Communist Party. At the same time, it represented an effort to resist what appeared to be an impending transformation of communism into social democracy. In that historical moment, there was no question about the urgency of de-Stalinization. The debate was between Right and Left de-Stalinizers. Althusser's tacit but nevertheless evident aim was to encourage de-Stalinization from the Left. This is why, in those rare instances in which he did publically venture political judgments, it was always to criticize the Right de-Stalinizers. He did so by calling their attempts to make sense of the Stalinist period, which he called the 'Stalinist deviation', un-Marxist. Thus he maintained that the idea of a 'cult of personality', a notion invoked by the Right de-Stalinizers and others to explain Stalinism, had no place in Marxist theory. It is significant too that Althusser defended his views not only by invoking passages from Marx and Lenin, but by reflecting on the political experience of these and other revolutionary figures. It is especially noteworthy that Mao Tse-tung was among the revolutionaries Althusser utilized for this purpose.

As remarked (in Chapter 2), until well into the 1970s, for many in the West, but especially in countries with significant communist parties, Maoism appeared to be the only viable political tradition historically continuous with Bolshevism that was also anti-Stalinist – in practice, though notoriously not in its self-representations. A French philosopher, like Althusser, dedicated to remaining in the Communist Party at all costs, could hardly declare himself a Maoist. But it was clear to all, from the outset, that, because he identified with Bolshevism, he gravitated toward Maoism while remaining within the communist fold, and that Maoist convictions helped to shape his thinking. This thinly disguised political commitment of Althusser's must be born in mind if we are to uncover the rational kernel of his thought.

The point, for Althusser, was to correct practice by theory – a Leninist position, especially when joined with the complementary conviction that practice shapes theory. In the days of *For Marx* and *Reading Capital*, Althusser thought that theory was decisive. The main political task was to get the theory right in order that it might guide practice effectively. In several subsequent 'self-criticisms', a term replete with Maoist connotations, he faulted this erstwhile 'theoreticism'. But it is plain that Althusser continued to think, as Lenin did, that 'without revolutionary theory there can be no revolutionary practice'. It is plain too that he remained determined to develop a 'revolutionary theory' in ways consonant not only with ways of thinking that were influential at the time, but also with Marx's writings and with the political practice of those magisterial figures, Lenin and Mao, whom he took to be genuine followers of Marx. In this sense, Althusser's thinking was *deeply* political; its rational kernel was formed by a certain, irreducibly political, view of the world. But this kernel will elude contemporary readers who remain fixed, as Althusser himself too often was and as his initial readership certainly was, on an outer, polemical shell shaped by immediate, 'conjunctural' circumstances. This is especially true nowadays, inasmuch as the context in which Althusser wrote, though close to us in time, has come to seem utterly foreign.

*   *   *

There are, in fact, two different Althusserian metaphilosophies: the one at work in *For Marx* and *Reading Capital*; the other expressly, though obscurely, advanced in Althusser's later writings. Indeed, it is in large part for his earlier views about philosophy that Althusser took himself to task in his 'self-criticisms'.[6] His original metaphilosophy, he claimed, was the root of the 'theoretical deviation' that marred his earlier work.

In *For Marx* and *Reading Capital,* Althusser's use of 'philosophy' was, in fact, ambiguous. On the one hand, the term referred to an historically specific 'ideological practice', allegedly rendered obsolete with the development of the Marxist science of society. At the same time, in those works, the term designated a type of 'theoretical practice', supposedly inaugurated by Marx. On each understanding, the Marxist science of society, which Althusser insisted on calling *historical materialism*, has profound implications for philosophy. We can see what these are, and also uncover some of the misunderstandings engendered by Althusser's ambiguities, if we reflect on the consequences for philosophy of these positions.

What Althusser might have called (but didn't) 'the spontaneous metaphilosophy of (academic) philosophers' goes roughly like this: philosophers investigate specifically philosophical topics – being and becoming, the nature of the good, beauty, justice and so on. To this end, they deploy their own characteristic methods. Philosophy is not a science. But, like the sciences, it has a 'history'; in other words, it advances towards a determinate end, the Truth. Thus, on the spontaneous view, philosophy is a cumulative and progressive discipline. Needless to say, progress is slow in coming. There have been few, if any, breakthroughs since its beginnings in ancient Greece. This is why working *within* the thought of, say, Plato or Aristotle is of continuing *philosophical*, not just historical, importance; while working through all but the most recent journal articles in, say, physics or biology is usually of value only to historians of science. But, even so, philosophy *can* progress, at least in principle.

Historical materialism – in Althusser's idiosyncratic sense – upsets this view. It turns philosophy from a path to knowledge into an 'object of knowledge', into something science *explains*. Therefore, the spontaneous view is wrong in one crucial respect – philosophy is not a way of knowing. But, of course, even if true, this is a non sequitur, at least if all Althusser meant was that a sociology of philosophy is possible. To explain a cognitive enterprise is not to impugn its legitimacy. A sociology of science is possible too; in fact, it has long been a thriving discipline. There is no reason to think that this fact undermines the integrity of science. Of course, it is possible, even so, that the Marxist science of society somehow undoes philosophy's credentials as a cognitive enterprise. But Althusser never explained how. It therefore appears that all he meant – or should have meant – by depicting philosophy as he did was that there are no extrascientific, distinctively philosophical ways of knowing; that, as the positivists maintained, science, and science alone, yields knowledge. If this was Althusser's point, it is fair to say that he made it in a disguised, if not meretricious, way. Whether he did so wittingly or not, it was plainly advantageous, in this instance, not to be forthright. As we know, 'positivism' has always been a term of reproach among Marxists, especially for those who, like Althusser, would assume an orthodox demeanor. It is not surprising, therefore, that Althusser would want to avoid the taint of association with this intellectual tradition.

But, however that may be, the conclusion he sought to convey was clear: that the Marxist science of society implies a new practice of philosophy; that old ways of doing philosophy cannot survive the coming of historical materialism (in Althusser's idiosyncratic sense of the term). Althusser maintained that, in opening up 'the continent of History' to science, Marx did more than just extend the methods and practices of existing science to new domains.[7] He also began a new scientific practice. And, like other theoretical revolutions of comparable importance – the opening up of the 'continent of mathematics' in ancient Greece, or the opening up of the 'continent of nature' in the Galilean Revolution of the seventeenth century – this way of knowing has profound implications for philosophy. Philosophy has always been what Althusser might have called 'a theory of the practice of ways of knowing'. So it should be again for the allegedly new way of knowing Marx discovered. To distinguish this new philosophy from its ancestor forms, Althusser was loathe to use the term 'philosophy' at all in *For Marx* and *Reading Capital*. He preferred to speak of *Theory* (with a capital 'T'). Or, to add to the confusion, he also appropriated the term 'dialectical materialism', using it interchangeably with 'Theory'. But by whatever name, the idea was that Marxist philosophy is a philosophy of Marxist social science – of historical materialism, as Althusser redefined it.

Leaving aside, for now, the claim that Marxist social science involves new ways of knowing, Althusser's metaphilosophical position is, in fact, fairly commonplace, even if it had never before been advanced in an explicitly Marxist framework. The idea is just that the progress of science generates puzzlements of a conceptual nature, and that philosophy is an effort to dissipate these puzzlements by restructuring the prevailing conceptual space. If the disturbance to received ways of thinking is sufficiently profound, the philosophical response will be correspondingly far-reaching. Thus the birth of Western philosophy in ancient Greece plausibly is seen as a response to the development of Greek mathematics; and the emergence of modern philosophy in the seventeenth and eighteenth centuries arguably was a response to the new sciences of nature. If historical materialism (in Althusser's sense) really is as novel as Althusser claimed, it too would call for a new philosophy, a 'Theory' of its 'practice'.

Althusser never repudiated this view of philosophy's relation to the sciences. What he 'corrected' in his later writings was the additional claim, never expressly asserted but implicit in the notion of Theory, that *only* the sciences determine philosophy. This supposedly mistaken claim is the root of 'the theoretical deviation' that Althusser came to think plagued *For Marx* and *Reading Capital*. These texts, he insisted, ignore philosophy's essentially political dimension. Accordingly, in the metaphilosophy he set out in *Lenin and Philosophy* and then in subsequent writings, philosophy is said to be 'doubly determined': by both science and politics (and, therefore, as Althusser obscurely but insistently maintained, by the economy too, though only 'in the last instance'.) This is why he claimed that the history of philosophy only apparently takes place *within* philosophy itself. Its 'real field' lies outside the philosophical realm altogether – in the history of the sciences and in political struggle.[8]

Philosophy 'intervenes' politically by representing political orientations in theoretical domains. It does so, characteristically, by advancing categories, theories, and theses. These have effects: they draw what Lenin called 'lines of demarcation' in the class struggle. This is the sense in which philosophy is 'partisan'. And this is why, contrary to the spontaneous view, philosophy has no 'object'. It has distinctive problems and themes, and characteristic methods. It has a tradition, and rules of the game. Philosophers, Althusser would concede, do not speak of just anything in any way they want. But there is not anything philosophy provides knowledge of. However, philosophy, in Althusser's view, does take a position with respect to knowledge – it is either *for* it or *against* it. This means, given Althusser's (tacit) support for this facet of positivist thinking, that it is either proscientific or else that it opposes science – and therefore knowledge too, even when its practitioners are unaware that this is the bearing of their categories, theories, and theses. This is the point of Althusser's appropriation of the claim Lenin advanced in the opening pages of *Materialism and Empirio-Criticism* that philosophy is always a war of tendencies – between materialism and idealism.

To some considerable extent, Althusser transformed this contention from a descriptive claim to a metaphilosophical thesis. One cannot fail to appreciate the polemical genius of this maneuver. Since it is empirically false that all philosophy is either materialist or idealist – since materialism and idealism are, in fact, creatures of an historically particular, though long-lasting, phase in the history of philosophy in the West – this position, understood descriptively, is plainly incorrect. How ingenious, therefore, to transform it into a claim that seems not only plausible, but profound! However, in this case, appearances are deceiving. Intentionally or not, in elaborating on the purportedly new view of philosophy somehow implicit in Lenin's political and theoretical practice, Althusser effectively reverted back, equivocally but unmistakably, to Lenin's actual position, according to which the doctrine of 'partisanship in philosophy' is just what it seems to be – a descriptive claim about actual philosophies. The account I will give here of Althusser's position will of necessity straddle the ambiguity that his account exploits.

In their traditional designations, both materialism and idealism are metaphysical doctrines that stake out ontological positions, accounts of what there is. Whenever we assert some claim that is either true or false, the materialist holds that our assertions are *about* a mind-independent reality, matter. This is what the idealist denies. For the idealist, the real is nonmaterial or ideal (mental). At least since Descartes, materialism has been advanced within a conceptual framework that privileges the epistemological question of determining the forms and limits of knowledge over ontological questions about the nature of the real. Descartes' principal concern, and a concern of many philosophers after him, was to defend knowledge from skeptical challenges; to justify the possibility of knowledge claims. To this end, Descartes established, at least to his own satisfaction, that we can know and therefore commit ourselves ontologically to the existence of a mind-independent reality. It is this reality, Descartes maintained, that the sciences of nature investigate. Contrary to the skeptical view, these sciences are therefore about what really is.

Descartes thought, in fact, that he had established the reality of two 'substances' – where substances, according to the received understanding, are fundamental categories of being. Again, this conclusion was epistemologically driven. By offering accounts of how we come to know the essential property of, on the one hand, our own existence as a thinking thing; and, on the other, of the world that we (intuitively) believe exists apart from our minds, Descartes concluded that there are two radically independent fundamental categories of being. Descartes called the substances he discovered in this way *thinking substance* or *mind,* and *extended substance* or *matter.* Matter, then, is essentially spatial (extended); and, as such, nonmental.

I will not rehearse the arguments that led Descartes to this dualistic ontology, nor the arguments that led those who followed in his wake to the two monistic ontologies, materialism and idealism, that Althusser, like Lenin, deemed central to the history of philosophy. However, it is important to bear in mind how, for Descartes and his successors, ontological questions were subordinated to epistemological ones. What is real for dualists, materialists, and idealists alike, is whatever can be known to be. Neither will I venture a judgment here about the cogency of this way of posing the problem of the nature of the real, except to suggest that, whatever its philosophical merit, it is unhelpful for capturing the concerns, spontaneous or otherwise, of modern scientific practice. For practicing scientists, the *possibility* of knowledge in the face of skeptical challenges is not a pressing issue. Neither therefore are the metaphysical disputes that arose centuries ago as philosophers grappled with this question. Scientists want to know what is true. They are indifferent to metaphysical doctrines about the substantial nature of what makes claims true or false. That is a 'conversation' that they have little interest in joining.

Althusser's insistence that the 'spontaneous philosophy' of scientists is *materialism,* read charitably, is a misleading way of making this point. But to ascribe this position to him, it is necessary, first, to peel away 'the outer polemical shell' of his formulation. It is not hard to see why that shell is there, given Althusser's conspicuous commitment to Marxist–Leninist orthodoxy. The Young Hegelians had already made an issue of materialism. By their own account, it was mainly in virtue of their materialism that their views differed from those of their Right Hegelian opponents, and from Hegel himself. As Marx turned away from expressly philosophical concerns in his later writings, this metaphysical commitment faded from view. But it was revived with a vengeance towards the end of the nineteenth century, as Marx's thought became transformed into a full-fledged and comprehensive body of doctrine. Thus, from the time of Engels and then, especially in the era of Kautsky and Plekhanov – in other words, in the generation that preceded Lenin's, the generation that developed classical Marxism – Marxism aligned itself unequivocally with the materialist solution to the ontological problem Descartes' work posed. Lenin's commitment to this doctrine then made it canonical, thanks to the prestige his endorsement carried after the Revolution he led.

The motivation for joining Marxism to materialism was always, to some degree, political. Throughout the nineteenth century, and well into the twentieth, materialism was identified, both in intellectual circles and in the popular imagination, with atheism, anticlericalism and revolutionary or at least progressive thought. Idealism, on the other hand, was thought to be on the side of God and country. These connections, which had preoccupied such eighteenth-century thinkers as Berkeley and Helvetius, were therefore part of the political common sense of the world in which Marxism emerged. It is hardly surprising, therefore, that Lenin claimed that Marxism continues the historical tradition of eighteenth-century materialism; or that, in reflecting on materialism, he emphasized those aspects of it that drew it in a Marxist direction – its hostility to religion, for example, and its affinities with revolutionary politics.

But, however understandable Lenin's identification with the materialist tradition in metaphysics was, it is unnecessary to link Marxism's fate to this ontological position. If nothing else, there is no reason why Marxists must be wedded to the Cartesian way of posing ontological problems. It should be noted too that, within the framework within which materialism and idealism contend, the materialist almost certainly had the weaker hand, as virtually every important philosopher, from the seventeenth century on, has recognized. The reason why is clear. What is material cannot be known as such; it can only be represented *in the mind*. There are, of course, ways materialists can attempt to accommodate to this fact. But, by most accounts, including some that enjoy prominence to this day, these ways are unsatisfactory. It was because he was persuaded that this was so that George Berkeley, Lenin's main non-contemporaneous target in *Materialism and Empirio-Criticism,* argued that matter cannot be known to exist, and therefore does not exist. For any philosopher who, following Descartes's lead, does ontology in an epistemologically driven way, this would have to be a compelling conclusion, if it could be sustained. It is noteworthy that no Marxist, including Lenin, ever refuted it directly. Instead, Lenin insisted that the choice between materialism and idealism was ultimately a political choice; in part because there are no conclusive nonpolitical reasons to adopt one or the other view. Even if one concludes that this was not a disingenuous stance on Lenin's part, it is plain that, notwithstanding his insistence to the contrary, its historical connection to post-Cartesian materialism is a problem for Marxism. Althusser could hardly ignore this fact. True to form, he therefore gave materialism a new meaning, while appearing to remain steadfastly Leninist.

Even so, there is a 'rational kernel' in Althusser's metaphilosophical claim. In opposing idealism, materialists do defend the idea that 'the object of knowledge' is mind-independent. In doing so, they articulate *realist* intuitions about the nature of science. Their guiding idea is that knowledge is about a reality that is as it is, regardless of how human beings apprehend it. Exactly how to articulate this thought and how to defend it have been matters of controversy at many points in philosophy's history. Althusser's 'materialism' adds little to our understanding of these issues. But his position *was* motivated by the same plausible intuition that fired the various forms of realism that have emerged throughout history – the idea that what grounds *objectivity* is the world itself, not our way(s) of apprehending it.

I would venture that it is its realist implications, as much as its connections with atheism or revolutionary politics, that motivated Marx's own commitment to materialism. So understood, being a materialist is indeed a way of siding with science. Either philosophy represents the integrity and objectivity of scientific knowledge in a realist way, or else it deems science dependent on something other than the way the world is, something 'merely mental'. If science is not constrained by a mind-independent reality in the way that realists suppose, scientific claims, even when they warrant unanimous assent, are ultimately arbitrary. This is what idealism implies. In this sense, it does oppose science. Materialism, on the other hand, is *for* science. But it expresses this position through the historically particular prism of Descartes' ontological program. However, this is unnecessary baggage. It is not necessary to be a post-Cartesian materialist to register support for its rational kernel. It is enough to be a realist *tout court*. For a realist, the aim of science is to uncover the mechanisms and processes that account for the observable world. This, on a realist view, is what science is about. The truth conditions for the assertions scientists make therefore depend on what these mechanisms and processes are. Thus it is the way reality is, not the way(s) we apprehend it, that make claims true or false. Had there been no *political* reason to express this conviction in the way he did, Althusser could have said nothing more. But, of course, he had a political reason to say more. He wanted to invoke the authority of Lenin.

Strictly speaking, realism is agnostic with respect to the contest between materialism and idealism. For materialists, all assertions with truth values are about matter. For idealists, all such assertions are about minds and their contents. Realism, however, only commits science ontologically to whatever entities, mechanisms or processes scientific theories discover. Whether this reality is material or mental, in the Cartesian sense, is not at issue. Thus one can be a realist with respect to numbers or protons or viruses – or modes of production – without taking any position at all on whether these entities are essentially extended and therefore material, or whether they are collections of ideas, as idealists would have it, or whether it even makes sense to inquire into their substantial nature, or to venture claims about what that nature *essentially* is.

That Althusser tacitly (and perhaps guilefully) took Marxism's allegiance to the materialist tradition to amount to nothing more than realism is suggested by his insistence that the distinction between materialism and idealism does not, in the end, refer to a contest between 'schools', organized around bodies of doctrine, but to conflicting 'tendencies'. Thus, in endorsing Lenin's claim that the opposition between materialism and idealism cuts across the entire history of philosophy, Althusser effectively proposed a new organizing principle for understanding 'philosophical practice'. On this view, materialist and idealist tendencies may be and, since Descartes' time, typically have been represented by positions that address the question of the substantial nature of the real. But they need not do so. For as Althusser (implicitly) redefined them, materialism and idealism are not ontological positions at all, but 'political interventions in the field of theory'. It goes without saying that this ostentatiously Leninist contention is, in fact, at some remove from Lenin's actual view, and from the understanding of other Marxists. But it is also at some remove from the erroneous descriptive claims they made.

According to the position Althusser imputed to Lenin, it will be rare, if ever, that one or another of these tendencies will be present to the complete exclusion of the other. More often, materialism and idealism will coexist, 'in relations of dominance'. It follows, then, that positions customarily designated materialist or idealist in virtue of their ontological commitments are not necessarily materialist or idealist in Althusser's sense. It all depends on their role in the 'theoretical conjuncture' in which they operate. Even Lenin's bugbear, Berkeleyan idealism, might count as materialist in a conjuncture dominated, say, by spiritualism or occultism. Then Berkeley's fidelity to common sense would represent a kind of partisanship for science. Likewise, orthodox dialectical materialism can be idealist – whenever it blocks the progress of science, as it did, for example, when Stalin, then the arbiter of Marxist–Leninist orthodoxy, endorsed the anti-Darwinian views of the agronomist T.D. Lyssenko, impeding the development of Soviet genetics.[9] Thus the 'eternal conflict' of materialism and idealism is not a dispute about metaphysical doctrines, after all. It is a conflict internal to philosophical practice – within, as much as between, schools of thought. Whether or not a philosophy is materialist depends, in the final analysis, on the theoretical and political context in which it operates – not on its commitments, if any, to one or another historically important views about substance. Tactfully, without making his opposition explicit, Althusser therefore sided against the philosophical system that Lenin actually did help to shape; the one that everyone, except the Althusserians, called 'dialectical materialism'.

Much less tactfully, he opposed positions taken by many of the best Marxist thinkers of the twentieth century. Their inclination, we know, was to join Marx's thought to Hegel's, while somehow identifying with the materialist camp. This was undeniably Marx's own position too, even after his epistemological break. But it is especially evident in Marx's early writings, the principal philosophical source of mid-twentieth-century 'Marxist humanism'. For the young Marx, objectivity was a 'moment' in the dialectical unfolding of relations between human subjects and the sensible world their *praxis* brings into being. It was 'the moment of political economy', captured by the (descriptive) 'laws' of economic science. But that moment will pass as capitalism is transformed into socialism. It will be dissolved into a higher, more transparent, unity of subject and object. At that point, science itself will be superseded. This position is plainly at odds with the positivism implicit in Althusser's thinking. For that reason, Althusser was quick to call it – and historicist Marxism generally – idealist. Thus it was Althusser's view that idealism had insinuated itself into Marxist thought; indeed, into Marx's own thought. Althusser then maintained that, if Marxist philosophy is to fulfill its mission, it must remove this infection. This was the task he assumed in his own efforts in Marxist philosophy.

For Althusser, progress in Marxism is progress in Marxist social science, in *historical materialism* (as he redefined the term). To be *for Marx* is therefore to be for science; and to be against science, even if only to seek its 'supersession', is to oppose the development and application of Marx's thought. The young Marx was therefore non- or even anti-Marxist. So too were Althusser's Marxist humanist contemporaries in the French Communist Party. By returning to the young Marx and, more generally, by adhering to the historicist tradition that had, to some extent, supplanted the genuine Marxism evident in some of Marx's own 'theoretical practice' and in the political practice of Lenin and other revolutionary figures, they advanced 'categories, theories and theses' that, in the existing conjuncture, threatened the prospect for a genuinely materialist theoretical practice. The task, therefore, was to draw a 'line of demarcation' against these manifestations of renascent idealism – so that revolutionary theory might survive and flourish.

In *What is to Be Done?* Lenin had famously proclaimed that revolutionary theory is indispensable for revolutionary practice. On this point, Althusser's agreement with Lenin was unequivocal. Thus, in his own view and in the view of his followers, the philosophical undertaking he had taken on was of great political urgency. In this respect, ironically, the Althusserians, in their own way, resonated with the revolutionary fervor of the young Marx. From their own, rarified perch, they, like so many others as the New Left waxed and waned, attempted to make history. Their self-designated charge was to forge a theory suitable for leading the proletariat to victory in the class struggle. Their predicament, however, was that somehow the proletariat had disappeared. Thus, even as they denied this fact with exceptional vigor, even as they protested against it too much, they shared the predicament of everyone, at the time, who endeavored to continue the Marxist project. They knew it too, at least 'unconsciously', for the kind of Marxism they went on to defend, albeit only programmatically, endeavored to retrieve Marx's core ideas even in the face of this undeniable truth.

4 The Break

'There is,' Althusser insisted,

> an unequivocal 'epistemological break' in Marx's work, which does in fact occur at the point where Marx himself locates it, in the book, unpublished in his lifetime, which is a critique of his erstwhile philosophical (ideological) consciousness: *The German Ideology*. The *Theses on Feuerbach,* which are only a few sentences long, mark out the earlier limit of this break, the point at which the new theoretical consciousness is already beginning to show through in the erstwhile consciousness and the erstwhile language, that is, *as necessarily ambiguous and unbalanced concepts.*[1]

This break, Althusser claimed before his metaphilosophy changed, consists in the founding of two distinct theoretical disciplines: Marxist social science ('historical materialism'), and the theory of that theory ('dialectical materialism'). Thus the epistemological break 'divides Marx's thought into two long essential periods: the "ideological" period before, and the scientific period after the break of 1845'.[2] Althusser then further divided these 'essential periods'. He identified a 'liberal–rationalist moment' (up to 1842) and a 'communalist–rationalist moment' (1842–45) on one side of the epistemological break; the works of the break itself (1845); and then the 'transitional works' (1845–57). Finally, there are the works of Marx's maturity (after 1857), of which the three volumes of *Capital* are the principal achievement. The details of these refinements in Althusser's account of Marx's intellectual trajectory need not concern us, however. What is at issue is the fundamental break alleged to have occurred in 1845.

Althusser's position appears to be, first of all, a textual thesis, a claim about the positions advanced in Marx's writings. As such, it is straightforward – and wrong. There is no doubt that 1845 was a pivotal year. Before it, Marx was a Young Hegelian, a 'critical critic'. After it, he turned his attention to political economy, sociology and history. After 1845 too, some of the concepts Marx developed in his later writings began to emerge. Thus it was in *The German Ideology* that he first periodized human history into discrete 'modes of production'. But a careful reading of Marx's writings supports nothing so momentous as the complete break Althusser proclaimed. Understood as a textual claim, the thesis of an epistemological break is, at best, an overstatement.

But, appearance to the contrary, Althusser's claim for the existence of an epistemological break was never exactly a claim about Marx's texts. It had to do instead, as he put it, with what these texts 'indicate'. For this thesis to be sustained, philologically adequate commentaries on Marx's writings or historically compelling accounts of the development of Marx's views are of only secondary importance. What is at issue instead are the consequences of a 'symptomatic reading'. Althusser's aim, set forth in *Reading Capital,* was to construct the *problematic* of Marx's writings – their underlying conceptual framework, the 'space' in which their positions and their 'silences' function significantly.[3] Whatever the surface similarities and differences of Marx's writings before and after 1845, Althusser's contention was that the year 1845 marked a change in Marx's problematic. For (mainly) polemical purposes, he depicted this change as a thoroughgoing transformation.

The notion of an epistemological break has come to be identified with Althusser's work. However, it is a borrowed concept. Its applicability to Marx was original, of course; but the groundwork had been amply laid. That Marx's thought before 1845 differed from what came later had been noted for a long time. This idea had even been advanced to oppose so-called Marxist humanism, which sought to find a basis for Marx's thought in his early writings. In *For Marx,* Althusser cited the authority of Auguste Cornu, 'a quiet, lone hero, who, unknown to French learning, spent many years in a minutely detailed study of the left neo-Hegelian movement and the Young Marx'.[4] But Cornu, a French communist scholar living in East Germany, was hardly Althusser's only source. Marxist orthodoxy, which developed at a time when Marx's early work was barely known, discounted his early writings; and this precedent was exploited by those who opposed the direction taken by the Marxist humanists of the 1950s and 1960s before Althusser did. In distinguishing the early from the later Marx and in siding with the latter against the former, Althusser, so far from breaking new ground, defended an almost standard position in communist circles.

However in depicting this difference as an 'epistemological break', Althusser did advance this view in a novel way. He cast it in terms that draw on the work of a towering figure in French academic life in the period preceding the 1960s – a teacher of

Althusser's, Gaston Bachelard.[5] It would not be far-fetched to say that Althusser's claim for an epistemological break represented an effort to execute a Bachelardian reading of Marx; and, in so doing, to justify Althusser's claim for the scientificity of Marxist social science. Bachelard cut an odd figure. On the one hand, he anticipated a postpositivist view of science, years in advance of the development of parallel views in English-speaking philosophy. But the insularity of French academic philosophy, Bachelard's intellectual milieu, left him unaware of or, at least, insensitive to the importance of many of the problems that concern contemporary philosophers. In the English-speaking world, philosophy had passed through a salutary, logical positivist phase long before views that resemble Bachelard's began to emerge. Its 'problematic' was therefore more developed and considerably more subtle than the 'space' into which Bachelard 'intervened'. Bachelard had good instincts. He drew sound conclusions. But his reflections on science seldom engaged what most philosophers today consider the main issues. Althusser's reading of Marx evinced similar shortcomings.

It was a central claim of Bachelard's that there is no general theory of knowledge into which particular scientific practices fit, and therefore no general criterion of scientificity. Thus he was among the first, in France or anywhere, to broach the prospect of understanding science philosophically by understanding it historically and sociologically. He maintained that, as a matter of fact, working criteria of scientificity are constituted by standards internal to the scientific communities in which different practices are sustained, not by philosophical fiat; and that, in view of the diversity of scientific methods in modern times, this is how it should be. In short, science is as science does.

But even as Bachelard insisted that there is no general philosophical criterion for scientificity, he did think that there are ways of ascertaining the soundness of scientific methods and even for differentiating science from non-science. His position verged on pragmatism. For Bachelard, what makes a purportedly scientific method scientific is its practical success, its 'knowledge effects'. Therefore, to differentiate science from non-science, one must look to the practical or technological consequences of the knowledge claims scientists advance. If a purported claim genuinely does yield knowledge, this fact will be indicated by the uses to which it can be put. Bachelard never identified what is true with what works in the way that genuine pragmatists did. But he did think that if a claim works, it is because it is true or, at least, approximately true. One can appreciate how Althusser, a Bachelardian in the academy and a Leninist in politics, intuited an otherwise unlikely affinity joining these figures. Unlikely as it might seem, he detected a Bachelardian resonance in the canonical Leninist claim that 'without revolutionary theory, there can be no revolutionary practice'. For both the philosopher and the revolutionary, the 'dialectic' between theory and practice is indispensable for shaping both theory and practice. Theory rightly guides practice; but practice, guided by theory, puts theory to the test.

This view of the relation between theory and practice is, of course, consistent with Bachelard's and Althusser's (implicit) denial of the logical positivists' claim for 'the unity of science', or at least with the (crude) version of that claim that holds that there is a single scientific method. On that view, science progresses continuously, by revising explanatory laws to take account of new evidence. Bachelard maintained instead that the sciences develop discontinuously, by overcoming 'epistemological obstacles'. Chief among these obstacles are prescientific modes of thought. All sciences therefore have identifiable beginnings; moments in which they break away from prescientific ways of thinking. All sciences are born in epistemological breaks. It is therefore wrong to hold, as positivists do, that science advances when new domains are somehow subsumed under the strictures of a general scientific method. No such method exists. Sciences come into being when what Althusser called a new 'theoretical practice' is launched.

This observation led Bachelard to identify what he took to be a general characteristic of science, one that obtains despite the diversity of scientific practices. Bachelard claimed that although scientific methods have no identifiable essence or core, they are all, in a sense that only suggestive metaphors can articulate, of a piece. Prescientific theory is overlaid with psychological concreteness, with analogies and images. Science, on the other hand, is 'abstract'. Bachelard counterposed this abstraction to what he called 'reverie', the dreamlike character of the 'discourse' of everyday experience – and also of prescientific theory and its cousins, poetry and art. Bachelard was, in fact, as much an aesthetician as a philosopher of science. He wrote two series of books: one devoted to the history and philosophy of science, the other to 'artistic reverie'. But these very different subjects come together in the doctrine of the epistemological break. To constitute itself as a science, discourse about some domain must break away from reverie. It must become abstract.

There is yet another characteristic of science, all science, that Bachelard stressed. It too contrasts with reverie. Unlike pre-science (and also, for that reason, unlike poetry and art) science is 'open'. Its answers are not 'pregiven'. Even its subject matter is never exhaustively fixed. The 'dialectic of reason and application' ensures that science will go through a series of 'recrystalizations', of what we might today call 'paradigm shifts', each of which redefines its basic concepts, its scope and the character of its scientificity.

Althusser took over Bachelard's position, but he also modified it. Bachelard viewed scientific practice and change psychologically. The epistemological obstacles he described existed in the minds of investigators. The pre-Althusserian notion of an epistemological break therefore had to do with changes in ways of thinking only. Althusser recast Bachelard's idea in a way that took issue with this contention. As a Marxist would, he sociologized and historicized it. For Althusser, epistemological obstacles were not so much ideas in the minds of investigators as 'effects' of the 'ideological instance' of 'social formations'. Thus he incorporated Bachelard's account of the origins of scientific thinking in particular domains into a conceptual framework Marxists could endorse. But the account itself remained intact. This is why Althusser was able to maintain that what preceded the epistemological break, the philosophical anthropology of the Young Hegelians, was a closed system of metaphorical connections, remote from and even opposed to the abstraction and openness characteristic of genuine science. And it is why he insisted that what began to emerge in Marx's writings after 1845 was a system of thought linked to other scientific practices not by its method, which he claimed was novel, but by its abstraction and openness.

Whether or not an epistemological break really can be found in Marx's work, it is clear that the claim has descriptive content. It asserts that the problematic of Marx's early writings differs from the problematic of his later writings; and that the former are a species of reverie, while the latter exhibit features characteristic of all scientific practices. However, at the same time, Althusser's position had a plainly political function. In the most provocative way imaginable, it drew a 'line of demarcation' between his own account of Marxist theory and the accounts of the Marxist humanists who, on the authority of Marx's early writings, effectively denied the scientific character of Marx's thought.[6]

As one might expect of a position formulated for maximum polemical effect, with a different end in view or in a different theoretical conjuncture, one could make virtually the same descriptive claim by proposing a nearly opposite thesis. Thus it could be held that Marx's intellectual development, though generally continuous, was punctuated by a series of conceptual breakthroughs that, in retrospect, create the appearance of discontinuities. Put this way, no serious student of Marx would disagree, though there would doubtless remain quibbles about the nature and extent or importance of these changes. It is worth remarking that Althusser very nearly came to admit that the doctrine set out so provocatively in *For Marx* and *Reading Capital* was misleadingly overstated. In his later writings, he seldom mentioned the epistemological break. When he did, the thesis was qualified in ways that are so far-reaching that, in retrospect, they seem almost comical. It was not just that Althusser stopped writing about textual differences between Marx's early and later work. He even stopped claiming that there was an unequivocal substitution of one problematic for another. More modestly, but also more plausibly, he came to hold that, after 1845, a new problematic was born, and that Marx's writings after that date are products of coexisting problematics, in uneasy and contradictory 'relations of domination'. Thus he effectively conceded that the philosophical anthropology of Marx's early work never entirely disappeared; that it 'operated' throughout the entire Marxist corpus, including *Capital*. It was just that, in *Capital* and other texts of Marx's maturity, it was subordinated to the radically nonanthropological problematic of a comprehensive social science. It came to be Althusser's view that nearly all of Marx's writings after 1845 were 'contradictory' in this respect. In fact, towards the end, the only texts that Althusser deemed exclusively 'Marxist' were *The Critique of the Gotha Program* and the *Marginal Notes on Wagner's 'Lehrbuch'*. The latter was seldom read and only barely known, even to scholars, before Althusser called attention to it; the former, though politically important, is a minor theoretical text.

It might seem that, in his later writings, Althusser weakened the claim for an epistemological break so thoroughly that it lost all its force. But this is not so. He did render it immune from textual refutation, inasmuch as evidence that contradicts it can always be written off as an effect of a subordinate problematic. But the claim for an epistemological break was never really a claim about texts. It was formulated in textual terms because, in the theoretical conjuncture in which it operated, it mattered to have the authority of Marx's writings on one's side. But what was at issue substantively was not the trajectory of Marx's intellectual development. It was the character of the theoretical tradition that identified with Marx. In order to oppose Marxist humanism and similar trends within the communist (and extracommunist Marxist) movement, Althusser 'displaced' the real question: transforming it into a question about Marx's intellectual history. Thus it is especially important, in this instance, to look through the outer polemical shell into the rational kernel. There the idea is just that Marxist social science, despite its novelty, is a scientific practice. The philosophical anthropology of the Young Hegelians, like other putative nonscientific or extra-scientific ways of knowing, is therefore *not* part of it.

We can finally see what is genuinely important in Althusser's position. Much of the debate on Marx in the century past addressed the question of the scientificity of his thought – typically with a view to disparaging Marxism. Too often, historicist Marxists tacitly accepted the arguments of Marxism's critics. They just drew different, antipositivist conclusions – turning Marxism's alleged shortcomings with respect to scientificity into a virtue. Sometimes, they would even disparage science itself in the name of a vaguely specified 'dialectical' way of knowing. What all sides in this debate assumed was that criteria of scientificity can be specified apart from scientific practice itself; in other words, that scientificity is a philosophical judgment on explanatory methods. Following Bachelard's lead, Althusser rejected this way of thinking, undercutting the discussion in progress – among Marxists, and between Marxists and their critics. In consequence, for anyone who took Althusser's account of the epistemological break to heart, a bone of contention disappeared. Questions about methodology remained, of course; but their importance was deflated. Even allowing that Marxist social science is somehow distinguished by its method, as Althusser insisted, this fact does not mark it off from other scientific practices. Like them, it has its own distinctive ways of being open and abstract. But on the core question of the scientificity of Marxism, the center of so much controversy, there was no longer anything to discuss. Claims for Marxism's scientificity were assured by its formal properties – its openness and abstraction – and by its knowledge effects.

Of course, Bachelard had physics and chemistry in mind when he advanced the idea of an epistemological break; sciences whose cognitive achievements were beyond dispute. He could therefore maintain that it would be presumptuous to impose philosophical standards of scientificity on them. He could argue as well that efforts to do so on the part of his contemporaries, the logical positivists or, of more immediate concern, the French philosopher Emile Myerson, were, if anything, more likely to generate epistemological obstacles than to advance science. But, in Althusser's use of the concept, it was 'historical materialism' or, more precisely, Marxist social science as he and his cothinkers understood it, not physics or chemistry, that was in contention. Just what this theoretical practice was remained obscure. But whatever it was, no one could claim that it had to its credit anything like the successes that abound in the sciences of nature. Even among Marxists, there was little agreement about what Marx had shown, and less about how to investigate social reality. There was, in short, no self-justifying consensus, as in physics and chemistry, forged by the progress of science itself. What justification, then, could there be for taking historical materialism's scientificity for granted? The question answers itself.

There is a certain irony in the fact that the Althusserians' programmatic account of historical materialism was perhaps the most disputed aspect of their work. It is especially telling that the most theoretically substantive essay in *Reading Capital* – written by Etienne Balibar, then a student of Althusser's – was entitled 'The Basic Concepts of Historical Materialism'. Had an epistemological break in Bachelard's sense occurred, it should have been unnecessary, except for didactic purposes, to say what the basic concepts of the new science are. But Balibar's contribution to *Reading Capital* was anything but didactic. It was as contentious as any of Althusser's own essays. It is worth noting too that Balibar subsequently modified many of the views presented in that essay.[7] One can only wonder, then, about an epistemological break that so few were aware of, and about which even the chosen few were unsure. Not only do we lack indisputable cognitive achievements; we do not even know unequivocally what the character of the new science is. In a word, the epistemological break that Althusser imputed to Marx was more of a wish than a reality.

But not entirely. For Marxism, as Althusser conceived it, did generate knowledge effects, or so he believed. These effects played a role in Althusser's thinking analogous to the role played by technological achievements in physics and chemistry in Bachelard's. They clarified the theory, and vindicated it. The knowledge effects Althusser had in mind were, of course, the Russian and Chinese

Revolutions, led by Lenin and Mao. These figures allegedly proved Marx right by applying his thought successfully. They therefore understood Max correctly – in a practical, though not always in a theoretical, way. Thus they merit the magisterial status Althusser accorded them. But, of course, this assumes that the Russian and Chinese Revolutions were indeed successful, and also that Marx was right, if not about literally everything then at least about how to make a revolution – to such an extent that failed revolutionary ventures undertaken in his name only show that Marxists can and do misunderstand Marx. No one today still endorses the first of these articles of faith, though, only a few decades ago, they were hardly controversial. The second is not much more secure. But, even at the time, the idea that Marx was somehow infallible – and that the task, therefore, is only to understand him correctly – could not be more out of line with what Bachelard called 'the spirit of science'. Paradoxically, it was because Althusser had this faith – or, at least, acted as if he did, for conjunctural political reasons – that he was able to treat historical materialism in the way that Bachelard treated chemistry and physics, and therefore to turn Marxism, implicitly but effectively, into a philosophy of (social) science. Had Althusser's own practice been more in line with what he claimed Marx's was, he would not have been able to 'import' Bachelard's notion into the Marxist fold.

*   *   *

In *For Marx* and *Reading Capital* Althusser insisted on a fundamental opposition between Hegel and Marx. Here, again, a political motivation was transparent. Althusser's opponents were all, in one way or another, Hegelian Marxists; Marxists who would 'correct' Marxist–Leninist orthodoxy by reviving Hegelian motifs in Marx's thought. But in just the way, and for just the reason, that Althusser came to mitigate the doctrine of an epistemological break, he also came to mitigate his rejection of Hegelianism. In this case too, he did so without exactly repudiating his earlier position. What he maintained, instead, was that the Hegel he had rejected in his own early work, the Hegel of the Young Hegelians, was not, in fact, the historical Hegel; and therefore that the Young Hegelians' Hegel, the Hegel to whom historicist Marxists appealed, was not the Hegel whose thinking Marx incorporated into his own.

In the Young Hegelian view, Hegel was not only an historicist but also a philosophical anthropologist. For their Hegel, then, all philosophical questions were to be conceived within the framework of a theory of the human subject, of Man and his essence. Throughout human history that essence is alienated (separated) from its subject, releasing a 'dialectic' of subject and object (objectified essence) that continues until the end (*telos*) of history is achieved. All the separated and fragmented aspects of human experience are *expressions* of human alienation. This is why they serve as indicators of the career of the human subject, passing through the stages of alienation (separation of subject and object) until, finally, unity is (re)attained. Marx's early writings aimed to exhibit this alienation in various aspects of human experience, and to reveal the inexorable process of its overcoming. They imply that the human subject *makes* history – that Man is both the author and victim of human alienation and the agent of its transformation into communism, the realm of Freedom.

This picture, in Althusser's view, represented the last gasp of prescientific reverie in Marxism's prehistory. It was a closed system of metaphors and analogies, suggestive perhaps and insightful but ultimately at odds with a practice suitable for achieving knowledge of social reality. Therefore, those who waved the banner of Hegel, like those who proclaimed that the early Marx was the true Marx, effectively denied the scientificity of Marx's thought. Thus the opposition to Hegel that was emblematic of Althusser's early work was yet another displaced opposition to tendencies among Marxists that he sought to combat: specifically, their disposition to deny the scientificity of Marxist social science.

Althusser came to insist, however, that there is another Hegel with whom Marx shared the deepest affinity. This was the Hegel who, as a holist, upheld the explanatory importance of the category of 'totality'; and who acknowledged the 'contradictory' character of this social whole. This *other* Hegel was the most important precursor of (genuine) Marxism, Althusser contended – because it was he who led Marx to his principal theoretical discovery: the idea that history is 'a process without a subject'.[8] In his later writings, Althusser claimed that this other Hegel was already a presence in *For Marx* and *Reading Capital*. He was not wrong. It is fair to say, in retrospect, that whatever polemical turns Althusser's opposition to historicist Marxism took, fidelity to the thinking of this other Hegel was indeed a constant fixture of his thought.

To see that this is so, it is instructive to recall Althusser's reflections in *For Marx* on the metaphor, dear to historicist Marxists, of 'reversal'; the claim that Marx 'stood Hegel on his feet', that 'the materialist dialectic' *reverses* Hegel's idealist dialectic. There are, in effect, two glosses in the Marxist literature on this image: a straightforward one, and an apparently more sophisticated Hegelian one. On the former view, Hegel discovered the structure of the Real, but misconstrued its substantial nature. It fell to Marx, then, to *extract* the account of that structure, the dialectic, away from the 'object' to which Hegel applied it (Spirit, the Idea), and to apply it to a different object (the economy or, perhaps what Althusser called 'concrete social practices'). On this view, Hegel was an idealist because he ascribed *the* dialectic to ideas. Marx was a materialist because he ascribed it to social practices. But the dialectic itself is neither materialist nor idealist. It is a method in search of a subject.

The Hegelian Marxists came to a similar conclusion, but without benefit of the metaphor of 'extraction'. Their view was that it makes no sense to extract a structure from one object, and then to transfer it to another. Georg Lukács's account of the emergence of the Marxist dialectic is exemplary. In the central essay of his masterwork, *History and Class Consciousness*, Lukács recounted how problems internal to Hegelian philosophy are only resolvable from within 'the standpoint of the proletariat', and how that standpoint can be realized only by the dialectical supersession, the *Aufhebung*, of the entire Hegelian system.[9] On his view, the transition from Hegel to Marx involved more than a change of ontology; *that* reversal is itself part of the dialectical process. But despite this difference, which he elaborated with considerable subtlety, the underlying thought remains: that there is a dialectical 'logic' common to both Hegel and Marx, and therefore that what separates Hegel from Marx ultimately redounds back to the quarrel between materialists and idealists. In the end, even Lukács was faithful to what had become almost a truism, established by Engels: that the entire battery of dialectical notions found in Hegel's philosophy – negation, supersession, dialectical contradiction, the identity of opposites – is evident in Marx's thinking too, and therefore that Marx's dialectic and Hegel's are essentially the same.[10]

Althusser faulted this conclusion on the grounds that it is insufficiently Hegelian. Following Hegel, Lukács understood that a method cannot exist independently of the theory that employs it. He realized that to 'extract' the dialectical method from the Hegelian system and then to deploy it elsewhere is to suppose a distinction between form and content, between structure and substance, that is probably incoherent and that, in any case, no true Hegelian can abide. But Lukács failed to recognize all the implications of this position and therefore, in the end, came to support the traditional, dogmatic understanding of 'standing Hegel on his feet'. Althusser too insisted that method and theory are inseparable; in part for Hegelian reasons of the kind Lukács invoked, but also because, following Bachelard, he was sensitive to how different types of discourse have different and often incommensurable problematics, and therefore incompatible methods. To extract a dialectical method from the Hegelian problematic and then to use it in a different theoretical space is an impossible undertaking. Because he was more genuinely orthodox than Althusser, Lukács failed to draw this conclusion. Because he was more disingenuous than Lukács, Althusser was able to wrap himself more effectively than Lukács did in the mantle of orthodoxy while, at the same time, being more genuinely Hegelian than Lukács was – drawing out all the implications of Hegel's contention that form and content, method and substance are inseparable. Thus he argued that there can be no dialectic that is, at the same time, *either* materialist *or* idealist. A 'line of demarcation' separates systems *and* methods; not systems *from* methods. One dialectic, applicable to two systems, is inconceivable. If there are indeed two systems, as all Marxists maintained, there must therefore be two dialectics. This is not to say that there cannot be historical or conceptual connections between them; for the two dialectics with which Althusser was concerned, Hegel's and Marx's, there plainly were. In *For Marx* and *Reading Capital*, Althusser understated and disparaged these connections; in his later writings, in a different polemical context, he acknowledged and celebrated them. But it remained a steadfast conviction of his that the metaphor of reversal in no way applies to the Hegel–Marx relation.

Thus Althusser's view of the Hegel–Marx relation, shorn of its outer shell, actually underwent very little change in the course of his writings. Whenever he emphasized their differences, it was always only to register a claim for the scientificity of Marx's thought. In this respect, what Althusser wrote about the Hegel–Marx relation ran in tandem with his account of the epistemological break. In fact, the two accounts converge. Althusser maintained that a materialist dialectic can no more result from a reversal of the idealist, Hegelian dialectic than a science is the opposite of the pre-science that precedes it. The connections between what fall on either side of an epistemological break are more complicated than that. So too, for the same reason, is the metaphor of reversal that the Young Hegelians and their successors invoked so promiscuously.

*   *   *

Inasmuch as the content and even the identity of Marxist social science was never satisfactorily established, the doctrine of the epistemological break was mainly a negative thesis: a claim about what Marxism is not. Marxism is not a philosophical anthropology, not a closed system of reverie built up out of metaphors and analogies. But what is the character of the open and abstract discourse that is supposed to have taken the place of the Young Hegelians' philosophical anthropology? Even in the absence of a full-fledged account, we can obtain at least a partial answer by focusing on the Hegel–Marx relation, as Althusser conceived it. To this end, it will be useful to turn to Althusser's account of what Hegel's dialectic and Marx's had in common. It was, in fact, to identify this shared content that Althusser made use of Marx's metaphor of the rational kernel and the outer shell. Marx had claimed that the Hegelian dialectic, despite its idealist shell, had a rational kernel. This kernel, Althusser insisted, is *the materialist dialectic*.

To understand what he had in mind, it will help to revisit the Hegelian dialectic. Schematically, it is a succession of 'moments': affirmation, negation, negation of the negation; or, according to a better-known formula, thesis, antithesis, and synthesis (or supersession, *Aufhebung*). The moment of affirmation is the moment of the in-itself. A reality presents itself; it is *there:* given, but not yet developed. The development of the in-itself consists in the process of its affirmation, the *becoming* of what it is. But this process is also, simultaneously, the development of negative elements, incompatible with and subversive of the process of affirmation, though internal to it and necessary for it. Thus, for a dominant class to develop, it must structure the entire society through the intermediary of another class – as capitalists do through the proletariat. But then their becoming dominant implies the formation of a dominated class, which has 'negative' bearing for their own affirmation. More generally, negations follow from affirmations. This is the sense of Hegel's declaration that negation is 'the *soul* of the content', the *motor* of the process of becoming. It is the moment of the 'out-of-self', of the exteriority and independence of negative elements. The moment of negation stands, then, as a distinct phase in the dialectical process; a phase that, as it develops, increasingly opposes the moment of affirmation.

This internally generated opposition is a 'contradiction'. An Hegelian contradiction is therefore the result of a division immanent in the process of development itself, in which a unity comes increasingly to stand against itself. So conceived, contradictions contrast with oppositions between independent entities or forces. Capitalists and workers oppose one another but, in the final analysis, they are not distinct entities in conflict. They are aspects of the same underlying reality – the class struggle as it unfolds throughout human history. A dialectical contradiction is the coexistence of these moments; a coexistence that is both inevitable and intrinsically unstable. The instability is resolved, finally, by the negation of the negation, the moment of the 'for-itself', in which each of the preceding moments is superseded or overcome – and therefore incorporated into a higher unity. What was opposed dialectically is resolved into a third moment that contains them both, but that also goes *beyond* them – conserving what they each in themselves represent, while moving to a higher stage in which their contradictory relation no longer obtains.

This movement continues until its end (*telos*) is achieved – Absolute Knowledge, in Hegel's case; communism, in Marx's. This side of that end, the same dialectical process continues to unfold. The third moment, the negation of the negation, becomes the first moment of a succeeding dialectical transformation which, in turn, engenders its own contradictions and supersessions. Hegel claimed to verify this process in his analyses of human history, philosophy and art. Since, for Hegel, everything ultimately is One, history, philosophy, art and everything else *express* the same underlying movement. And since the One unfolds according to the dialectical process, the resolution of contradictions, wherever they might arise, is inevitable. Thus it was Hegel's position that there are no contradictions without solutions. At the end of history, everything will be resolved, and everything will be retained.

The end of history is not the end of chronological time. The idea, instead, is that whatever happens as subsequent (chronological) time unfolds is in some sense already settled. New contradictions may appear, but they are already resolved. They develop, as Hegel said, empirically and locally – without historical significance. This is the sense in which, for the Right Hegelians and perhaps also for Hegel himself, history culminated with the Prussian state; a state that Hegel thought would continue to exist indefinitely. It is also what the Left Hegelians had in mind when they conceived of communism as humanity's destiny. Under communism, history, but not chronological time, would come to an end – giving way to a permanent 'realm of freedom'.

*   *   *

How does this dialectic, on Althusser's reading of it, function? To answer this question, it will be useful to look briefly at Althusser's account of Hegel's claim that a state based on principles of Right, a *Rechtstaat*, 'resolves' the contradictions of civil society.[11] According to Althusser, it was this position of Hegel's that the young Marx appropriated and developed into a 'critique' of the state itself, as the penultimate, not the final, stage in the overcoming of human alienation.[12] Following Rousseau, civil society, on Hegel's view, is the locus of contradictions between individuals – motivated by egoism and a desire for recognition, and coexisting in a milieu of scarcity. It is also, Hegel added, an arena in which contradictions exist between groups of individuals or, as he recognized before Marx, social classes. The state, Hegel then argued, reconciles these contradictions and resolves them in the sphere of the 'universal' through the category of Right (*Recht*). After this resolution, individuals may still be in competition with each other for everything. The quest for mutual recognition and esteem may still go on unabated. Even classes may persist with workers selling their capacity to labor, capitalists organizing production, and bureaucrats managing public affairs. Inasmuch as the interests of these classes remain at least somewhat opposed, class oppositions may persist as well. But these oppositions will be of a derivative or secondary importance from the standpoint of human history. They will no longer move history along. In the *Rechtstaat*, the state governed by principles of Right (*Recht*), their driving force is superseded.

Hegel's idea was not just that the *Rechtstaat* neutralizes the virulence of class oppositions by superintending and controlling them. It was also, mainly, that, in the *Rechtstaat*, different classes each realize certain aspects of a stable, unified whole. Hegel called these aspects 'determinations'. Opposed in civil society, classes are reconciled in the *Rechtstaat* because the *Rechtstaat* requires workers and capitalists for its material survival, and bureaucrats to direct public affairs. Workers, capitalists, and bureaucrats – along with all other components of civil society – are therefore, in Hegel's view, determinations of the *Rechtstaat* – that is, aspects or necessary manifestations of it. This is why the Right Hegelians, as conservative defenders of Order and declared opponents of revolutionary change, took sustenance in Hegel's philosophy of history. For Hegel, whatever is is indispensable from the point of view of the unfolding of the dialectical process through which Reason becomes increasingly manifest in the actual, the world of appearance. At the end of this process, when the subject–object opposition is overcome and Reason is fully in control, whatever is carries, as it were, the mandate of history. Therefore, if history culminates in the *Rechtstaat*, and if the existing Prussian state instantiates that ideal, it is what Reason requires. Whoever seeks to overthrow it is an enemy of Reason itself.

Left Hegelians had a different view of the historical bearing of the Prussian state. For them, it was not the end of history, but the last of the old regimes, destined to be overthrown by a social revolution that would at last bring history to its end (*telos*). But all Hegelians agreed that, once the end of history is attained, oppositions that remain, including class oppositions, would no longer be mortal, dialectical contradictions. They would only be disturbances in a secure and rational social order in which fundamental divisions have been overcome. Marx faulted the notion of a *Rechtstaat* on the grounds that it failed to express this ideal adequately; and, like all Left Hegelians, he categorically denied that the Prussian state had risen even to this level. But he never questioned Hegel's ideal itself. When the young Marx challenged the notion that the Prussian state was the end of history, he did so on Hegelian grounds, for reasons that Hegelians would understand, even if the vast majority of them did not accept their applicability in this instance. In much the way that Althusser faulted Hegelian Marxists, like Lukács, for not acknowledging the full implications of the positions they held, the young Marx took the Right Hegelians to task for being insufficiently Hegelian. Althusser thought that the Hegelian Marxists failed to break away from idealism for reasons that were at least partly political. Marx's (implicit) explanation for the failure of the Right Hegelians to recognize the true implications of Hegel's philosophy of history was of a similar stripe. He thought that the Right Hegelians misunderstood Hegel for reasons that were mainly ideological. They were blinded to the consequences of their convictions because they were more committed to blocking the impending German revolution than to following Hegel's ideas through to their conclusion. Because they wanted to maintain the status quo, they mistook the status quo for the end of history

*   *   *

On Althusser's telling of Hegel's story, the *Rechtstaat* is the *essence* of which society and its contradictions are forms of appearance.[13] A problem, then, is to reconcile this claim with the Hegelian view that Truth is not given once and for all, that it *emerges* through the development and overcoming of contradictions. These views are at odds because the distinction between essence and appearance harkens back to the Platonic tradition, in which *essences* remain constant throughout the flux of time. The key to dissolving this tension, Althusser reasoned, is to develop an appropriate concept of the *totality* or, more specifically, of the social whole. Althusser maintained that, in this endeavor, Hegel had already shown the way.

For Hegel, because all is One, the real is totalizing and global. It was this thought that allowed him, unlike his predecessors, to construe the essence–appearance distinction dynamically; to see the difference between essence and appearance as a *process*. Nowhere is this more evident than in the philosophy of Right (*Recht*). Determinations express the social whole at particular times and places. For example, in the present 'moment', the worker represents the state in the sphere of work – the state works *through* the worker. A similar relation holds for all the other classes that comprise civil society. Each determination is necessary for the totality to manifest itself. But no particular determination expresses the totality completely; the Whole *requires* all of its parts. But the parts themselves, as determinations of the Whole, are always in flux; affirmation and negation shape their trajectories. Their essential natures therefore reveal themselves as their contradictions are superseded. It is the negation of the negation that determines, in retrospect, what was essence and what was appearance. Essences themselves therefore rise and fall – to be incorporated into ever higher unities in the dialectical process that history expresses. In the end, each and every determination is thoroughly superseded. Then, finally, the totality presents itself *as the totality that it is.*

Althusser claimed that, at every stage in this process, a relation of *expressive causality* joins the totality to its determinations. This relation is the key to the idealist dialectic. To *express*, in the sense Althusser intended, is to realize or materialize something that in one way or another preexists its expression. However, for Hegel – on Althusser's reading, even in *For Marx* – the underlying reality that appearance expresses is never a fixed substance, as it was for Feuerbach and the other Young Hegelians, including the 'pre-Marxist' Marx.[14] What is expressed is a process – in which an ever developing Truth affirms itself, then develops and in that movement negates itself, only to be recuperated in a higher order affirmation. Each of these moments expresses one of the determinations of the ever-unfolding totality or whole. Thus 'the Hegelian whole', as Althusser put it, has a 'spiritual' unity in which 'all differences are only posed to be negated'. They 'never exist for themselves', but have instead only a 'semblance of an independent existence'. Althusser went on to say that 'since they never manifest anything but the unity of the simple internal principle alienated in them, they are practically equal among themselves as the alienated phenomena of this principle'.[15] The totality, then, is just the unfolding of a process that everything phenomenal illustrates. Its essence, therefore, is the process itself. In this sense, there is only 'becoming'. For there *is* nothing, ultimately, apart from its coming to be. Thus, for Hegel, history, like the process it expresses, is a *process without a subject.*

As history unfolds, it realizes or makes evident what is already there but not yet accessible to consciousness. Outcomes are therefore predetermined. The teleology of the system is intrinsic to its inner principle. The Hegelian totality is a monad, a metaphysically independent entity, in which all change is and can only be self-development. But unlike the well-known monads of Leibniz's metaphysics, the Hegelian monad is not a substance. It has no content at all. It *is* its own principle of change. As Hegel declared – in his system, 'the principle is the end, the end is the principle'. Its self-development consists in its becoming evident to itself – in its own expanding *self-consciousness.*

Human alienation is a consequence of the internal development of this principle. Althusser conceded that this genuinely Hegelian category, in certain of its aspects, was taken over by the Young Hegelians. But, for them and therefore also for the pre-Marxist Marx, alienation was still an essentialist notion. Their view was that there is an essence, a human essence, from which the subject of history, Man, is alienated. This essence therefore exists apart from the process of its alienation and overcoming. Human history, for the

Young Hegelians, is the story of the career of this suprahistorical subject. It is a process *with* a subject, the human subject. This is why Althusser identified the Young Hegelianism that preceded the epistemological break with Marxist Humanism, and inveighed against them both together.

Althusser's contention was that the *humanist* understanding of Hegel is both conceptually untenable and historically incorrect. Characteristically, he confounded these claims, insisting only that Hegel's principal philosophical advance was to 'exclude the subject'. Althusser never quite elaborated on this claim in a way that clarified it enough to make it susceptible to rational adjudication. But he did succeed in identifying an ambiguity in the Young Hegelians' concept of *alienation.* On the one hand, they put that category to work to reveal the vicissitudes and fate of the human essence. But, on the other, because the category points away from any notion of a transhistorical human essence, they prepared the way for the idea that the epistemological break would finally liberate from its outer, polemical shell: the idea of a process without a subject.

$$*\quad *\quad *$$

What, then, did Marx learn from Hegel?

According to Althusser, the first thing he learned was *theory*. But Althusser used this term in an idiosyncratic way – and also in a misleading way, inasmuch as he also used 'theory' to designate a type of philosophical practice (see Chapter 3). But, when focusing on Marx's debt to Hegel, Althusser identified *theory* with *holism*. Thus he claimed that, from Hegel, Marx learned to relate apparently isolated elements of situations to one another, to organize otherwise undifferentiated experience, and to conceive of what science reveals as an integrated whole, in movement and 'determined by a principle'. The materialist dialectic, like its idealist ancestor and rival, is a totalizing structure. The rational kernel of the Hegelian dialectic therefore includes a refusal to isolate elements in explanatory contexts. To explain a phenomenon, Althusser insisted, is to relate it to the totality of which it is a part and in which it operates. One thing that Marx learned from Hegel, then, was holism, as the term is customarily understood.

From Hegel too, Marx took over the idea that contradictions are real and in principle explainable. Outside the Hegelian ambit, the idea that the real is contradictory, or that contradictions can be explained – rather than diagnosed and then dismissed – is unthinkable. But for Hegel, reality genuinely is contradictory (this side of the end of history), and contradictions are therefore appropriate explananda. Althusser deployed considerable ingenuity in attempting to specify what he called a materialist notion of contradiction. His account suffers from irremediable obscurities.[16] Still, it is illuminating to see what he attempted. In his efforts to identify a specifically Marxist concept of contradiction, Althusser borrowed freely from non-Hegelian and non-Marxist sources – from Lacanian psychoanalysis and from the 'structuralism' that flourished in France in the 1960s. He appears to have taken the scientificity of these sources for granted; something hardly anyone would do today. Nevertheless, drawing on these strains of thought, Althusser concluded that the concept of *overdetermination,* a concept he ascribed to Freud, best captures Marx's idea.

Presumably, an effect is overdetermined when it is the outcome of more than one cause, any one of which would be sufficient for bringing it about. Althusser never quite made this or any other gloss on overdetermination sufficiently clear. What he did instead was to clarify what contradiction, understood as overdermination, is *not.* It is not, like an Hegelian contradiction, an ever unfolding division into opposites within a single unity. Rather, it has to do with 'complex structural instabilities and determinations'. One looks in vain in Althusser's writings for a clearer – or, failing that, a more suggestive – statement. Ironically, analytical Marxism, born in part in reaction to the influence of Althusserianism in Britain in the 1970s, would eventually provide a clear and plausible reconstruction of Marx's notion of contradiction that might have served Althusser's purpose. But Althusser himself never did anything of the sort, despite the attention he lavished on the topic. He did insist, however, that, for Marx, contradictions are real, and possible objects of investigation. Thus he concluded that another thing that Marx learned from Hegel was a sense of the importance of contradictions or, as he put it, 'a sense of the movement of the whole'.[17]

*   *   *

Adherents of the metaphor of reversal implicitly rejected Althusser's account of how Hegel educated Marx. For them, history has a subject, the human subject. For some of them, this subject is incarnated in individual human beings; for others, in the working class as the representative of the human race; for yet others in some idealized notion of humanity itself – such as the 'species being' that, following Feuerbach, the Marx of the 1844 *Paris Manuscripts* invoked. But, on Althusser's view, to suppose that the subject of history can be specified in any way at all is to misrepresent Hegel's thought. It is to dehistoricize his understanding of essence and appearance. For Hegel, the idea was always that the opposition of subject and object is a manifestation of a process *which is itself the real subject*.

This was, Althusser maintained, a potentially materialist insight. But its materialist implications were bound to remain obscure before Marx's epistemological break. The Young Hegelians, including Marx, were idealists without knowing it, because they put the dialectic to use in a philosophical anthropology. They can be forgiven for that, inasmuch as they had no better way to grasp the significance of the 'facts' that concerned them. Still their problematic was a muddle – partly because they misunderstood Hegel, but also because they had yet to cross the threshold into Marxist social science. Neither had Hegel himself, of course. His idealism, at least, was not similarly confused; and, presumably, he understood his own intentions. But Hegel's thinking, taken in its totality, nevertheless also threatens to lead us down the wrong track for the same reason that Young Hegelian criticism does – because it too assumes the absence of an explanatory program of the kind Marx would discover. Hegel was an idealist of the old school; he genuinely did endorse a post-Cartesian idealist ontology. Thus he insisted that all aspects of human experience dissolve into a single Idea, which they then all express. In this way, Hegel joined the notion of a process without a subject to an ontological claim about the nature of the Real. In Althusser's view, this was understandable *before* the epistemological break – before Marxist social science revealed new ways of connecting the part to the whole, and of grasping the movement of the process through which the totality progressively unfolds. But after the epistemological break, it became inexcusable.

Before Marxist social science emerged, there was no alternative to the notion of expressive causality. This, Althusser observed, is the idea that underwrites the idealist misappropriation of Hegel's discovery. This was as much true for Hegel himself as for the Young Hegelians. Since, in Hegel's own case, everything expresses the same underlying (ever evolving) Idea, it follows that it is the Idea itself that is realized through the unfolding of the dialectical process; that what that process reveals is the Idea in its various determinations.

Within the discourse Hegel developed, this is a way of maintaining that the real subject is *the logic of the movement*. Once that discourse is made obsolete, in virtue of the epistemological break, we are left with the conclusion Althusser endorsed – that there is *only* a process without a subject. But, again, to arrive at that point, we must have at hand an alternative to expressive causality, one that makes 'the continent of History' susceptible to scientific exploration. This is what the epistemological break provided.

*   *   *

It was characteristic of Althusser that he was an incisive critic of what he opposed, at the same time that he was vague or negligent or both in elaborating positive proposals. This was as true of the idea of a process without a subject as of any other of his other contentions. Stripped to its core, what Althusser opposed was the notion of the subject assumed in the philosophical anthropology of the Young Hegelians. On this much, he was emphatic and clear. But because he was much less clear about what the doctrine implies, it is easy to misunderstand even his negative claims. Althusser's opaque and tortured language exacerbated the problem. Thus even a careful reader might have the impression that Althusser somehow opposed the very idea of a subject – even one that is, so to speak, nonsubstantive. He did not – as the following, characteristically obscure but revealing passage explains:

> ... For what is logic? The science of the Idea, i.e. the exposition of its concept, *the concept of a process of alienation without a subject*, in other words, the concept of the process of self-alienation which, considered in its totality, is nothing but the Idea. Thus conceived, Logic, or the concept of the Idea, is the dialectic, the 'path' of the process as a process, the 'absolute method'. If Logic is nothing but the concept of the Idea (of the process of alienation without a subject), it is then the concept of this strange subject we are looking for. But the fact that this subject is only the concept of the *process of alienation itself*, in other words, this subject is the dialectic, i.e. the very movement of the negation of the negation, reveals the extraordinary paradox of Hegel. The process of alienation without a subject (or the dialectic) is the only subject recognized by Hegel. There is no subject to the process: *it is the process itself which is a subject in so far as it does not have a subject.*[18]

In other words, an account of change that is not internal to a pregiven subject is not only unexceptionable; it is the rational kernel of Hegel's thought. In the materialist dialectic, this idea finally comes into its own. But it was already implicit in Hegelian idealism. Marx therefore owed a considerable debt to Hegel, despite the impression *For Marx* and *Reading Capital* conveyed. So, far from breaking away from its Hegelian roots, Marx's mature thinking stood on Hegel's intuition about the kind of process history is. Had Marx consistently and vigilantly paid heed to the implications of his own thought, his writings would have unequivocally reflected this fact. Because he did not, and because so many of his followers have gone astray, it was Althusser's mission to recover this achievement of Marx's and to see it through to the end.

*   *   *

However, what Althusser had to say about Marx's position after the epistemological break was much less clear, and much less helpful, than his account of what Marxism is *not*. The picture he presented was too philosophical (in the manner of French philosophy of that period) and, despite his gestures towards Bachelardian philosophy of science, almost entirely bereft of sustained reflections on actual social scientific practice. In a word, the account of the materialist dialectic one finds in Althusser's writings was dangerously, if not fatally, obscure. It had an a priori and stipulative character that had almost nothing to do with ongoing social scientific research, Marxist or otherwise. No doubt the paucity of indisputable progress in an historical materialist vein was at least partly responsible. It was as if, having proclaimed an epistemological break in the absence of evidence that one had occurred, there was nothing to do but hide behind grand philosophical poses. It is worth remarking that Althusser effectively conceded this point when he claimed that reflecting on the political practice of Lenin and Mao and other revolutionaries, who supposedly understood Marx better than anyone else, was the best way to uncover the nature of the materialist dialectic. Towards the end, Althusser even claimed that these revolutionary figures were better guides to Marxist theory than *Capital* and other works of Marx's maturity. Evidently, practicing historical materialists, including the no longer young Marx some of the time, did not understood Marx well enough.

A brief look at Althusser's account of causality will suffice to indicate the shortcomings of his elaboration of the materialist dialectic. In his view, the kinds of causes historical materialism identifies are not, for the most part, 'linear'. Althusser never explained what he meant by this description, but the general idea is plain – Marxists, in Althusser's view, are not much interested in *sufficient conditions* (where A is sufficient for B, if whenever A occurs, B occurs). Thus what Althusser seems to have had in mind when he faulted linear causality was roughly the understanding of causality that the scientific revolution of the seventeenth century brought to the fore. Althusser's claim, it seems, was that historical materialism makes use of a different idea – one that somehow eschews any notion of unique causal determinations.

Since he never satisfactorily explained what this alternative to the standard view might be, and since he certainly never teased it out of ongoing Marxist social scientific practice, it is fair to speculate that, in pressing this point, Althusser was, again, articulating a political position in a philosophical guise. Indeed, it seems, in retrospect, that what motivated his treatment of causality was, in large part, of a piece with the attack on 'vulgar Marxism' that was emblematic of Western Marxism from the 1920s on. In context, this amounted to an attack on Soviet Marxism and therefore, by implication, on official communism generally. Althusser advanced this case by insisting that, whenever linear causality is assumed, the way is open to 'economic determinism', the idea that the economy exclusively determines everything else. He faulted this view for the familiar reason – that it reduces all struggles to economic struggles, in contravention of Marx's sense of the importance of politics (for which he found evidence in Lenin's political practice) and ideology (for which he found evidence in Mao Tse-tung's). All Western Marxists opposed economic determinism on similar grounds, even if they were less inclined than Althusser to mask their opposition to Soviet orthodoxy, and the system it helped to sustain, by staking out a Leninist or Maoist pedigree for their views.

The search for 'linear' causes leads, Althusser insisted, to *economism*, the idea that the development of productive forces alone, not economic development in conjunction with political efforts to transform social relations, is sufficient for the transformation of society from capitalism to communism. Economism, Althusser maintained, lies at the root of the political failings of the communist movement; not least 'the Stalinist deviation'.[19] He insisted too that

its deleterious effects stem from the fact that it is intrinsically un-
dialectical. By this, he seems to have meant, among other things,
that it is insufficiently 'theoretical' or, rather, holistic – that the
category of totality plays no role in economic determinist explana
tions because economic determinism does not take account of the
effect of the whole upon its parts. Economism is dialectically
deficient too because where it holds sway, contradiction drops away.
Even if the term is retained, it can only designate simple and direct
oppositions. Contradictions as 'complex registers of structural instabilities' become unintelligible. Thus economic determinism makes it
impossible to incorporate the rational kernel of the Hegelian
dialectic into what Lenin called 'the soul of Marxism' – 'the concrete
analysis of concrete situations'.

Structural casuality is holistic, just as expressive causality is. But in
other respects, the two notions contrast markedly, or so one would
infer from what Althusser says *against* the rival view. Althusser
maintained that Marx was the first to deploy the idea of structural
causality. He insisted too that, for Marx, unlike Hegel and the
Hegelian Marxists, the totality is not causally efficacious because its
determinations 'express' it. Althusser advanced this contention with
hardly any argument, but his rationale is nevertheless apparent.
Expressive causality is incompatible with some of the central claims
of Marxist social science – particularly those that accord priority to
the economic level. Where it is assumed, it is natural, and perhaps
even necessary, to view each determination, each expression of an
underlying essence, as a coequal part of the social whole. There is
therefore no way to assign causal and explanatory preeminence to
production over distribution or to the economic base over the legal
and political superstructure and forms of consciousness. Althusser
reproached the young Marx on this account. He and his coauthors
in *Reading Capital* maintained that the problematic of the (1844)
Paris Manuscripts makes it impossible to account for how some levels
dominate others.[20] Either the economy is conflated with the totality
of human life (through the categories of production and exchange)
or else it is depicted as one of many expressions of human alienation.
The worker becomes Man as such; and the class struggle is identified
with the human condition. Althusser objected to each of these alternatives. Against them, he offered a motley of philosophical and
political considerations – according, as was his wont, the greatest
weight to what he took to be the (implicit) politics of self-identified
Marxisms that, wittingly or not, deploy the category of expressive

causality. He claimed that, in denying the specificity of class struggle, they support 'opportunism' – presumably by deflating the Leninist and Maoist sense of the importance of political and ideological struggles. And he maintained that their way of opposing the 'mechanistic' posture of economic determinists and other dogmatists who subscribe to linear understandings of causality implies the philosophical anthropology Marx came to reject. Thus they encourage the explanatory practice pioneered by the Young Hegelians, according to which the objective is not to discover real causal determinations, but to make individuals take consciousness of the ways that particular determinations of the social totality express the whole. In practice, this amounts to concocting analogies in light of which analogized elements are understood to express the totality they represent. Theoretical practice therefore devolves into an exercise of the practitioner's ingenuity in finding similarities linking very different kinds of phenomena, while politics turns into a futile effort to represent general human interests from an enlightened perspective beyond classes and their struggles. Nothing, Althusser insisted, could be further from the Leninist (and therefore Marxist) idea – not just in its political implications, but also in its opposition to science or, what comes to the same thing, in its idealist adulteration of Marx's thought.

What, then, *is* the concept of causality proper to Marxist social science? Althusser called it *structural causality*. But, in his writings, this concept was more intimated than elaborated. What Althusser proposed was a notion that somehow accounts for the intervention of the whole on its elements, and for relations between 'regional structures' (such as the 'economic level') and global structures ('social formations'). But what that notion might be, he never quite said. Instead, he provided intriguing promises and intimations of a position, along with fragments of arguments. Thus he said that his intent was to elaborate upon Engels's claim that the economy is 'determining in the last instance', and to show how the last instance 'never occurs'; in other words, to show how it is never (or almost never?) the case that the economy causes political or ideological effects in a linear way. He maintained that causes determine outcomes through 'the conditioning of the complex structured whole', and that the concrete is always complex. Everything conditions everything else, not by expressing it but by somehow causing it. Again, though, the question is how. For all his bluster, Althusser had no answer. What he did, instead, was to declare that the task of Marxist social science is to give an account of this complexity, and to claim that doing so is indispensable for enabling a political practice based on a 'concrete analysis' of 'concrete situations'.

This much, however, is relatively clear. The concrete analysis of concrete situations involves a category of totality, of the complex structured whole, in which each element plays a causally efficacious role. What is to be explained is comprehensible to the extent that it is understood in its relation to this totality; not as expressive of it, but as somehow conditioned by it and its various configurations. For the whole just is a system of elements and relations of elements. There is no subject – or, more precisely, no substantive subject – in it, beyond it, or lurking beneath it. This is the sense of Althusser's claim, repeated throughout *For Marx* and *Reading Capital*, that the entire existence of the materialist dialectic consists in its effects. The whole is the system – and nothing more. It is as a system that it brings about its effects.

Thus Althusser's thinking was of a piece with those structuralisms that purported to explain phenomena (of language, ethnography, psychoanalysis, literature, and so on) by appeal to unseen theoretical structures. For Althusser, it was an article of faith that causality is seldom, if ever, transparent; that the 'complex effect' of the whole upon particular elements is not empirically presented. As he would say, in his characteristic but unnecessarily paradoxical way, the structural cause is 'always absent'. The point, then, for Marxist social science is to discover the real causal determinations that account for what can be observed; to look beneath the veil of appearance into the realm of real (but unseeable) causal structures. This is what the structuralists tried to do, and it is what Althusser claimed Marx did, whether he knew it or not.

But unlike other structuralists, Althusser never elaborated an account of these determinations. His reflections on Marx's own positions and on those of the revolutionary leaders who supposedly understood Marx correctly underwrote an attack on historicist Marxism, but not a theoretically developed alternative to it. It almost seems as if Althusser proposed the idea of structural causality only to castigate the explanatory practice of the Marxist humanists. In any case, the concept remained obscure. However much he or his followers may have insisted otherwise, structural causality was a placeholder term, at best.

But even in its unelaborated state, this notion of Althusser's allowed him to declare pertinent two related, generally Maoist, notions that, by his lights, make sense only if structural causality is assumed: the concept of 'the relative autonomy' or independence of 'instances', and the idea of differential historical times. In Althusser's view, not all levels or determinations of the complex structured whole need be, as it were, in sync. Social formations can and typically do embody elements that must be understood not only in relation to the whole, but also in relation to their own internal dynamics. These dynamics can and typically do proceed at different rates. These thoughts, though much discussed, also remained undeveloped. They come together, however, in Althusser's insistence on the political indispensability of the idea of 'the uneven development of contradictions' – an obscure doctrine, of unmistakable Maoist origin, that Althusser smuggled in, not very surreptitiously, under the cover of Leninist orthodoxy.

*   *   *

By the standards that analytical Marxism would impose, Althusser's work was sadly deficient. But it would be unwise to dismiss it on that account. Althusser provided a critique of philosophical anthropology in its Marxist version that is of continuing interest and importance. In doing so, he endeavored to show how those who would turn Marxism into a philosophical anthropology implicitly deny its scientificity, thereby rendering a Leninist politics impossible. In these respects, his work genuinely was animated by a commitment to Leninism. What he showed is what many historicist Marxists would have readily conceded: that the program they endorsed is incompatible with Lenin's understanding of theory and its relation to practice. This was reason enough for Althusser to conclude that philosophical anthropology must go. Lenin, after all, understood Marx best.

But, of course, Althusser never *justified* this conviction – not even to the extent of defending his claim for the scientificity of Marxism. Instead, he assumed that a science of history was the issue of an epistemological break, in much the way that Bachelard assumed the scientificity of modern physics and chemistry. But whereas Bachelard's assumption was warranted by the cognitive achievements of those sciences and by the technological advances that follow from them, Althusser's assumption was an act of faith – one that would become nearly impossible to sustain, even as an illusion, once Maoism revealed its true colors, and once the heady days of New Left optimism had passed.

Even as he proclaimed its centrality, Althusser had hardly anything helpful to say about what Marxist social science should be. Impatiently and mistakenly, he assumed that that issue was already settled. But he did show, as a Leninist should, what must be done – for Marxism to have a future. Despite his own intentions, and (probably) unbeknownst to himself, Althusser's work demonstrated that the task ahead is to reconstruct positions – based on Marx's thinking, wherever possible – that are amenable to rational adjudication, development and, if necessary, revision or abandonment, as in any other intellectual enterprise with scientific pretensions. A Marxist philosopher has no alternative when, as Althusser knew but would never quite admit, a philosophy representing the worldview of the proletariat is not an option. Thus he pointed the way towards the normalization of Marxism. Ironically, it fell to the analytical Marxists, philosophers and social scientists at some remove from Althusser and his concerns, to execute this proposal. They too drew on sources outside the Marxist tradition. But they were more inclined than Althusser was to ignore Marxism's Hegelian roots and, in consequence, to avoid almost completely the problematic of twentieth-century continental philosophy. Theirs was the wiser strategy for implementing the program Althusser's work suggests.

The lesson to be learned from Althusser is that Marxism needs an epistemological break. But that break cannot simply be declared; it must be accomplished. The task, therefore, is to make the claim for an epistemological break true. To that end, Althusser's account of the materialist dialectic is of little use. Insofar as he engaged the relevant issues, his efforts fell short. This was partly due to his adherence to continental philosophical styles. But it was also a consequence of the fact that he remained fixed in the political and theoretical culture of historicist Marxism, a terrain unsuited to the kind of theoretical practice he endorsed. These were not problems for the analytical Marxists. They were creatures of an academy that didn't so much float above the fray that engulfed the socialist movement as ignore it altogether. Arguably, in their 'conjuncture', this was a condition for the possibility of the advances they made. But it was also a state of affairs to be regretted. Because they were accountable to political, not academic, constituencies, both historicist and Althusserian Marxists had to grapple with the problems caused by the all-too-evident loss of a revolutionary agent. By the time Althusser's Marxism erupted on the scene, the battle was already lost. If a proletariat had ever existed in the way that Marx and his immediate cothinkers envisioned, by the mid-twentieth century, it was gone. But since Althusser was adamant in maintaining an identification with Marxist orthodoxy, this fact, if he and his followers perceived it at all, failed to register – except obliquely, between the lines of texts that, on the surface, ostentatiously advanced proletarian positions 'in the field of theory'. From today's vantage point, Althusser's willful blindness or meretricious guile in this matter gives his work an almost antiquarian flavor. It makes it an unsuitable basis for reviving socialist theory. But at the same time, it provides a link to a past from which analytical Marxism would all but lose contact – a past rich with resources, both theoretical and political, that any future Left ignores at its peril.

Moreover, Althusser's views, shorn of their polemical outer shell, do point those who would revive the socialist tradition in the same direction that analytical Marxism does. Both opposed historicist Marxism; both sought to normalize Marxist social science by treating it as a science among others, albeit one with conceptual resources that others lack and therefore with discoveries to its credit that elude the rest. But Althusserianism was more than just a histrionic precursor of what would come later. For all its shortcomings, it suggested a way of breaking with historicist Marxism while remaining part of the larger socialist movement as it has existed since its inception more than a century and a half ago. Analytical Marxism would fall short in this respect. Again, this was probably a blessing. Had analytical Marxists not been sequestered in the universities, we would probably not now have at hand a body of theoretical work that can help to renew socialist theory in the conditions that currently obtain. But were there to be a new wave of analytical Marxism, and were it as disconnected from the socialist tradition as its predecessor was, it too, in all likelihood, would fail to move socialism forward, no matter how trenchant the theory it produced. To advance liberty, equality and fraternity, it is necessary to break out of the confines of academic life; and, for that, an organic connection to traditional socialism is probably indispensable. A revived Marxism that stands on the shoulders of analytical Marxist philosophy, as any future Marxism must, risks irrelevance if it fails to make that link. Against that possibility, it remains useful to reflect on Althusser's work, obscure and unsatisfactory as it was. Thanks to its substantive affinities with analytical Marxism and its integral role in Marxist politics as it existed in the days before the New Left sputtered into oblivion, it is the best available corrective for analytical Marxism's own most glaring shortcoming – its 'academic deviation'.

5   The Analytical Turn

Analytical Marxism was indeed an academic phenomenon. But it was never the dominant current among self-identified academic Marxists. That title must go to Althusser's self-described successors who claimed somehow to join Marxism with one or another strain of 'postmodern' theory. Unlike Althusser, however, postmodern Marxists reject many of the fundamental assumptions that Marx and his closest cothinkers shared with other intellectual heirs of the Enlightenment; not least among them, a dedication to representing the world as it really is, not as it might be 'constructed' out of particular 'discursive practices'. Therefore their Marxisms had – and continue to have – little connection with the letter or spirit of Marx's work. The analytical Marxists, on the other hand, genuinely were Marxists, albeit of an academic type. And unlike the postmodernists with whom they coexisted, they exhibited an intellectual seriousness equal to the best philosophy and social science of the time. It is therefore this minority tendency that deserves attention here, not the more popular versions of Marxism that continue, to this day, to find sustenance in certain academic precincts. Analytical Marxism is of great importance if Marxism is to have a future; postmodern Marxism is not. Ironically, it is fair to enlist Althusser in support of this judgment. What is living in his thinking is consistent with and continued by analytical Marxism. Postmodern Marxisms, on the other hand, build on the obscurantist, programmatic and confused side of Althusser's work.

The story of analytical Marxism is a short one. It begins in the decade that spanned the years 1968 to 1978, and continues for roughly the next decade and a half. In retrospect, this story has a paradoxical aspect. On the one hand, despite the intentions of its founders, analytical Marxism came to reinforce the impression that Marxism is finished as a distinct intellectual tendency. It did so not just in acquiescence to the spirit of the age, but for reasons grounded in arguments. Work in an analytical Marxist vein therefore poses a challenge to anyone who thinks that Marxism does have a future. It especially challenges a conviction that lies at the heart of Marxist political theory – that a regime *beyond* the conceptual horizons of mainstream liberalism is both feasible and desirable. At the same time, analytical Marxist work uncovered what the living core of the

Marxist theoretical tradition is. One might therefore say that, without realizing it, the analytical Marxists saved Marxism by destroying it; that they breathed new life into the Marxist project, even as they came eventually – and regretfully – to the conclusion that they were its gravediggers.

For all appearances, however, analytical Marxism does seem to have done Marxism in – by collapsing it into mainstream liberal philosophy and mainstream social science. This was not the original intention; nor is it a conclusion that most analytical Marxists welcomed. It is worth noting that no important analytical Marxist has become an apostate, as so many erstwhile Marxists of earlier generations or of other intellectual tendencies had. Even as they more or less self-consciously abandoned Marxism, the analytical Marxists saw themselves remaining true to its spirit. There was nothing disingenuous in this belief. But the analytical Marxists' own assessment(s) of Marxism's prospects need not be taken at face value. After analytical Marxism, it is clearer than it ever was what Marxism had been about all along. Thanks to the analytical Marxists too, it is plain that Marx left the world theoretical resources, unavailable elsewhere, that are of continuing vitality and urgency.

Among other things, Marx provided means for grasping the difference between forms of social organization that are achievable in principle, and visions of ideal arrangements that are inaccessible and therefore dangerous to endorse. Marxists, we know, had always been scientific socialists – proponents of the view that socialist convictions are grounded in a theory of history. Thus they opposed *utopian* socialisms that envisioned ideal arrangements apart from, and sometimes in blatant disregard of, accounts of the real course of historical change; socialisms that argue for socialism mainly or exclusively on moral grounds. An overriding objective of the first analytical Marxists was to defend scientific socialism. Revealingly, the foremost defender of this view, G.A. Cohen, the author of the seminal *Karl Marx's Theory of History: A Defence* has argued recently that the utopian socialists were right, after all.[1] I will maintain, against this latest assessment of Cohen's, that the traditional view was correct; that Marxism, and Marxism alone, joins a defensible account of what is historically feasible with a vision of ideal social, political and economic arrangements. I will argue, in other words, that, despite what many analytical Marxists have come to believe, the original intention motivating analytical Marxism was sounder than the new consensus.

Analytical Marxism came into being in British and American universities. Indirectly, it arose in consequence of the student movements that came to a head, briefly, in the spring of 1968. Thus it owed its existence to the New Left – or, more precisely, to the desire of a handful of student militants, trained in analytical philosophy and empirical social science, to join their theoretical interests to their political convictions. But the New Left was a worldwide phenomenon. Analytical Marxism was a culturally specific and institutionally structured manifestation of this larger political moment. To understand analytical Marxism, it is therefore necessary to reflect not only on the larger political context, but also on Marxism's career in the university culture of the English-speaking world. To see the forest for the trees, it will be best to paint this picture with a broad brush. What follows is therefore intended only to convey a sense of what the analytical Marxists did – with a view to showing, on the one hand, how they contributed to the current dominance of liberal political philosophy; and, on the other, how their work can help to restore Marx's vision of a social order beyond liberalism.[2]

*   *   *

To a degree that is unparalleled elsewhere in the West, the English-speaking world and especially the United States never had significant political or intellectual movements identified with Marxism. Anglophone philosophers and social scientists of the generation of 1968 who were moved to identify with Marxism, whether for reasons of intellectual commitment or out of a sense of solidarity with others in struggle or for some combination of these reasons, therefore had hardly any tradition to continue, in marked contrast to their counterparts elsewhere. They also had less reason to join political parties identified with Marxism, communist or otherwise. Thus the panoply of concerns lying just beneath the surface of Althusser's writings had almost no resonance in the work of the analytical Marxists. If analytical Marxists were accountable to anyone or anything, it was to their own internalized disciplinary standards, not to political constituencies of any kind.

As remarked, before analytical Marxism, theoretical work in a Marxist vein was almost always linked to partisan political concerns. Althusser's case was no exception. Analytical Marxism, however, was as free floating as any other philosophical enterprise. This state of affairs was plainly in tension with the political motivations that brought the majority of its practitioners into its fold. But it did leave them free to invent themselves and to follow their own course. In this, they were abetted by the fact that they could begin with a nearly clean slate. English-speaking academic life was very little affected by historicist tendencies of any kind. Historicist Marxism therefore encountered difficulties gaining a foothold in the larger intellectual culture. This helps to explain why the English-speaking world generally was very little affected by any of the intellectual tendencies we now call Western Marxism,[3] and why English-speaking contributions even to official communist doctrine were marginal and derivative. There were, of course, influential European émigrés on American soil during and after World War II, and also Trotskyists and independent Marxist theorists. In Great Britain, there were important historians, such as E.P. Thompson and Christopher Hill, who founded a tradition of Marxist historiography that enjoyed a certain influence by the early 1960s. But, in the main, analytical Marxism represented a fresh start, very little encumbered by what had gone on before.

The kinds of Marxism that were attractive, at first, to New Left militants were varieties of Western Marxism imported from Germany and France. Thus Althusserian Marxism enjoyed a certain vogue, especially in Britain. But, in the end, Western Marxism proved intractably difficult to integrate into the prevailing intellectual culture, especially as political fervor waned and, along with it, uncritical enthusiasm for *anything* bearing a Marxist pedigree. Just as the earlier emigration of Western Marxists, fleeing Naziism and war, had little lasting influence on the mainstream intellectual culture of the United States or Great Britain, this later importation of Western Marxism also failed to take hold, except on the fringes of intellectual life. The reason why is easy to discern. Western Marxism drew on intellectual currents that were, on the whole, unfamiliar in the English-speaking world – neo-Hegelianism, phenomenology, existentialism and, in Althusser's case, structuralism. Unlike logical positivism, another continental import of roughly the same vintage, these doctrines were uncongenial to Anglo-American sensibilities, except again on the margins. Western Marxists were proficient at grand theorizing and programmatic formulations. But, as Althusser's example attests, they were more inclined to posture than to argue. In the end, they did not do all that much that was recognizably philosophical to philosophers schooled in the analytic tradition, where the reigning inclination was to look on grand theorizing and programmatic pronouncements with suspicion, and to greet the appearance of profundity with skepticism bordering on derision. The sociology and economics that Western Marxism underwrote were, if anything, even more discordant with Anglophone academic sensibilities.

In the 1950s and 1960s, the cutting edge of philosophical work in the English-speaking world consisted in painstaking investigations of ordinary speech, guided by the conviction that most, if not all, long-standing philosophical problems were consequences of linguistic confusions, awaiting dissolution through careful analysis. Ordinary language philosophy had passed from the scene by the time the New Left flourished, but the spirit that motivated it remained in force. Then, as now, mainstream philosophers in the English-speaking world preferred to engage in tasks that appear pedestrian from the Olympian vantage point continental philosophers assumed – discerning conceptual structures, making distinctions (where appropriate), collapsing distinctions (where they are inappropriately drawn), and marshaling clear and sound arguments. To anyone trained in this tradition, continental philosophy seems hopelessly pretentious and obscure. Because it drew on these currents, Western Marxism courted a similar judgment.

That this understanding took time to register was a consequence of two related phenomena, the one psychological, the other political. By the late 1960s, the *need* for an ideology consonant with prevailing attitudes was keenly felt on the Left. Everyone assumed that *some* version of Marxism must fit that description. In those days too, when many student radicals thought 'the arm of criticism' about to pass into 'the criticism of arms', there was little appetite for protracted intellectual undertakings, especially those of a piece with ordinary academic exercises.[4] Novice socialist militants therefore wanted to be Marxists, and they wanted their Marxism ready-made. But desire is the root of denial. Add impressive Franco-German credentials and the possibilities for self-deception become almost limitless. In retrospect, it seems odd that the intra-Marxist debates of the 1970s between historicists and Althusserians were, in part, debates about which side was more rigorous. The oddity is only partly a consequence of the fact that the intellectual heirs of these tendencies, the postmodernists, characteristically renounce rigor (along with science) – in practice, and often in theory too. The more astonishing fact is that the obvious answer, *none of the above*, failed to impress itself on the participants. For there was at hand, in the disciplinary standards commonplace in Anglo-American universities, a standard of rigor that none of the parties in these debates began to approach. Everyone should have known this. But so ardent was the desire to assume the mantle of revolutionary Marxism, that hardly anyone acknowledged this incontrovertible fact.

There was also a more political reason why so many welcomed Western Marxism enthusiastically. The student movements of the period were directed, in the first instance, against the institutions in which students found themselves, the universities. In the United States, where radical students were motivated mainly by the struggle for racial equality and by opposition to the Vietnam War, institutional racism and university involvement with the military were therefore the principal arenas of contestation. It was natural, in these circumstances, to oppose the intellectual culture of the institution one was fighting against. For many, this attitude took a nihilistic turn, away from intellectual work altogether, into the realm of the emerging counterculture or into workerist politics. But, for some, particularly those who looked forward to university careers, the temptation of an alternative intellectual style readily at hand was irresistible. No matter that this alternative was taken from what was, in the end, only a different academy. All the better, in fact, inasmuch as the alternative was vested with the prestige of German and French culture, a condition that played well against the lingering sense of intellectual insecurity that continued to plague Anglophone, and especially American, academics in the humanities and social sciences. Elsewhere, where the underlying psychological and political dynamics differed, the theoretical deficit experienced by would-be Marxists was much the same. The temptations of Western Marxism were therefore nearly as lively as in the United States. Western Marxism, in one or another of its many forms, therefore came to be embraced by student militants everywhere.[5]

In time, though, the political motivation faded into oblivion and so too did the need of would-be Marxists to deceive themselves about the merits of the Western Marxisms to which they had been drawn. As interest in Marxism generally waned, interest in Western Marxism subsided too. Some descendants of the Frankfurt School continued to enjoy a certain standing among academics with philosophical training. But the figure in that tradition who is taken most seriously today, Jürgen Habermas, has come to distance himself from the Marxist past of his intellectual forebears and to ally himself instead with the Anglo-American liberal tradition.

Otherwise, apart from a few vestigial remnants, Western Marxism has passed from the scene.

*   *   *

Contemporaneously, liberal political philosophy underwent a renaissance. In the period immediately preceding the 1960s, after logical positivism and ordinary language philosophy had deflated philosophy's pretensions generally, political philosophy seemed especially spent.[6] Then, in 1971, John Rawls published *A Theory of Justice,* putting that impression definitively to rest.[7] Rawls's masterpiece revived political philosophy and set its subsequent course. Ironically, the Rawlsian turn in academic political philosophy shaped the course of analytical Marxism from its inception – even when its principal objective was still only to reconstruct and defend Marxist orthodoxy.

Marxist credentials have never been helpful to anglophone academics, and no one ever imagined that Marxism was about to become a ticket to academic success in the English-speaking world. Unlike what may have been the case elsewhere, the impulse motivating a Marxist identification on the part of those who would become analytical Marxists was never academic opportunism. It was to advance Marxism by defending Marx's views; an objective that required, first of all, that they be stated clearly and in a form in which they could be rationally assessed. Close reading and, where necessary, imaginative philosophical reconstruction therefore became the order of the day. The guiding conviction was that Marx's positions would survive even the most stringent critical assessments; in other words, that Marx's views were generally sound. Guided by this thought, attention focused on a number of issues important in the Marxism of the period preceding the Russian Revolution. Of these, one especially, the problem of justice, coincided with the question that Rawls had made Topic A in mainstream political philosophy.[8] The coincidence was not accidental. Philosophers working in a field in which Rawls's influence was already paramount, cut their teeth on the topic they knew best.

Orthodox Marxists had always denied that justice was a transhistorical 'critical' concept, a standard against which socioeconomic structures could be assessed. Their view was that ideas of justice were superstructural and therefore relative to economic structures or modes of production. Injustices can arise *within* capitalism, in the sense that institutional arrangements or social practices can offend identifiable capitalist norms of what justice requires. But capitalism itself can be neither just nor unjust. Among the first analytical Marxist ventures were efforts to prove the orthodox view right or, failing that, to show how a suitable transhistorical concept of justice could be integrated into the larger theoretical structure Marx contrived.[9] From the outset, then, there was an effort to draw Marx and Rawls together. The connection was not merely topical. It carried over into styles and standards of argumentation as well. For the first time, philosophers working on Marxist themes approached their subject in the way that philosophers working on other issues did. In this respect, the debate on Marxist justice anticipated what would follow.

The idea, again, was to interrogate Marx's positions, not Rawls's or any other liberal's, and to debate the question of justice from within a Marxist framework. But in doing so, it was necessary, in the circumstances, to deal with Rawlsian justice and therefore with liberal political theory generally. Inevitably this engagement took place on the latter's terrain. Analytical Marxism was in its infancy. Liberal political philosophy was a mature intellectual discipline, undergoing a renaissance. And because it was firmly entrenched in the academy, it had the weight of that embattled but established institution behind it. In contrast, analytical Marxism's place in the university was tenuous, at best. If there was to be a Marxist voice in ongoing, academic discussions of justice, it could therefore only be on terms that the institution in which these discussions took place already acknowledged.

In retrospect, the superior position Rawlsian liberalism enjoyed may have worked to the advantage of the Left, at least if it is fair to hold that socialist theory, Marxist or otherwise, was bound to suffer major setbacks in the period that ensued. Rawlsian liberalism breathed new life into egalitarian theory and therefore into a core component, arguably *the* core component, of socialist ideology. This fact may seem paradoxical in view of the separate histories of liberalism and socialism. But Rawls's work forced a rethinking of the long-standing view of the relation between liberal theory and egalitarianism.

The methodological affinity joining early analytical Marxist ventures in the theory of justice to mainstream philosophy was, at first, more accidental than deliberate. Those who engaged Marx on justice knew no other way to do philosophy. Even had they wanted to join the historicist tradition, it is not clear how they might have done so. The issues involved in the academic debates of the period were too focused on details and arguments for any grand but obscure style of theorizing to be deployed. Thus Marxism became *one* voice among many in an ecumenical philosophical discussion already in progress. In time, it became clear that it was not a different *kind* of voice. Eventually, a virtue was made of this observation. The methodological affinity joining analytical Marxism to mainstream philosophy gave rise to a substantive claim, one to which nearly all analytical Marxists subscribed.

*   *   *

That claim is that *there is no distinctive Marxist methodology*. This conviction separates analytical Marxism from historicist currents of all varieties. Indeed, if there was one point on which orthodox Marxists and Western Marxists agreed, it was that Marx, following Hegel, developed a *dialectical* methodology that distinguishes Marxism from 'bourgeois' science and philosophy. We have seen that, wittingly or not, Althusser deviated from the consensus view – by insisting that Marx's materialist dialectic was not at all like Hegel's idealist dialectic. To be sure, Althusser was fatally vague about the nature of Marx's method. For all the attention he lavished on the subject, he only managed to say clearly what it is *not*. But inasmuch as he proclaimed it scientific, and insofar as his understanding of science, following Bachelard's, was roughly in line with standard views, Althusser too, implicitly but effectively, dispatched the idea of a distinctive Marxist methodology. However, as we have seen, insofar as he was not being disingenuous, he did so unwittingly. Officially, Althusser was emphatic in asserting the theoretical novelty of the materialist dialectic. In this sense, even he was of one mind with other Western Marxists.

More generally, the idea that Marxism is distinguished by its method was widely assumed throughout the entire intellectual culture. Thus opponents of Marxism faulted Marx and the Marxists precisely on these grounds. They claimed that the method Marxists deployed violated norms of legitimate scientific practice. A well-known exponent of this view was Karl Popper.[10] Many less distinguished thinkers agreed with him. But no one took the Marxists' claims for methodological distinctiveness to task. Rather, on that unsubstantiated doctrine, everyone agreed. It is therefore fair to observe that, before analytical Marxism, the idea that there is a distinctive Marxist methodology was a dogma to which nearly everyone, Marxist or not, subscribed.

However it soon became clear to those who looked at the tradition with philosophical detachment that this claim is ambiguous at best. If the aim of Marx's investigations of 'the laws of motion of capitalist society' and of his various other explanatory projects was consistent with the aims of modern science generally, as Marx himself maintained[11] – if, in other words, what Marx wanted to do was to discover the real causal determinants of the phenomena he investigated – then the idea would be that Marx contrived or at least deployed a novel and distinctive way of executing this task: of forming concepts, constructing theories, corroborating hypotheses and so on. No one has ever shown that this is the case. On the other hand, if a different sort of objective is supposed, then Marxism's methodological novelty would have to be understood in light of this aim, whatever it might be. This is what most believers in Marxism's methodological distinctiveness appear to have had in mind. But the Western Marxists, including Althusser, were, at best, unhelpful in identifying an alternative explanatory objective, and so were their orthodox opponents. There is therefore no reason not to take Marx at his word, and to acknowledge that the explanatory aim of Marxist social science is indeed the discovery of real causal determinations. Those who would insist otherwise shoulder the burden of proof. Their first move in discharging this burden must be to identify what alternative explanatory aim Marx might have had in mind. So far, no one has.

The dialectical method has been defended countless times. But the proof lies in the elaboration of the program, not in its declaration. The analytical Marxists came to realize that dialectical explanations either restate what can be expressed in unexceptionable ways, or else are unintelligible and therefore not explanatory at all. The lesson is plain: if there were an explanatorily useful dialectical method, it ought by now to have become apparent. That it has not is good reason to conclude that, at best, the dialectic is a way of organizing and directing thinking at a pretheoretic level. A heuristic device of this sort is not to be despised. But it is no royal road to truths inaccessible to modern science.

Analytical Marxists came to this conclusion reluctantly. Their intent, at first, was only to reconstruct and defend Marxist orthodoxy. That Marx was a dialectical materialist is an orthodox claim. It is true that Marx never used the expression. But he identified with the idea throughout his life, not just before the epistemological break Althusser identified in his work. Thus, even in *Capital*, at the same time that he asserted his affinity with modern science, Marx represented himself as a dialectician in the Hegelian tradition, faulting his rivals for their shortcomings in this regard.[12] Was this a 'creative tension' in Marx's thinking or a simple confusion? Perhaps both. In any case, analytical Marxists who concerned themselves with questions of method sought, at first, to rehabilitate dialectical logic, not to debunk it.[13] What transpired in the course of doing so anticipated what would happen in so many other areas – the operation succeeded (more or less), but the patient died.

For an analytical Marxist, to defend a position, it is necessary, first, to translate it into terms that bear scrutiny according to the most demanding disciplinary standards in philosophy or in an appropriate social science. Marx's positions have turned out to be remarkably amenable to this kind of treatment.[14] Before analytical Marxism, Marx's views were thought to differ qualitatively from mainstream positions, to follow from a different and perhaps incommensurable paradigm. Marxist theoretical work was also thought to imply conclusions that mainstream theorists would, in many cases, reject – not only for political reasons or because of ideological resistance, but on grounds that depend on their own theoretical commitments. These assumptions can no longer be sustained. In making Marx's views acceptable in the way that analytical Marxists did, Marxism became a voice among others in ongoing debates.

*   *   *

This conclusion upsets received understandings. But it is not the whole story. For there is a component of Marxist orthodoxy that does lie outside the scope of mainstream thinking – Marx's theory of history, 'historical materialism' in its traditional, not its Althusserian, sense. As we have seen, this aspect of Marxist orthodoxy had always been definitive of Marxist thought; it was what distinguished scientific from utopian socialism.

Historical materialism was nearly of as much concern to early analytical Marxism as justice was. But with the publication in 1978 of Cohen's *Karl Marx's Theory of History* the topic assumed a preeminent importance. For Marx, the inner workings of capitalism and other modes of production are only intelligible as part of an endogenous process of development and transformation. Historical materialism provides an account of this process. Cohen naturalized this theory, assimilating it into the intellectual mainstream. As remarked (in Chapter 2), he showed, in doing so, how Marx's theory of history, unlike Hegel's, is not *teleological*. This result speaks to the issue that Althusser had made central, the question of Marxism's scientificity. Scientists from at least the seventeenth century on had rejected the notion of teleological causality, the idea that to explain a phenomenon is to discover the 'end' or *telos* towards which it tends. Historical materialism, on Cohen's reconstruction, joins that consensus. Cohen made it clear that Marxism is equipped to supply and defend an account of history's structure and direction that in no way compromises modern understandings of causality and explanation. Notwithstanding the polemical outer shell that was never far from Althusser's theoretical proclamations, this was what Althusser wanted to do as well. The difference is that Althusser only talked obscurely and programmatically about doing it; Cohen actually did it.

We have seen too how contemporary historiography proceeds on the assumption that there are no significant theoretical constraints on what counts as an object of historical inquiry or as an historical explanation. Not unrelatedly, it also supposes that there is nothing enlightening to say about history's structure and direction. Past events, no matter how they are individuated or categorized, are susceptible to causal explanations. But history itself cannot be explained. One cannot even concoct a trivial account of history's structure and direction by conjoining all particular explanations. To do so, it would be necessary, first, to have a theoretically well-motivated way of marking off events and therefore of identifying discrete explanations to join together. But in the atheoretical view of modern historiography, this is impossible. Even if we allow (almost) anything to count as an explanation, there is no theoretical warrant for dividing the world up into exhaustive and mutually exclusive events and therefore no justification for joining these explanations together.

Historians can, of course, impute structure and directionality to aspects of the past. When they do so, however, they are only imposing categories that accord with their own or others' interests or with received understandings. This is not the same thing as discovering real properties of past events or collections of events. Therefore, when they deal with trends or when they otherwise generalize over long swatches of time, it is not because they have discovered real structural or directional properties of human history. It is because they have certain extratheoretical interests that shape the narratives they construct.

Hegel's philosophy of history was, of course, the immediate precursor of Marx's own attempt to make sense of history as such. From Hegel, Marx gained the conviction that human history has a real, not an imputed, structure and direction. But in abandoning Hegel's project of explaining history teleologically, Marx was obliged to forsake the idea that historical events have meanings. In history, as in nature, meanings can only be specified in relation to *ends*; if the latter go, so too must the former. For Marx, therefore, history is as meaningless as nature is now thought to be. Like nature too, it has properties that are independent of investigators' interests, properties that await discovery. Cohen, like Marx, was persuaded that, despite his teleology, Hegel had succeeded in grasping aspects of real history. But his vestigial commitment to teleological explanations in history distorted his insights. Marx's achievement, in Cohen's view, was to set Hegel right in this respect, without succumbing to the atheoreticism emblematic of contemporary historiography. Thus Marx did stand Hegel 'on his feet', after all. He did so, however, not by somehow applying the dialectic to the right substance, matter, but by integrating Hegel's rational intuitions about human history into an explanatory program consonant with modern scientific practice.

Any theory that purports to be part of the larger enterprise of modern science is in principle susceptible to revision. According to one widely accepted view, the more foundational a theory is, the less likely it is to change through the ordinary procedures of what Thomas Kuhn called 'normal science'.[15] In extreme cases, fundamental theoretical frameworks may sometimes be recalcitrant to all but thoroughgoing 'scientific revolutions'. But even theories that are not overthrown undergo revision over time. Historical materialism was no exception. Once it was elaborated in a way that invited scrutiny and assessment, it came under attack and began to fall.

For all their differences, Western Marxisms were of one mind in distancing themselves from Marx's theory of history. Their objections were mainly political. They faulted the implicit fatalism of classical historical materialism. In their view, historical materialism's account of history's structure and direction implied that what happens in history happens inevitably. This thought, they insisted, denies human agency its due. More generally, it deflates the importance of political practice in moving history along. If the end is already given, one can perhaps hasten its coming or shape its nature in marginal ways, but nothing can fundamentally alter the eventual outcome. This, it seemed to them, was a recipe for quiescence; for awaiting the revolution, not making it. But the historical materialism Western Marxists faulted was not exactly the historical materialism Cohen defended. As reconstructed by Cohen and others, historical materialism is a theory pitched at a very high level of abstraction that predicts only what *could* happen in human history or, more precisely, what would happen *ceteris absentibus*, in the absence of countervailing forces. It does not prophecy what is bound to come. Thus its commitment to historical inevitability is not nearly as vulnerable to the concerns that led so many twentieth-century Marxists to distance themselves from Marxism's core theoretical discovery.[16] Perhaps for this reason and perhaps also because it was introduced in a period that was already politically quiescent, the analytical Marxists' version of historical materialism failed to elicit the kinds of criticisms that earlier accounts had drawn upon themselves. In the discussions it generated, the worries of the Western Marxists were largely ignored. Attention focused instead on such issues as the adequacy of Cohen's recourse to functional explanations, and on other matters of a generally technical and apolitical nature.

Even so, it seemed for a while that Marxist philosophy would revive by returning to its classical roots. This hope soon faded, however. Subject to relentless criticism, some of it from Cohen himself, many historical materialist claims came to seem indefensible. No one maintained that the theory ought to be cast aside. But the historical materialism that emerged in the wake of the scrutiny Cohen's work spawned was a considerably attenuated version of Marx's theory.

Analytical Marxism began with the implicit understanding that Marxism is not methodologically distinctive, a claim it went on to vindicate. It offered the promise, though, of defensible substantive claims that would distinguish Marxism from 'bourgeois' theory. But as historical materialism's explanatory pretensions were progressively retracted, this expectation too diminished. This increasingly evident state of affairs added to an emerging consensus that, to this day, is more tacit than explicit. The idea is not quite that Marxism has suffered an historical defeat in the way that communism did.

No analytical Marxist came to the conclusion that Marx's positions were no longer worth taking seriously. It was rather that, as the *Communist Manifesto* said of 'all that is solid' in bourgeois society, Marxism seemed to have 'melted into air'. What once appeared to be an alternative to bourgeois ways of apprehending the world vanished, almost without a trace. This is analytical Marxism's unintended legacy, or at least the part of it that is apparent for now.

As remarked, the turmoil that attended repudiations of Marxism in generations past never surfaced in the wake of these developments. Perhaps analytical Marxism was too academic to arouse fundamental passions in the way that earlier strains of Marxist theorizing had. In any case, its internal trajectory gave rise to disappointments, not betrayals. But, for Marxism itself, the effect was more devastating than earlier defections from the Marxist camp had been. For analytical Marxists were driven by ostensibly timeless, rationally compelling arguments, not passing moral or political concerns. If, from this purview, Marxism melts into air, then it is done for indeed.

What happened to historical materialism paralleled developments elsewhere. Thanks to the work of John Roemer and others, Marxist political economy, which everyone had regarded as an alternative to mainstream, neoclassical economics, collapsed into its putative rival.[17] Marxist sociology suffered a similar fate. If there is no distinctive Marxist methodology in the social sciences, then Marxist sociology is, at most, a framework for generating explanations – one that, following Marx's own example, accords explanatory priority to class structure and class conflict or, more precisely, to the understanding of class structure and class conflict that Marx developed.[18] But, then, it is an open question how explanatory class analysis is for the range of phenomena sociologists investigate. There is no doubt that it explains a great deal.[19] But unless there is a theoretically well motivated reason to privilege it, one cannot say that it explains the most important or most fundamental things. Historical materialism does supply grounds for according explanatory preeminence to class analysis. But as it came increasingly under attack, this rationale seemed to evaporate too. Class analysis therefore came to look like nothing more than one explanatory strategy among others. No one denied its importance. But neither did anyone who had passed through the analytical Marxist cauldron any longer insist that it is somehow an alternative to mainstream sociology. In this domain too, then, without setting out to do anything of the sort, the analytical Marxists effectively folded Marxism into its ostensible rival.

*   *   *

Faute de mieux, analytical Marxists eventually came to make a case for Marxism's theoretical integrity on the terrain of normative theory. This stand is doubly ironic. The first irony is a consequence of analytical Marxism's political detachment. Having executed a radical divorce of Marxist theory from its political roots, the analytical Marxists arrived at the conclusion that the one thing that keeps Marxism from melting into air, that keeps it an *ism,* is its valuational commitments. But since these commitments imply a dedication to changing the world in the way Marxists have always envisioned, it follows that Marxism is distinguished by its politics, after all. From their apolitical vantage point, the analytical Marxists brought politics back in, and even placed it at center stage.

The second irony arises out of the analytical Marxists' initial interest in defending orthodox positions. Classical Marxism derogated normative concerns. Its socialism, again, was scientific, not utopian. Accordingly, the historical materialism analytical Marxists inherited relegated normative considerations to the same category as the legal and political superstructure, thereby denying them any independent role in moving history along. So too did Cohen, at first. To be sure, his defense of historical materialism was friendlier to normative theorizing than was the norm among proponents of historical materialism in the heydays of the Second and Third Internationals. This is hardly surprising: as a political philosopher; normative theory was (and is) Cohen's main professional interest. But it was only in the course of *criticizing* the theory he had reconstructed that Cohen and others created a space, within Marxism, for normative theory as such. The idea that Marxism's distinctiveness lies with its normative commitments suggested itself to analytical Marxists because they failed in their original purpose, because they were not able to defend a more classical view. It should always have been plain, however, that this was a desperate move. The idea that Marxism is distinguished by its valuational commitments simply does not bear scrutiny.

After his epistemological break, Marx was not much interested in normative theory, except in one crucial respect. He remained a steadfast opponent of applications of *moral* theory in class-divided societies. No doubt, this stance was partly pragmatic; Marx struggled against utopian socialisms unrelentingly. But there was also a rational kernel contained within the outer, polemical shell of Marx's express position. To begin to extract this kernel, we must first distinguish moral theory from normative theory generally. Let us therefore say, following much precedent, that a moral theory is a normative theory that adopts the moral point of view.[20] This is the point of view implicit in the Golden Rule and epitomized in Kant's categorical imperative, the point of view of generality or universality.[21] The Golden Rule tells us 'to do unto others' as we would have others 'do unto ourselves'. It tells us, in other words, that in deliberating on alternative courses of action, what matters is not what differentiates us from one another, but what we have in common. Thus we are enjoined to deliberate in an impartial or agent-neutral way – from the vantage point of agency as such, rather than from our own perspectives as agents. The moral point of view is obviously not appropriate in all contexts. In ordering from a menu in a restaurant, where nothing depends on one's order except what food one will be served, it would be pointless to act on universalizable principles. In that case, it only makes sense to order what one would prefer to eat; in other words, to deliberate and then to act in an agent-specific way. But in deliberating, say, on whether to pay one's bill after having eaten, moral deliberation does have a place. If Kant was right, it enjoins us to act on principles that we could will all agents to act upon.

Marx had something to say *about* this deliberative stance – not so much in its applications to individual conduct, however, as in its role in organizing and defending institutional arrangements. He did not take issue with universalizability as such. In fact, in his early writings, Marx faulted existing social, political and especially economic arrangements from precisely this point of view. Whatever Althusserians might believe, there is no reason to think that, on this matter, he ever did or ought to have changed his mind. Quite the contrary. Throughout his life, Marx insisted that claims for universality in class-divided societies are almost always *false* and also *tendentious* in the sense that they promote the particular interests of the economically dominant class. It was for this reason that, even after his epistemological break, Marx never stopped taking issue with the notion of *Recht*, of universal principles implemented in social and political institutions. In Marx's view, the *Rechtstaat* and the theory that sustains it, moral theory, plays a systematic role in the class struggle. It is only under communism, when systemic social divisions generally and class divisions in particular will have disappeared, that institutions can genuinely implement universal ideals. Thus Marx was not a critic of moral theory as such. In his view, a genuinely moral order is a human possibility and a worthy objective. What he denounced was applications of moral theory *in existing social and political circumstances* – not just in particular instances but, this side of communism, in nearly all cases. This claim, if true, has enormous implications for normative social and political philosophy. But, even programmatically, it does not imply an alternative to moral theory.

Marx had almost nothing directly to say about the bases of normative evaluation. However, he was not shy about condemning economic, social and political arrangements in normative and even moralistic terms. Arguably, then, he did have views on the subject, even if they have to be teased out of his writings on other subjects. Marx's normative commitments have, in fact, received a great deal of attention in recent years, thanks to the analytical Marxists. It has become plain that, following Aristotle's lead, but then historicizing Aristotle's idea, Marx valued *self-realization,* the actualization of his- torically situated human potentialities. He assessed social, political and economic arrangements according to how well they serve this end. It is equally plain that Marx accorded central importance to a particular notion of *community*, evident earlier in the political philosophy of Rousseau and, implicitly, in the republican tradition in seventeenth- and eighteenth-century political thought. Above all, Marx valued autonomy. In his view, it was precisely this idea of freedom that took a wrong turn, as it were, into Hegel's philosophy of Right; and it is this idea that will finally become feasible under communism, when the *Rechtstaat,* along with other defining insti- tutions of bourgeois society, will have withered away.[22]

But, again, these commitments hardly comprise a distinctive normative theory. The idea that a Marx*ism* can be concocted out of Marx's valuational commitments is therefore illusory. Thus the last stand of the analytical Marxists fared no better than the rest. With nowhere else to retreat, some analytical Marxists drew the apparently unavoidable conclusion: that analytical Marxism, despite itself, has brought Marxism itself to its end.

*   *   *

The value that served as the principal point of contact between liberalism and Marxism, as liberalism took a Rawlsian turn and as Marxism, having taken an analytical turn, became increasingly ensconced under the Rawlsian tent, was *equality*. Therein too lies an irony. For, throughout their respective histories, both liberalism and Marxism have evinced ambivalence, if not hostility, towards this ideal. The first liberals were concerned mainly to defend property rights – above all, the right to accumulate property privately and without limitation. They were therefore antiegalitarian, according to the usual understanding of the term. Marxists too characteristically disparaged egalitarianism, though their views about the distribution of the economic surplus plainly had egalitarian implications. In part, Marxists distanced themselves from egalitarians in order to differentiate their own objectives from those of utopian socialists. But they had a more substantive reason as well. Marx's goal was communism, a society of a radically new and different kind. In the dialectical language of historicist Marxism, communism is the 'negation' of capitalism. But income equality or, more generally, resource equality does not require the negation of capitalism. In principle, it can be realized under capitalism through progressive taxation, state-organized redistribution, and other, related social policies. So too can any other likely egalitarian objective.

More generally, if, by 'socialism', we mean an economic system in which 'social property' replaces private property in society's principal means of production, then, if all socialists want is equality, socialism would be, at best, only a means to the desired end.[23] But, then, it is an open question how efficacious this means is. It could turn out that, in some or perhaps even in all instances, there are better ways to realize the end in view. Then, paradoxically, socialism would be unnecessary for obtaining what socialists want. Marxists could still insist that, in real-world conditions, socialist property relations are useful for achieving the objectives they and Rawlsian liberals share. They might even argue that, for some especially pertinent range of cases, they are indispensable. But, then, socialism would still be nothing more than a strategy egalitarians might pursue. As with other imaginable strategies, its suitability would depend entirely on circumstances of time and place.

This conclusion, if sustained, would mark the end of socialism as a distinct political ideology dedicated to advancing the long-standing project, launched in the aftermath of the French Revolution, of radical *social*, not just political, transformation from the bottom up – at least to the extent that scientific socialism came to exercise hegemony over the socialist cause. It would also signal the demise of Marxism's – and therefore socialism's – commitment to communism; to a vision of ideal social and political arrangements beyond the purview of liberal political philosophy.

*   *   *

Part of the explanation for the fact that the analytical Marxists were so ready to give up on communism almost certainly has to do with the professional culture and disciplinary styles to which they held themselves accountable. Analytical Marxism was free from disabling political ties. But analytical Marxists were very susceptible to certain *déformations profesionelles*. This state of affairs helped to bring about the subsidence of analytical Marxism as an intellectual current. Insofar as analytical Marxism raised Marxist theory to a new level, its demise helped, in turn, to speed the decline of Marxism itself in those circles that fostered work in an analytical Marxist vein.

Philosophy was the most influential of the academic disciplines that shaped analytical Marxism. To oversimplify just a little, one might even say that analytical Marxism just was analytical philosophy applied to Marxist themes. But philosophy apart, the academic discipline that, more than any other, influenced analytical Marxism substantively was economics, the most technical of the social sciences and the most self-consciously rigorous in its standards. Analytical Marxism enjoyed, on the whole, a beneficial relationship with economic theory. But there are, even so, perennial features of mainstream economic theory that found their way into analytical Marxism – to its detriment.

Of these, perhaps the most important is a tendency to focus on what can be modeled formally; and therefore, all too often, to sacrifice substantive insights and explanatory power for the sake of theoretical elegance and formal precision. This temptation undoubtedly played some role in leading analytical Marxists to focus more on equality than on the values that moved Marx directly – self-realization, community and autonomy. Mainstream economics is mainly about the distribution and redistribution of resources. Equality therefore falls within its purview. Thanks to decades of work on the topic, it is plain that the idea can be modeled in ways that genuinely do advance understanding. Self-realization, community, and autonomy have received less attention and are, in any case, less susceptible to formal modeling than equality is. It is not surprising, therefore, that those who are prone to internalize the standards of the economics profession would emphasize this value at the expense of the others

There is also a more subtle consequence of the affinities joining analytical Marxism to academic economics. The economics profession promotes the explanatory efficacy of rational choice explanations that apply, in principle, to economic interactions generally and even to aspects of life that are not literally economic. Even so, what economic analysis explains best are market arrangements in regimes of private property. In dealing with equality, therefore, it is natural for economists, like liberal egalitarians, to assume that measures enhancing equality involve the *redistribution* of privately owned goods; that capitalist markets distribute assets that the state then redistributes in accord with one or another egalitarian ideal. Valuational commitments that imply institutional arrangements that are noncapitalist or nonstatist fit uneasily, if at all, into this problematic. Thus communism, as Marx understood it, resists incorporation into the economist's explanatory framework.

Finally, economic theory is hospitable to *methodological individualism*, a view about explanation proposed earlier in this century by philosophers of a deliberately anti-Marxist bent and then revived by the analytical Marxists.[24] In this case, the irony is extreme. Marx famously inveighed against the 'individualism' of the classical economists and contractarian political philosophers, heaping scorn on their efforts to conceive individuals abstracted from their social relations. In the middle years of the twentieth century, the principal defenders of methodological individualism, Karl Popper and Friedrich von Hayek, took Marx at his word, faulting him on this account. They promoted methodological individualism as an alternative to Marxism. Writers sympathetic to Marxism responded in kind. But for some analytical Marxists, this debate was wrongheaded. What matters, in their view, is that social scientists risk falling into error when they formulate explanations that fail to take account of the individual-level 'mechanisms', psychological or otherwise, through which social factors become causally efficacious. Elster's methodological individualism, in particular, was motivated by the thought that social scientists are obliged, whenever possible, 'to look under the hood', to identify the microfoundational means through which social effects are realized. No matter, then, that the older generation of methodological individualists was motivated by a politics inimical to socialism. Their view of explanation was basically correct, and therefore ought, as far as possible, to be incorporated into the Marxist fold. It was the conventional wisdom among historicist Marxists – and their non-Marxist opponents that Marx set Hegel 'on his feet', putting the dialectical method that Hegel had devised for an idealist metaphysics to good materialist use. Following this precedent, we might say that Elster performed a similar operation on Popper and Hayek. He maintained that it is because many Marxist explanations *are* susceptible to methodological individualist reconstructions that they are generally sound.

There is no need here to take on the eminently contestable views of Elster and his cothinkers on explanation in the social sciences.[25] But it is fair to observe, even so, that a penchant for explanations that satisfy methodological individualist constraints encourages a disposition to focus on normative concerns that are compatible with an individualist outlook. The liberal understanding of equality fits this description because it focuses on *individuals'* holdings. In the liberal view, equality is achieved when individuals have equal shares of the right distribuand, whatever it might be. The values that mattered more to Marx accord less well with this sensibility. This is plainly the case for community. Communal interests are irreducible to the interests of individual members of communities.[26] But it is also true for self-realization and autonomy, as Marx understood these notions. For Marx as for Aristotle, to self-realize is, among other things, to become a social and political being, an integral part of a political community. For Marx as for Kant, to be autonomous is to act in harmony with other free beings, to become 'self-legislating members of a republic of ends', integral components of an harmonious, internally coordinated association of rational beings.

To be sure, methodological individualism is a view about explanation only. It is therefore compatible, strictly speaking, with a wide range of normative commitments. But it is psychologically in tension with positions that are not individualistic. It is curious that Elster, who did so much to investigate the philosophical implications of such phenomena as cognitive dissonance and denial, set out a view of Marx's normative commitments that coincides roughly with the picture sketched here.[27] Unlike Roemer, Elster never claimed, even implicitly, that Marx would have been a liberal egalitarian, if only he had better understood what he and other socialists wanted. Instead, Elster reconstructed and defended Marx's commitment to self-realization and, to a lesser degree, to autonomy and community. He did so, moreover, without suggesting that the normative commitments implicit in Marx's work were in any way at odds with sound explanatory practice. But to endorse these values and methodological individualism at the same time is to court cognitive dissonance or to invite denial. In Elster's case, the way out of this unhappy situation was, as he might say, 'essentially a by-product' of changes in his intellectual interests. Quietly, Elster abandoned Marxism. Others, like Roemer, buffeted by similar tensions but intent on maintaining continuity with the Marxist political tradition, endeavored to fit normative concerns that better conform to an individualist worldview, the concerns of liberal egalitarians, into a Marxist framework. The immediate result of this *démarche* was a rather tepid and politically unfeasible proposal addressed, in the main, to formerly Soviet-style societies in transition to capitalism, to maintain a form of 'socialist' property relations – the better to achieve the values liberal egalitarians promote.[28]

*   *   *

Unlike the historicists and Althusserians, with their grand but obscure theoretical pretensions, the analytical Marxists did yeomen's labor clarifying and assessing Marx's ideas. In doing so, they came, for the most part, quietly but definitively, to fold Marxism into liberal political philosophy and empirical social science. But notwithstanding this unforeseen development, it remains the case, as we will see, that the core of the Marxist program not only survives analytical scrutiny, but emerges strengthened by it. Analytical Marxism – or, rather, its first (and, so far, only) phase – has perhaps melted into air. But it has left a legacy on which to rebuild.

Thus analytical Marxism's fate is not the same as that of other tendencies in Marxist thought. Historicist Marxism survives, barely, at the margins of the intellectual culture; after Althusserian and analytical Marxism, it is, in all likelihood, irrelevant to any foreseeable Marxist revival, even if it somehow continues on for an indefinite period. Althusserian Marxism, historicist Marxism's first important rival, today seems a relic of an already remote past. Its former practitioners, when not trying to make sense of their 'erstwhile philosophical consciences', have gone on to other projects. It is as if their Althusserian days were a phase they long ago outgrew.[29] To the degree that expressly Althusserian motifs survive, it is because they have become incorporated into postmodern

'Theory'; a manifestly wrong turn for anyone who imagines a future for Marxism. Still, despite this unhappy and ironic twist, the Althusserian moment did set Marxism on a sounder course than it had previously taken. But Althusserianism remains too slight and obscure a basis for future generations to build upon.

Not so analytical Marxism. Like the erstwhile Althusserians, most analytical Marxists have gone on to other things. But even if they stopped being Marxists, they never stopped being analytic. Neither have they lost interest in Marx. The idea that there is a still recognizably Marxist voice that merits a place in ongoing academic discussions lingers, however faintly. In fact, analytical Marxism never quite died. Instead, like a good soldier, it faded away. It may therefore yet be possible to take up where the analytical Marxists left off or, failing that, to incorporate some of the findings of what may someday seem to have been the first wave of analtyical Marxist thinking into future philosophical and social scientific work of a distinctively Marxist kind.

It would therefore be misleading to conclude that analytical Marxism killed Marxism off in order to save it; and that it then quickly withered away itself. This conclusion would be wrong in roughly the way that both sides in the debate about Marx's epistemological break are wrong. In each instance, there is a descriptive claim advanced by proponents of one or another position that ought not to be controversial, and then differences in emphases – occasioned, in part, by extraphilosophical, political exigencies – that turn an otherwise sound thesis into a polemical pose. In providing this sketch of the trajectory of the analytical moment in Marxist thought, I have tried not to pose, though I must confess to a polemical intent. My aim has been to suggest that the analytical Marxists gave up the specter of communism too easily; that, contrary to what almost everyone nowadays believes, Marx did point the way to a defensible vision of ideal social, political and economic arrangements beyond the purview of liberal theory. This is a claim with descriptive content as well as polemical force. I elaborate on aspects of it in the next chapter.

6   The Legacy

For more than a century, Marxists led a long march that only recently fell into disarray. But that march can reconstitute itself and resume its forward journey. Perhaps, some day, it will successfully conclude. From a contemporary vantage point, this hope must seem quixotic. But it is a good bet – because the real-world factors that engendered a yearning for socialism (and its final phase, communism) are as much in force as they ever were, albeit on a global scale and in ever changing conditions. The Left, especially the socialist Left, is down but it is not out; in all likelihood, it will revive. But will the next Left march under the banner of 'Marxism'? The taint of the Soviet experience, along with so many other burdens of history, make this prospect uncertain. Is there a chance, then, that Marx's work will be ignored or, if studied, treated only as an historical artifact? It is not impossible. But it would be unfortunate if this becomes Marxism's future. For it would then be necessary to rediscover what Marxists already knew. There are several reasons why this is so. They are implicit in the preceding account of analytical Marxism's trajectory. In this final chapter, I elaborate on them.

*   *   *

It nowadays appears that historical materialism has had its day in the sun. Its prominence in small but influential academic circles has been over for more than a decade. Key tenets of the orthodox view were put to the test, and many of them were found wanting. Nevertheless, the theory itself remains generally intact. It may not explain all that its defenders once thought that it did, but it still explains a great deal. It shows what real property relations are materially possible, and therefore what economic structures are on the historical agenda. Suitably qualified, it also shows how 'legal and political superstructures' and 'forms of consciousness' are explained by 'the economic base' that sustains them. These positions have important implications for political theory – and for real-world politics – that have been only barely explored.

That interest in historical materialism has waned is partly a consequence of the fact that the theory challenges some of the principal assumptions of mainstream liberalism and the social sciences associated with it. Therefore, despite its brief efflorescence, it lapsed – in part, because it ran against the grain of the culture that sustained it. I have suggested, however, that analytical Marxism's journey into liberalism was impelled as much by extraphilosophical factors as by rationally compelling arguments. Certainly, no analytical Marxist ever provided good reasons to think that a political theory consonant with historical materialist positions, a political theory suitable to a scientific socialism, would somehow be untenable. Such a theory would, however, run counter to the belief that there is no alternative to liberalism. This is the academic version of the view, now endemic throughout the larger political culture, that there is no significantly different and still desirable alternative to the institutional arrangements in place in liberal democratic countries. Both claims are wrong. But both threaten to become self-fulfilling prophesies. For anyone who thinks it important that Marxism have a future – or, even if it doesn't, that socialist theory be renewed – there is therefore some urgency in returning historical materialism to center stage; and in reflecting, as analytical Marxists once did, on its implications.

*　*　*

Historical materialism aims to account for history's structure and direction by identifying a causal process internal to human history, an endogenous process, that supplies history with a determinate trajectory or, strictly speaking, that would do so in the absence of countervailing exogenous causes. It is important to acknowledge this limitation on the theory's explanatory power. It is one thing to identify an endogenous process and something else to maintain that it explains phenomena it would explain if no other factors intervened. It might be the case, for example, that all organisms are genetically programmed to die eventually, but that within particular populations deaths may be caused by circumstances other than the execution of this program in some or all cases. Perhaps an environmental toxin kills off all members of the population before death sets in, as it otherwise would. Then, undoubtedly, the fact that the organisms are programmed to die would explain *something*. It might, for example, explain, at least in part, the nature of the organisms' life stages or even their vulnerability to the toxins that killed them. But it would not explain why some or all of the organisms died. Similarly, there is good reason to think that Marx's theory of history explains *something* of why history has taken the course that it has; why capitalism, once introduced, has been so successful and what its possible futures may be. But Marx was probably wrong to maintain, as he claimed in the Preface to the 1859 *Critique of Political Economy*, that it explains actual epochal historical transformations. With respect to that explanandum, it may explain something; but contingent and exogenous factors are very likely more important.

Historical materialism purports to identify real natural kind divisions within human history, and to explain movement from one natural kind division to another. This is a very strong ambition. In chemistry, the periodic table of elements provides an account of the natural kind divisions of matter. In specifying what the *elements* are, it identifies all the ways that matter can be. Thus it provides a 'map' of possibilities. But the periodic table is only a map. Chemistry finds no reason to predict movement, *ceteris absentibus*, from one element to another. Historical materialism does. Not only does it propose an account of possible modes of production or economic structures, a map describing all the ways modes of production can be; it also predicts movement, of an irreversible and progressive kind, from one point on the map to another. As in chemistry, it requires a body of theory even to conceptualize the possibilities. That there is such a thing as a capitalist mode of production is hardly self-evident.[1]

It was widely assumed by the end of the eighteenth century that a major transformation of European, especially British, society was taking place, and that economic changes were central to the changes in progress. There was, however, considerable disagreement about how to characterize these changes and about how to account for them. Major technological transformations in manufacturing, the so-called Industrial Revolution, clearly had a great deal to do with the emerging social order, a fact not lost on contemporary thinkers. So too did changes in the organization of production processes, especially the increasing division of labor. But the claim that changes in real property relations, in control and revenue rights over productive resources, is the key to understanding the great transformation then taking place was an idea that was distinctively Marx's.

Of course, this claim must be qualified; no idea is completely new. The utopian socialists, especially the French ones, had already made forms of property central to their thinking about ideal social arrangements. They despised private property, upholding social ownership in its stead. Marx followed their lead. This is why Lenin identified French socialism, along with British political economy and German philosophy, as one of the roots from which Marx's thought sprang.[2] But even the utopian socialists did not grasp how economic structures or modes of production constitute distinct, historically specific, ways of organizing human societies. They named what they opposed *capitalism*, and they called what they proposed *socialism*. But, from Marx's standpoint, they had an inadequate understanding of both. If he was right, they can hardly be blamed. As remarked, the idea of an economic structure or mode of production is unintuitive. Thus, it would be difficult to imagine someone for whom the concept of capitalism was not already well established thinking, say, that fifteenth-century Italian city states and the developed economies of the early twenty-first century fall under the same theoretical designation. But this is just what Marx's theory of history implies. Marx contended that the modes of production he first identified in that ostensibly 'transitional' work, *The German Ideology* – feudalism, capitalism, and socialism, among others – are real, natural kind divisions of human history, and that understanding their internal functioning is indispensable for grasping the course of history itself.

*   *   *

In support of this contention, it will be well, finally, to turn to historical materialism itself; to the account of history's structure and direction that underwrites the idea of a scientific socialism. To that end, it will be necessary, first, to clarify the terminology Marx used.

An *economic structure* or *mode of production* is a set of real (as distinct from juridical) property relations,[3] where 'property' designates a bundle of control and revenue rights over productive resources. In precapitalist societies, there is private ownership of persons and things. Chattel slavery, of the sort that existed in the American South before the Civil War, is a clear example of ownership of other persons. So too, in a somewhat gentler way, was European feudalism – where lords had property rights in (some of) their serfs' labor. Under capitalism, there is private ownership of external things, but not of other persons. In communist societies, as Marx envisioned them, neither other persons nor external productive resources are privately owned – though personal property would still exist. The abolition of private property in major external productive resources is also a distinguishing feature of *socialism*, communism's 'first phase'.

Production relations or *social relations of production* designate effective control and/or revenue rights over productive assets. They are distinguished from *productive forces* or *forces of production*. These terms designate technology in the broadest sense, that by means of which human beings engage in productive activities. Thus means of production like tools and instruments, the organization of the production process, and even knowledge, insofar as it figures in production, are included among the productive forces. An *economic structure* or *mode of production* may then be defined as a set of production relations. The chief explanatory claim of Marx's theory of history, its first Master Thesis, is, as Cohen put it, that *the level of development of productive forces* explains *the nature of the economic structure.*

Cohen also made it plain that *explains* in this context means '*functionally* explains'. Functional explanations are genuine causal explanations, unlike the teleological explanations of the historicist Marxists. Where *X* explains *Y* functionally, *X* and *Y* causally affect one another. But, at the same time, there is an explanatory asymmetry. Consider, for example, the causal connection between a furnace and the ambient temperature in a room heated by that furnace and regulated by a thermostat. Thanks to the workings of the thermostat, the temperature in the room causally affects the operation of the furnace, and the operation of the furnace causally affects the temperature in the room. But it is the function of the furnace to regulate the room temperature; it is not the function of the room temperature to regulate the operation of the furnace. The same relation holds in the theory of evolution by natural selection. Natural selection is an optimizing mechanism that explains why, for example, giraffes have long necks. Within the population of giraffe ancestors, those individuals who had longer necks, thanks to random variations in neck size, had an advantage over individuals with shorter necks. They were more successful at obtaining nourishment from leaves that grow on tall trees, and therefore had a better chance of surviving to reproductive age. Thus they produced more offspring. In consequence, their descendants came to be more prevalent in later giraffe generations than the descendants of shorter-necked giraffes. In this way, giraffes generally came to have longer necks than their ancestors did. If this explanation is correct, there is a causal interaction between the long necks of giraffes and the trees whose leaves giraffes eat. But there is, once again, an explanatory asymmetry. The function of giraffes' long necks is to obtain the leaves that grow on tall trees; it is not the function of the trees or their leaves to lengthen giraffes' necks.

Because the theory of evolution by natural selection is well supported by evidence, functional explanations are well established in the biological sciences. But, as Elster and others were quick to point out, their role in the social sciences is more dubious. Social scientists, Elster lamented, are inclined to offer functional explanations with reckless abandon, and without regard to establishing genuine causal connections. It is inordinately tempting, it seems, to infer from the fact that because X benefits Y, that X stands in a functional relation to Y. Elster maintained that, since it is easy to confound benefits with functional relations, it is imperative to demand of those who would proffer functional explanations that they provide an account of the mechanism(s) through which the functional relations they purport to have discovered are achieved. For this reason, he impugned Cohen's account of historical materialism for its failure to identify feedback mechanisms, analogous to thermostats and natural selection, that account for the functional relations the theory asserts.[4] It came to be acknowledged, in the wave of discussion launched by Elster's reactions to Cohen's work that Marx indeed fell short on this account; that he had very little helpful to say about *how* forces of production explain relations of production, but not vice versa. But it also came to be generally recognized that this shortcoming does not render Marx's theory false – especially if, in each case of an epochal historical transformation, a plausible causal story can be told that explains why one mode of production succeeded another. Still, the absence of a developed account of the mechanisms through which there is movement along the map of historical possibilities is a concern that persisted for as long as interest in historical materialism did. Thus historical materialism is in roughly the situation of biology before Darwin. Before Darwin discovered natural selection, investigators could truthfully say that giraffes have long necks *because* it helps them obtain food. But they either had no idea how this functional relation was achieved or else they had a false idea; they believed, for example, that God designed giraffes' necks for this purpose.

There is a second Master Thesis of historical materialism, according to Cohen's reconstruction: that *economic structures or modes of production explain legal and political superstructures and also ways of thinking or forms of consciousness*. In this case too, 'explains' means *functionally explains*. The contention, then, is that the legal

and political superstructure, the state and its laws, and forms of consciousness help to *stabilize* and *reproduce* the economic base. The
state and its laws and forms of consciousness are as they are because
the economic base needs them to be that way in order to sustain and
reproduce itself. This is why, in the usual case, real and juridical
property relations coincide.

In his later reflections on the theory he had reconstructed and
defended, Cohen pointed out, contrary to the standard Marxist view
and to Marx's own understanding as well, that there is no
compelling reason to interpret what Marx said about the relation
between superstructural phenomena and the economic base in an
'inclusive' way.[5] In other words, to sustain the claim that forces
(functionally) explain relations of production, it is not necessary to
maintain that there are economic explanations for *all* noneconomic
phenomena. Such a claim is not only unnecessary; it is false. It is
possible, of course, that anything having to do with the state or law
or forms of consciousness can be explained by reference to its role in
stabilizing and reproducing the mode of production. But is it even
remotely plausible, for example, that there is such an explanation
for why Kant formulated the categorical imperative in the way he
did or why the Mona Lisa smiles? Surely, the answer is No. It is
possible, of course, that *anything* can be explained in the way that
inclusive historical materialists suppose. But it is plainly not the case
that *everything* actually is.

Cohen therefore suggested that historical materialists need only
hold that economic structures functionally explain those
noneconomic phenomena that affect social relations of production
in ways that impinge upon the endogenous historical dynamic that
historical materialism's first Master Thesis identifies. Cohen calls this
view *restricted* historical materialism, in contrast to the *inclusive*
historical materialism of orthodox Marxism and of Marx himself.
For inclusive historical materialists, Marx's theory of history
comprises two distinct claims, each asserting a functional relation –
forces of production (technology, broadly conceived) functionally
explain relations of production (real property relations), and then
these relations (or, rather, sets of production relations) functionally
explain the legal and political superstructure (the law and the state)
and forms of consciousness. Restricted historical materialists endorse
these theses too. But, for them, they are joined in a way that they are
not for inclusive historical materialists. For restricted historical
materialists, what falls within the scope of the second Thesis cannot

be specified independently of the first, in the way that it can for inclusive historical materialists. For inclusive historical materialists, there is an historical materialist explanation for *everything* that has to do with the state and law and forms of consciousness. On the restricted view, historical materialism only explains phenomena to the extent that they affect the endogenous dynamic process that, *ceteris absentibus*, moves history along.

Because many aspects of political life have nothing to do with the connection between forces and relations of production, they fall outside the purview of Marx's theory of history altogether. So too, presumably, does most of the intellectual, artistic, religious and scientific history of the human race. Unlike inclusive historical materialism, restricted historical materialism is not a theory of everything historical. It is therefore much weaker in its explanatory pretensions. But it is also far more plausible, and much less vulnerable to facile refutation. Thus it would not embarrass restricted historical materialism, as it would the inclusive version of the theory, if, as Max Weber famously argued, the 'Protestant ethic' was largely a consequence of Protestant theology (rather than of economic causes),[6] or if there is no plausible historical materialist explanation for why, say, a particular legislative assembly requires the presence of half (as opposed to a third or two-thirds) of its members for a quorum. Unless these explananda somehow impinge on the underlying historical materialist dynamic, they have nothing to do with historical materialism's second Master Thesis. Historical materialism therefore has nothing to offer in the way of explanations for them.

*   *   *

Even so, in conjunction with the historical materialist view of history's structure and direction, restricted historical materialism has important implications for political philosophy. Above all, it underwrites the claim that the state form of political organization is not an eternal human necessity. It is instead a creature of a 'moment' in human history, spanning roughly the period from the emergence and consolidation of the capitalist mode of production to the dawn of the end of class divisions under communism. In its time, the state may indeed be indispensable for realizing urgent human interests. It may be necessary for order, as Hobbes believed; and perhaps also to advance (distributive) justice, in the way that liberal egalitarians, like

Rawls, suppose. It may even be necessary, after capitalism is abolished, to move people along to a point where communism becomes feasible, as Marxists, unlike anarchists, have always believed. But, if Marx was right, people will eventually be able to do without states. As productive forces develop and as appropriate economic and political changes take place, either automatically or as a result of deliberate state policies, the urgent and otherwise ineluctable needs to which the state responds will pass. Then, under communism, there will be no state at all.

*   *   *

Almost everything Marx wrote bore in one way or another on the state, especially in the last three decades of his life. But the theory he would go on to elaborate was already implicit in some of the claims he and Engels advanced in the *Communist Manifesto*. There, the general outline of a distinctively Marxist political theory, consonant with Marx's theory of history and with his developing understanding of political economy, is already evident. As will become apparent, Marx's account of the state transcends the frontiers of liberal political philosophy. It is therefore not surprising that analytical Marxists were, on the whole, inattentive to this aspect of his thinking.[7] In this respect, the Althusserians compiled a better record.[8]

In the *Communist Manifesto*, Marx and Engels characterized the state mainly by focusing on what it does, not on how it operates. Throughout history, they claimed, the state organizes the *economically* dominant class into a *ruling* class – overcoming internal divisions that would otherwise render it unable to dominate subordinate classes and to sustain the mode of production from which it benefits; while, at the same time, encouraging internal divisions within subordinate classes that might otherwise threaten its rule. The state, they insisted, does so through historically specific institutions. Thus it is a tenet of Marx's political theory – and an implication of historical materialism's second Master Thesis – that the nature of the state, its institutional form, varies according to the kind of economic structure or mode of production it superintends. There is a distinctively capitalist state; and, although Marx had little to say about it, there is also a distinctive form of the state appropriate for the social order that is destined to supersede capitalism, socialism – the first phase of communism, the final mode of production.

As Althusser would have it, Lenin, in this respect at least, understood Marx best – albeit only in theory, and at a time when he was unencumbered by the requirements of leading a real-world revolutionary state. In his well-known tract *The State and Revolution,* written in the months preceding the Bolshevik Revolution, Lenin famously maintained that all states are 'dictatorships'.[9] Obviously, Lenin's thesis is false if 'dictatorship' is understood to designate a form of government in which an individual or group of individuals rules at is own discretion, without the checks and balances of parliamentary or judicial institutions. But this is not what Lenin meant. As he observed, Marx, in his writings on the (failed) Paris Commune of 1871, described representative democracy, ostensibly dictatorship's opposite, as the characteristic form of the class dictatorship of the bourgeoisie. And, in the same period, Marx called the direct democratic institutions concocted spontaneously by the workers who established and (briefly) maintained the Paris Commune the first historical example of a proletarian class dictatorship. The rationale for this usage becomes clear when we realize that, following the precedent set by Rousseau in *The Social Contract,* what Marx had in mind was the *state,* not the *government.* The term 'state' designates the political entity itself, not the institutional apparatus, the 'government', through which it executes its will. Marx's contention, then, was that, in the final analysis, state power is unconstrained in just the way that most political philosophers had always thought it was; that it rests ultimately on force – not on laws or customs, or on the consent of the governed. In calling states 'dictatorships', Lenin, like Marx and Engels before him, implied that state power, everywhere and in all its forms, is rule based on extralegal and extraconsensual violence. This terminology was misleading; indeed, dangerously so, in view of what would be made of 'the dictatorship of the proletariat' after the Bolshevik Revolution. But the point behind it is, if anything, standard in the political theory of the past several centuries.[10] The idea that force is the foundation of the state has been the dominant view, at least since the time of Hobbes and, before him, Jean Bodin and Niccolo Machiavelli. Where Marx, Engels and Lenin diverged from the mainstream, in ways that go beyond their unfortunate choice of words, was not in holding that states are dictatorships, but in claiming that they are always *class* dictatorships; dictatorships of the economically dominant class or class coalition.

It would not be far-fetched to say that Marx's central theoretical claim amounts, unwittingly, to a recasting of the interest-based case for states developed by Hobbes in a few widely celebrated pages of the *Leviathan*.[11] For Hobbes, individuals in a state of nature are incapable of coordinating their behaviors in ways that accord with their interests. By doing what is individually best, they unintentionally generate radically suboptimal outcomes; they improve themselves to ruin in a generalized 'war of all against all'. The way out of this unhappy state of affairs is to establish a state by instituting sovereignty, a power sufficiently mighty to coordinate individuals' behaviors through the use or threat of force. Sovereignty therefore solves a Prisoners' Dilemma problem that exists because the payoff structure individuals confront in its absence is such that, by maximizing their own utility, they find themselves worse off than they might otherwise be. The sovereign changes the payoff structure individuals confront, in a way that makes it irrational for them always to do what would be individually best in a state of nature. Subjects of a sovereign must adjust their behaviors to accord with the sovereign's commands. They must, in other words, maximize utility against a background of laws, coercively enforced. This constraint, in Hobbes's view, makes all individuals better off.

Marx's (implicit) revision of Hobbes's case for sovereignty followed from his contention that state power is the power of a social class or coalition of classes. For Hobbes, the point of departure for thinking about political institutions was the individual conceived atomistically, apart from any social relations. For Marx, on the other hand, the fundamental unit of society, even for purposes of political theory, was social classes. From his vantage point, then, there is no notion of a general, interindividual coordination problem for the state to solve. But there is a class coordination problem. Herein lies a crucial difference. Classes, unlike atomic individuals, are not mired in a war of all against all. This is not because the interests of classes are in harmony. Quite the contrary. It is because for a state of nature to be a state of war, potential combatants must be, as Hobbes insisted, relatively equal to one another in the amount of force they can bring to bear in pursuit of their interests. This condition does not obtain between classes – thanks to the economic structure. Among the classes whose interests stand opposed, some (usually one) are powerful enough to dominate the rest. Some (usually one) are in a position to take unfair advantage; to *exploit*, the others. Therefore the interclass coordination problem that exists in class-divided societies does not mimic the condition that led Hobbes to propose the institution of sovereignty. In class-divided societies, there is no war of all against all that everyone seeks to escape. Rather, the economic structure or mode of production itself establishes an order, one that the beneficiaries of the regime in place – and, thanks to the way forms of consciousness relate to the economic base, not only them! – seek to reproduce indefinitely. The role of the state in establishing order is therefore secondary or derivative in just the way that historical materialism's second Master Thesis claims. Its role is not to establish order, but to maintain and reproduce the order established by the economic structure. In the final analysis, it does so – as all political theorists, not only Hobbes, would agree – through the use or threat of force.

To discharge this mission, there is an intraclass or, more precisely, an intra–ruling class coordination problem, similar to the one Hobbes identified for individuals generally, that must somehow be solved. Among the exploiters, individuals and coalitions of individuals have conflicting interests. But they also have a common interest, analogous to the interest in peace that individuals in a Hobbesian state of nature share. Specifically, everyone in the economically dominant class has an interest in maintaining the existing system of exploitation, for it is only in virtue of this system that they are economically dominant. The state is the means through which they act on this interest. It is what allows the economically dominant class to overcome its own internal coordination problem, its (potential) *intra*class war of all against all, the better to wage war, class war, against subordinate classes. Thus the state is the mechanism through which exploiters organize their own class dictatorship. As Marx and Engels proclaimed in the *Communist Manifesto*, it is 'the executive committee' of the entire ruling class.

This contention is at odds not only with liberal political philosophy, but with all strains of political thought that, following Hobbes's lead, see the state as a solution to an interindividual coordination problem. For nearly everyone who is not a Marxist, how (or how best) to achieve interindividual coordination is the fundamental problem of political life. For nearly everyone, therefore, states are not class states. They are states of an undifferentiated citizenry. Liberals are part of this consensus; indeed, for many decades, they have constituted overwhelmingly the main part. Marxists fall outside the post-Hobbesian consensus altogether.

It should be noted that Marx's thesis pertains, in the first instance, to *ruling* classes. It would therefore embarrass the theory profoundly if a Marxist account of the ruling class under capitalism proved untenable. But the theory can survive the absence of a classical proletariat in 'bourgeois society'. Indeed, the idea that the state is 'the executive committee' of the entire ruling class implies a profound rethinking of the standard understanding of the proletariat and its class dictatorship. This is because it is consistent with Marx's express position – and is in fact the case, as Marx himself implied as early as the *Communist Manifesto* – that subordinate classes also face intraclass coordination problems, problems that are exacerbated by the class dictatorship that enforces their subordination. This was a perennial theme in the analyses of political events that Marx composed in the later decades of his life. By the 1860s, when he helped to found the First International, Marx had come to believe that, under capitalism, working-class political parties can help to counter the state's role in decapacitating the working class. He also came to regard working-class parties as indispensable tools for organizing the conquest of state power – something that, following the precedent established in 1789 in France, he thought prerequisite for any imaginable social revolution. But until subordinate classes succeed in their historical mission, working-class parties can only do so much to unify the working class, the bearers of socialist and, eventually, communist social relations. It is only *after* the conquest of state power that the intraclass coordination problems workers confront can finally be solved. More generally, it is only by organizing its own class dictatorship that a previously subordinate class is able, finally, to act coherently in its own interest – to become what some historicist Marxists would call a 'class-for-itself'. Therefore, until the construction of communism is under way under the aegis of a proletarian class dictatorship, the proletariat, in the sense of the term that matters for Marx's political theory, *does not yet exist*. The victims of capitalist exploitation, the direct producers, are indeed potential bearers of new social relations. No doubt too, the less they have to lose, the more likely they are to actualize this potentiality. At the limit, they probably are most mobilizable if they 'have nothing to lose but their chains'. But, strictly speaking, the theory does not entail that direct producers stand 'outcast and starving' prior to taking hold of the state. Their degree of 'integration' is a problem for Marxist politics, not for Marxist political theory. For the latter, the direct producers need only be capable, in principle, of moving society along to its next and final stage.

It should also be observed that, after a socialist revolution, for the very first time in human history, the ruling class's interest is not to perpetuate its rule indefinitely, but to overcome class divisions altogether. The proletariat rules in order to dissolve itself and, in doing so, to forge precisely what the liberals and the others wrongly assume possible this side of communism – a genuinely undifferentiated citizenry.

*   *   *

Thus the idea of a proletarian class dictatorship, in the sense that Marx intended it, has nothing to do with dictatorial forms of government or one party rule, or with the wholesale transgression of human rights with which it came to be associated after the Bolshevik Revolution. As remarked, Marx's and Lenin's model for the dictatorship of the proletariat was the radically democratized social order that emerged spontaneously in the Paris Commune. For them, radical democracy is emblematic of the dictatorship of the proletariat. Dictatorial government – governing structures of the kind that everyone nowadays rightly opposes – may sometimes be necessary *in extremis*, when circumstances are extraordinarily dire. But it is always inimical to the mission and tendency of a workers' state.

Even so, the idea of a proletarian class dictatorship resurrects a tension between democratic commitments and liberalism that was once keenly felt, but that has lain buried for roughly the past century and a half. The problem is just that, in the end, no matter how democratic its form of governance may be, a proletarian class dictatorship is at odds with liberal norms. In a word, its implementation involves restrictions on the rights of former exploiters and other social strata with interests detrimental to the interests of direct producers. It therefore requires what liberals oppose – in principle, if not always consistently in practice: the *unequal* distribution of fundamental rights.

Thus a proletarian class dictatorship is not a *Rechtstaat*, a state in which all individuals stand equally before universal principles of Right. We have already seen how it was Marx's view that, before communism, no state can be a genuine *Rechtstaat*. It can proclaim itself one, and even appear to be what it claims it is, at least for a while. But, when it does so, appearances are deceiving – and, worse,

counteremancipatory. If it is true that states are always class dictatorships, then equal citizenship is impossible – now and for as long
as states exist. This was Marx's view in his prebreak, Feuerbachian
period too. In his early writings, however, Marx formulated this
thought in a way that accorded with the philosophical preoccupa-
tions of the Young Hegelians. In the *Communist Manifesto* and then
in his reflections on actual political events, he framed it in a way
that is consistent instead with the bodies of theory he was in the
course of developing. But, whatever the context or larger agenda,
Marx's contention throughout his life – on both sides of the epistemological break – was that in class-divided societies pretensions
of equality are always ultimately shams. Liberal representative
democracies, class dictatorships of the bourgeoisie, proclaim
equality, the better to organize the domination of the many by the
few. Proletarian class dictatorships are no truer to Hegel's ideal. But
they are, at least, more transparent in their transgression of it. More
importantly, they aim to establish the conditions under which the
kind of order Hegel envisioned might actually become possible. It is
for the sake of this goal that they expressly proclaim inequality, to
the advantage of the many and to the detriment of the few. They
must do so, Marx believed, in order to be able to superintend the
transition to the true equality of a classless society.

Ironically, then, if Marx was right, at the same time that
communism is not a utopian dream, the *Rechtstaat*, the liberal ideal,
is. It is an unrealizable form of political association. The conditions
for its possibility are humanly feasible, of course. But as they come
into being, the *Rechtstaat* – and, more generally the state form of
political organization – becomes increasingly superfluous. As
communism is achieved, systemic class divisions disappear. So too,
therefore, does the mechanism that exists to sustain them. This is
why, as Marx famously put it, the state that succeeds the capitalist
state – the state that superintends the transition from socialism,
communism's first phase, to full-fledged communism – 'withers
away'. As it fulfills its historic mission, it disappears for want of a
sufficient reason for being. It was the burden of historical
materialism's first Master Thesis to show that, as productive forces
develop, *this* prospect actually does come onto the historical agenda;
and therefore that, in this sense, communism is historically feasible.
But the *Rechtstaat* is never historically feasible. It is like the Messiah
in Kafka's parable: '...[who] will come only when he is no longer
necessary ... not on the last day, but on the very last'.[12]

*   *   *

The dictatorship of the proletariat, as conceived, by Marx and by the Lenin of *The State and Revolution*, is therefore the *last* state in a process that culminates in statelessness. Its role is to maintain the class power of the working class as its members overcome the effects of human alienation, and as the task of producing use values devolves to humanity generally; or, in the words of the *Internationale*, as 'the international working class becomes the human race'. Mainly through the educative effects of direct democratic governance – but also, because it is still a state, through its distinctive means of coercion – the dictatorship of the proletariat progressively undoes the conditions that make it necessary and possible.

Beyond this very general description, Marx had little to say about the nature of a proletarian class dictatorship. His reflections, such as they were, were scattered throughout his political writings, especially in his reflections on the failed Commune. They consist largely of speculations about its institutional forms. This focus is well chosen from an historical materialist point of view; historical materialism's second Master Thesis implies that different institutional forms are appropriate for different class dictatorships. Even so, focusing on Marx's express accounts of institutional arrangements can be misleading. For it was Marx's view that proletarian class rule does not strictly require *any* particular set of institutions. This is why, for example, the political program proposed in the *Communist Manifesto* seems so odd to readers nowadays. Some of the measures Marx and Engels proposed there – the establishment of a progressive income tax, for example, or the centralization of the means of communication and transport in the hands of the state – have been tried long ago by capitalist states. They seem innocuous nowadays. Others, like the abolition of private property in land and the 'gradual abolition of all distinctions between town and country by a more equitable distribution of the population over the countryside' seem hopelessly utopian (in the sense of historically unrealizable). But whatever their merits or shortcomings, these measures were put forth as a program for an impending German revolution, the one that did in fact erupt in 1848. Marx and Engels never thought of them as anything other than demands appropriate for a particular time and place. In other times and places, different, even opposing, measures might be correspondingly apt. The same is true of Marx's other, post-Commune recommendations on institutional forms. Of course, liberals too can be flexible about institutions. But theirs is a pragmatic flexibility. Liberalism implies a politics of muddling through, of proceeding in a vaguely progressive direction, but without any vision of an alternative end in view. Marx's politics, on the other hand, sets its course by what historical materialism identifies: the natural kind divisions of human history, their trajectory, and their (possible) destination.

Thus Marx's writings leave the nature of postcapitalist institutional arrangements largely unspecified. It could hardly be otherwise, given the indeterminacy that necessarily attaches to an issue so thoroughly conjunctural. Still, there is at least one general implication for states in socialist societies that follows from Marx's theory of history and its associated political theory. Inasmuch as it is implied by these core theoretical commitments, it is not surprising that it resonates throughout Marx's scattered reflections on socialism and communism. It has to do with the historical dynamic of the institutional arrangements of proletarian class dictatorships. Since the proletariat has no interest in maintaining itself as a class, since its interest instead is to abolish class divisions altogether, state institutions in a proletarian class dictatorship ought to aim, as far as possible, at undoing the conditions that make them necessary. In this respect, they contrast with the institutional forms of other class dictatorships, including those that incorporate liberal principles, as the best 'bourgeois class dictatorships' characteristically do. Other class dictatorships develop institutions that tend to reproduce themselves indefinitely. They do not even try to undo the conditions that make the state form of political organization necessary. Liberalism is no exception. In this respect, perhaps more than any other, it is at odds with what is genuinely distinctive in Marx's thought.

One can, of course, debate the feasibility and desirability of institutions of the kind that Marx suggested, institutions that are progressively self-effacing. An obvious concern is whether they can sustain the kinds of safeguards against tyranny that liberalism, to its everlasting credit, introduced into the political arena.[13] But liberals have nothing constructive to say about eliminating the need for states. That prospect lies beyond the pale of their conceptual horizons. Notwithstanding the analytical Marxists' best efforts to turn Marxism into liberalism, and not forgetting the considerable successes they registered in that endeavor, this fact, by itself, suffices to make it impossible completely to incorporate within the liberal fold a political philosophy shaped by its historical and conceptual links to Marx's theory of history.

*   *   *

Thus, on the face of it, Marx's contention that statelessness is feasible contradicts the statism endemic to all strains of modern political philosophy, including liberalism. But there is a sense in which Marx and mainstream statists agree. Hobbes, the founding father of statism, maintained that the state is a transhistorical human necessity in consequence of ineluctable facts about human nature and the human condition. Marx agreed that these factors render anarchy, uncoerced cooperation, impossible – for persons living in societies marked by class divisions. But because Marx thought that a classless society is a human possibility, he would implicitly qualify the premise from which Hobbes's statist conclusion follows. In Marx's view, the aspects of human nature and the human condition that make states necessary are powerful and pervasive. But they are not timeless in the way that Hobbes and those who follow in his wake assume. As forces of production develop, the human condition, and perhaps human nature too, can change. Beyond a certain achievable threshold, the Hobbesian premise would no longer obtain. Therefore, neither would the conclusion it underwrites. Thus the statist's case becomes weaker as communism becomes ever more materially possible – that is, as the development of productive forces progressively emancipates humankind from the thrall of scarcity. Then, with class divisions superseded and the state 'withering away' for want of a sufficient reason, the anarchists' ideal, uncoerced cooperation, comes onto the historical agenda. This is a prospect that liberalism is ill equipped to contemplate. But it informs every aspect of Marx's thinking about the state in socialist societies.

*   *   *

Restricted historical materialism, in conjunction with the claim that economic structures rise and fall to track ever increasing levels of technological development, also provides a deeper understanding than previously available of the role of class struggle in Marx's political theory. As we have seen, historical materialism is not the 'worldview' of a class with 'universal chains' – a class that has, in fact, gone missing. It is a theory of historical possibilities opened up by the development of 'productive forces'. If capitalism is indeed the final precommunist (and therefore presocialist) mode of production, and if it is indeed distinguished from other economic structures in the way that Marx thought, by its real property relations, then, so long as capitalism exists, there is in principle a revolutionary agent at the ready – comprised of all the victims of the property relations in place. There remains, of course, the enormous problem of motivating these agents; a problem that proved intractable in the days of the New Left. But there is no reason, grounded in political theory, why the revolutionary agent must resemble the classical proletariat of orthodox Marxism. The bearers of new social relations must be direct producers. But, even so, in cultural and other ways, they need not be all that much like the working classes of industrialized societies as they existed until fairly recently. All that is necessary, strictly speaking, is that they have an interest in changing the economic structure fundamentally in the way that historical materialism's first Master Thesis predicts, and that they have the capacity to do so.

Thus there is a way, after all, to retain Marxism's view of capitalism's (possible) future in a world in which the class Marxism ostensibly represented no longer exists. Marx's notion of class struggle is sufficiently robust to survive fundamental changes in the class structure of industrialized societies – including changes that make the prospects for class politics today very different from what they were in Marx's time and in the decades that followed. In this way, it provides theoretical resources for addressing the problem that Althusser grappled with implicitly, even as he officially denied its salience; and that, in its political practice, the New Left confronted and failed to resolve.   In this respect too, Marxism contrasts with liberal political philosophy. For liberalism excludes the class struggle entirely from its purview.

Liberalism's focus is, as it were, entirely superstructural. Underlying (class) power relations fall outside its scope. This is a theoretical difference with important practical implications. It is what turns liberalism away from political orientations that would radically alter existing property relations. And it is what leads even progressive liberal philosophers, like Rawls, and like the liberal egalitarians that so many former analytical Marxists have become, to address social problems in a way that underwrites the long-standing liberal penchant to engineer away society's ills, and to discount the prospect of revolutionizing away the conditions that make these ills inevitable. For Marxists, these conditions have always had to do, in the main, with the capitalist mode of production. Accordingly, in its political orientation as well as in its theoretical commitments, Marxism is anticapitalist to its core. Arguably, as Rawls once suggested and as analytical Marxists like Roemer effectively demonstrated, liberals can be socialists too.[14] But a liberal socialist political theory would be liberal for principled reasons, and socialist only contingently. It would be socialist to the extent that its proponents advance reasons to believe that socialist property relations are instrumental for realizing liberal aims. Marx's contention, implicit in the idea of communism, that there are reasons for socialism (and, ultimately, communism) that transcend liberal horizons – reasons that have to do with the nature of communal life and the kinds of relationships that are humanly possible – implies a very different kind of socialist theory.

*   *   *

It should nevertheless be plain, in light of analytical Marxist work, that Marxism does not so much oppose liberalism as go beyond it; and that liberalism can be a progressive political philosophy, just as it was at its inception. Those who look forward to a revived Left should therefore take care not to follow the example of the New Left by casting undue aspersions on it. This is true even for those who think that the highest priority at the present moment is to revive political imagination. Compared to socialism, liberalism has never been an inspirational ideology. But the fact that it is bereft of any theoretically grounded account of the forms and limits of political arrangements – and of any notion of alternatives to liberal 'bourgeois class dictatorships' capable of advancing the values of the historical Left – does not entail that liberal societies must be as depleted of political vision as they have become. Liberals can again become allies of a reinvigorated socialist vanguard in a revived Left.

Still, it must not be forgotten that an exclusively liberal political orientation does foreclose thinking about far-reaching alternatives. This is why it is fair to conclude that even liberal egalitarianism is unlikely to reignite a genuinely radical political vision – especially now, when it has fallen so thoroughly under the sway of the American model. Having taken a liberal turn, 'first-wave' analytical Marxism implicated itself in this unhappy state of affairs. It made itself part of the problem. But it does not have to be that way. In bringing Marx's theories of history and the state to center stage, and in putting these theories – or, at least, reconstructed versions of them – on a sound footing, analytical Marxism left a legacy that points in a very different, more salutary, direction. Perhaps, in the not too distant future, philosophers and others determined to move *beyond* liberalism will put this legacy to use.

*   *   *

Analytical Marxism's strength, its determination to reconstruct Marx's views in terms consistent with the best philosophy and social science of the time, was also its weakness. For in making Marxist theory accountable to the academic constituencies with which its exponents identified, the analytical Marxists, despite their own findings, succumbed to prevailing professional deformations – to the point, eventually, that they came to deny what was genuinely distinctive and timely in Marx's thought. The idea that the economic base must be socialist and eventually communist if human beings are to make the social world as good as it can be was one of Marx's signal contributions to political philosophy. So too was the idea, implicit in this larger conviction, that the principal victims of the old order must be both the bearers of new social relations and the agents of social change. This understanding is central to Marx's notion of communism, and of the politics necessary for establishing and sustaining it. It should be evident, to all who have not surrendered to the spirit of the present moment, that, in the aftermath of the analytical Marxist turn, this core Marxist insight is not only left standing; it has survived strengthened. Therefore, contrary to what nowadays appears, not only to its practitioners but also to most observers of the scene, analytical Marxism, so far from killing Marxism off, actually provided a basis for revitalizing the Marxist theoretical tradition, just as its proponents initially hoped it would. In the same spirit that animated the Althusserians, but far more effectively, analytical Marxists rediscovered and then reinforced the foundation of a theory and practice beyond liberalism, grounded in Marx's thought, and previously accessible, if at all, only through the opaque and distorting lense of historicist theory.

Conclusion:
A Future for Marxism?

The world desperately needs the socialist tradition to revive. The odds that it will are good. The conditions that brought the historical Left into being persist; if anything, they have intensified and expanded on a global scale. This can hardly fail to have an effect. Already, there are stirrings; perhaps, in a few years time, it will seem in retrospect that a revival is, even now, under way. But a Left without socialism, without a dedication to carrying the project launched in 1789 to its culmination, can hardly rise above the laudable but balefully inadequate meliorism that, alone among socialist goals, survived the collapse of the New Left. As the triumphalism that attended the end of communism fades, the idea that liberal democracy is the end of history no longer resonates as it did – especially in the face of the countless horrors wrought throughout the world by the imperial overreach of the United States, the one remaining superpower and also, by its own reckoning, the paradigmatic liberal democratic state. Intellectual life has yet to catch up with this emerging sensibility. In the universities especially, liberalism, in one or another version, is very nearly all there is. Thus liberal egalitarianism now finds itself bearing the full burden of the Left's historical mission. But there are signs that it is dawning, even in academic circles, that however considerable liberalism's merits may be, its conceptual framework is not adequate to the task at hand; and therefore that the old ideal of changing life radically for the better must come back onto the political agenda. There is therefore hope that the will to constitute a *socialist* Left will again assert itself – first, in the academy, but then also, much more importantly, in the larger political culture.

I have tried here to restore the idea – evident in Marx's writings before his epistemological break, but foreign to the thinking of the majority of those who would later identify with Marxism – that liberalism is not so much wrong as incomplete, and that it is therefore insufficient for realizing the values the historical Left drew from the Revolution in France – liberty, equality and fraternity. If this assessment is sound, it would imply just what Marxists have always believed: that communism, not liberal democracy, is the end of history. To this I would add, contrary to what was the conventional view before analytical Marxism, that socialism's historical rival is not liberalism at all. It is what might be called nostalgic premodernism, epitomized in the various 'fundamentalisms' that identify with the world's religions. In recent decades – thanks to disingenuous and ill-conceived Western meddling, the dissolution of the old bipolar world order, and the collapse of a genuinely Left alternative to endemic oppression – this plague has been loosed upon the world. The danger is plain. Unlike liberalism and even (post-French Revolutionary) conservatism, these ideologies – and that is what they are, however much they may present themselves as something unworldly and therefore extrapolitical – are not merely inadequate for realizing the emancipatory project that engaged the historical Left. They are detrimental to it.

With this in mind, I would venture that those who, in the interwar period and subsequently, posed the alternative 'socialism or barbarism' were right. Of course, the barbarisms they feared were fascism, socialism's bastard cousin, and, in some cases, 'totalitarianism', a category that included both fascism and Soviet communism. This concern was well-founded. The twentieth century, the century of total war and the industrialization of mass murder, may well appear, in retrospect, to have been an age of barbarism. But the twentieth century's barbarisms were specific to an historical moment that has passed. The barbarisms that threaten today, with their nostalgia for premodern ways of thinking and being, represent, if anything, an even more egregious reaction to the ineluctable course of modernity.[1] They call for a reversion to the tribal passions and animosities, and to the superstitious concerns, of ages past. This is a species of barbarism that, unlike fascism or totalitarianism, is overtly hostile to the secularism emblematic of all serious social and political thought since, at least, the seventeenth century. For the time being, in many parts of the world, this reactionary movement appears to have bested the continuators of the Enlightenment tradition; elsewhere it is an enduring danger. Thus Marx was right about this too. Enlightenment is not enough to root out the dead weight of the past. For that, it is necessary to change the world in the ways that Enlightened theory suggests – to forge a form of life in which the scourges of twentieth and twenty-first century political life are definitively and irreversibly superseded. Marx thought that only a triumphant socialism could excise the demons of his own time. It is fair to speculate that he would have thought the same for our own.

Thus the world needs a Left, a socialist Left – indeed, a victorious socialist Left – urgently. But the fact that this need exists does not imply that it will be met. It only enhances the prospect. I have suggested that the odds that a socialist Left will reemerge are good. I would add that the odds that it will triumph eventually, as historical materialism predicts *ceteris absentibus*, are, at the very least, far stronger than is nowadays everywhere assumed.

What, though, of Marxism itself? Can it revive after its decades-long connection with Soviet communism and with a host of other political movements that are now, deservedly or not, nearly as defunct? Can it survive after the scrutiny accorded it by its best defenders? Here, I would not hazard odds. But I have tried to suggest that a revived analytical Marxism – a second wave, as it were – is not out of the question. Appearances notwithstanding, the main obstacles in its way are political, not theoretical. It is not impossible, therefore, that the pendulum will swing back, and that a Marxist identification will again become timely. The intellectual world works that way: what was discredited yesterday often comes back tomorrow, strengthened, and in many ways superior to what holds sway today. But whatever happens, it would be unfortunate in the extreme if the substantive achievements of the first wave of analytical Marxist thought remain lodged entirely under liberalism's broad tent. If they do, a revived socialist Left will have to rediscover what the Marxists already knew.

I have had little to say here about Marxist political economy or about Marxist social science, as they too passed through the analytical Marxist crucible. What appears to be the case in these domains is that Marx's views turn out to have been generally sound. Marx, it seems, anticipated positions and modes of analysis that the mainstream would discover only decades later. It seems too that much of what Marx said can be 'translated' into terms that mainstream economists and sociologists can recognize as their own. The consensus view, though, is that there is not much left to be learned from Marx – that what he did, however estimable and however advanced it may have been for its time and place, can now be done better in other ways. I will not venture an opinion on whether this assessment is correct – except to note that, in the past, the prescience of the 'old mole' has been rediscovered time and again. It would be premature, at best, to conclude that, after analytical

Marxism, there are better reasons now than there were decades ago to think that this time, finally, Marxism's relevance to the progress of social science is exhausted. Thanks to their Hegelian roots – in other words, to their connections to an intellectual tradition dedicated to an holistic purchase on the real – Marx's explanatory projects evince a concern with the whole that is uncommon in mainstream economics and sociology. This focus may yet prove crucial to gaining knowledge that would otherwise be inaccessible.

Marxism's focus on the whole may also point the way to a distinctive and continuing contribution to normative theory. I have remarked that the normative commitments implicit in Marx's thought, his dedication to self-realization, autonomy and community – and, more ambivalently, to equality – do not amount to a distinctive ideology; partly because Marx's understanding of these notions, community partially excepted, is no different from understandings encountered in the Aristotelian, Kantian and republican traditions. But, in light of what has now become clear, second-wave analytical Marxist work, if it materializes, is poised to find that there may indeed be a distinctive Marxist way of putting these valuational commitments together, and that this 'voice' can have important political consequences. Just as liberalism tends to support a reformist political practice supportive of received institutional arrangements, Marxism, even in the reconstituted version that may someday emerge, will in all likelihood again underwrite what is sorely needed today – a politics that promotes genuinely structural changes and, at the limit, the radical transformation of the Old Regime. Again, this is not enough to warrant calling Marxism a distinctive normative theory, let alone a political ideology. But in conjunction with those aspects of Marx's thought that genuinely are unique, and that transcend the horizons of other problematics, Marx's particular understandings and emphases may someday help to restore the political configuration that existed long ago – when there still was a flourishing Left, with liberal and socialist components, guided by a vision supplied, ultimately, by its socialist wing.

Marxist political theory genuinely is unique and vital. There may be other bodies of theory, derived from Marx's thinking, that are as well. Even in its restricted version, historical materialism has implications for the analysis of forms of consciousness, just as it does for the superstructure itself – that is, for the state and the law. I have not had much to say here about this prospect because my focus has been on recent Marxist philosophy, on Althusserian and analytical

Marxism, not cultural criticism. To be sure, Althusser did famously discuss ideology. But his account of what he called the 'ideological state apparatus' had more to do with political theory – with the state and its institutional forms – than with forms of consciousness per se.[2] As one would expect, Althusser's analysis followed the lead of revolutionary figures in the Marxist tradition, filtered through his own ingenious philosophical imagination. In this case, his principal, though largely unacknowledged, sources were Antonio Gramsci and Mao Tse-tung, leaders who sought, in various ways, to enlist struggles in and over culture in their larger efforts to overthrow capitalism and then – in Mao's case, at least officially – to build a socialist order. Althusser did, in addition, venture a few more direct remarks on cultural subjects. But these issues were peripheral to his central concerns. The analytical Marxists had even less to say about forms of consciousness. Perhaps, though, if analytical Marxism does enjoy a second wave, or even if it has continuators who do not adopt a Marxist identification, some of the implications of historical materialism's second Master Thesis, as they pertain to cultural issues, will finally be broached. This, however, remains a task for the future.

But, whether or not this comes to pass, the main legacy of analytical Marxism, for now and the foreseeable future, is its account of what is historically possible and of what humanity's destiny can be. This is a perspective that lies beyond the ken of other descendant versions of the ideologies that emerged in the aftermath of the French Revolution, including liberalism at its most egalitarian. None of them, except Marxism, have any inkling of a possible communist future. I submit, however, that it is precisely this idea that is indispensable for restoring and then advancing the political imagination of a renascent Left – making it possible, again, to unify what would otherwise be a motley of well-meaning, but mainly reactive, causes into a movement with a serious prospect of changing life for the better, definitively and irreversibly. That has always been Marxism's mission, a fact that remained evident, even as the designation, like the designation 'liberal democracy', came to be implicated in some of humanity's greatest tragedies and crimes. It is a mission that can be resumed. The best way, no doubt, would be to take up where analytical Marxism left off. But if it remains the case, for an indefinite future, that a Marxist identification is a liability, and if, for this or any other reason, the next Left distances itself from it, then the mission can be resumed in other ways. What matters is just that it be resumed – that Marxism or, if need be, some functional equivalent be made to have a future.

Notes

INTRODUCTION TO PART I

1. 'So-called' because although its ostensible targets – in the first instance, Islamicist militants – are indeed terrorists of the worst kind, it is being waged by a superpower, the United States, which, along with its allies and client states, projects power through terror – that is, through violence directed mainly at non-combatant populations.
2. The idea that history has ended with the triumph of the West was famously proclaimed by Francis Fukuyama in the early 1990s and, for reasons that remain mysterious, taken seriously immediately thereafter by influential thinkers of the Left. See Francis Fukuyama, *The End of History and the Last Man* (New York: Free Press, 1992). However, just a decade after its proclamation, Fukuyama's thesis appears more than a little outdated. What seems to be on the rise today, even in the erstwhile First and Second Worlds, is premodern, religious fanaticism – not liberal democracy or any other modern, secular political project.
3. See E.P. Thompson et al., *Out of Apathy* (London: Stevens, 1960).
4. See, for example, Daniel Bell, *The End of Ideology: On the Exhaustion of Political Ideas in the Fifties* (New York: Free Press, 1962).
5. Sigmund Freud, *The Future of an Illusion* (1927) in James Strachey, ed., *The Standard Edition of the Complete Psychological Works of Sigmund Freud*, vol. 21 (London: The Hogarth Press, 1961).

CHAPTER 1

1. This is, of course, the view originally argued by Alexis de Tocqueville a century and a half ago in *The Old Regime and the Revolution*, François Furet and Françoise Mélonio, eds. (Chicago: University of Chicago Press, 1998). The contemporary revival of Tocqueville's assessment of the French Revolution owes most to the work of François Furet. See, especially, *The French Revolution and the Creation of Modern Political Culture* (Oxford and New York: Pergamon Press, 1987–94).
2. Thomas Hobbes, *Leviathan*, Michael Oakeshott, ed. (Oxford: Basil Blackwell, n.d.) Originally published in 1651. See especially ch. 13.
3. See St. Augustine, *The City of God* (New York: Random House, 1950). Written A.D. 413–26.
4. See Edmund Burke, *Reflections on the Revolution in France,* Connor Cruise O'Brien, ed. (London: Penguin, 1968) and Tocqueville, *Old Regime*.
5. See Michael Oakeshott, 'Political Education', in *Rationalism and Politics* (London: Methuen, 1962).
6. See Edmund Burke, *On the American Revolution: Selected Speeches and Letters*, Elliott Robert Barkan, ed. (New York: Harper and Row, 1966); and Alexis de Tocqueville, *Democracy in America*, edited and translated by Harvey Mansfield and Delba Winthrop (Chicago: University of Chicago Press, 2000).

7. For Locke's views on religious toleration, see his *First Letter on Toleration* (New York: Library of Liberal Arts, 1950). For his views on slavery, private property and market exchange, see his *Second Treatise of Government*, first published in 1690, C.B. Macpherson, ed. (Indianapolis, Ind., Hackett, 1980), especially chs. 4 and 5.

8. In the Introduction to *The Critique of Hegel's 'Philosophy of Right'*, first published in the *Deutsch-Französische Jahrbücher* of February 1844, Marx declared: 'Germany, which likes to get to the bottom of things, can only make a revolution which upsets *the whole order* of things. The *emancipation* of Germany will be an *emancipation of man*. Philosophy is the *head* of this emancipation, and the *proletariat* is its heart. Philosophy can only be realized by the abolition of the proletariat, and the proletarian can only be abolished by the realization of philosophy.'

9. In practice, however, liberals acquiesce in and even encourage substantial deviations from the ideal – more often, revealingly, in substance than in form. This is especially true in the electoral arena, and nowhere more than in the United States, where constitutional and legislative provisions work together to insure extraordinary inequalities of political influence, at the same time that the principle of one person one vote is generally respected.

10. See, however, *The Defense of Gracchus Babeuf: Before the High Court of Vendôme*, edited and translated by John Anthony Scott (New York: Schocken, 1972).

11. Presumably, though, for socialists and other income and wealth egalitarians, income and wealth equality are only proxies for what they really want when they call for material equality. After all, income and wealth are, at best, only means, imperfect ones at that, for attaining whatever might be thought to matter fundamentally. This claim holds as much for those who think that justice regulates the distribution of resources, as for those who think it regulates the distribution of well-being or anything else that could plausibly be held to matter intrinsically. However, it will suffice, for the present purpose, to focus on these proxies. If nothing else, income and wealth equality are tractable notions, while it is far from clear what material equality, understood more deeply, involves. The problem, in short, is that making persons equal in some respect almost always makes them unequal in other respects. Thus equalizing resources is bound to generate inequalities in, say, happiness – and vice versa – because people differ in the ways that resources affect their levels of happiness. Thus an individual with inexpensive tastes will require less income than one with expensive tastes to reach an equal level of happiness. This is the problem that generates the so-called 'equality of what?' debate. For a brief overview of some of the contending positions in that literature, see my *Rethinking Liberal Equality: From a Utopian Point of View* (Ithaca, N.Y.; Cornell University Press, 1998), esp. pp. 43–51. For the present purpose, it is unnecessary to wade into these troubled waters, however: first, because income and wealth equality convey the general (admittedly problematic) idea of material equality well enough, but also, more importantly, because whatever distribuand one might favor in the 'equality of what?'

debate, it is almost certainly the case that the best (and perhaps the only feasible and/or acceptable) way to attain it is through a more equal distribution of income and wealth.

12. This is essentially the view set forth by Joseph Schumpeter in *Capitalism, Socialism, and Democracy* (New York: Harper and Row, 1942). See too my *Rethinking Liberal Equality*, ch. 4.

13. See, especially, Chapter 6 below.

14. See Leszek Kolakowski (P.S. Falla, trans.), *Main Currents of Marxism*, vol. 2 'The Golden Age', (Oxford: Oxford University Press, 1978).

15. See Friedrich Engels' letter to Conrad Schmidt (August 5, 1890) in Marx and Engels, *Selected Correspondence* (Moscow: Progress Publishers, 1955), pp. 415–16. Engels wrote: '... just as Marx used to say, commenting on the French "Marxists" of the late seventies: "All I know is that I am not a Marxist (... *que je ne suis pas marxiste*)".'

16. G.A. Cohen has recently made a similar claim, though with a more approving assessment of its implications. See *If You're an Egalitarian, How Come You're So Rich?* (Cambridge, Mass.: Harvard University Press, 2000.)

17. More's *Utopia* introduced the term into the English language and, from there, into all the languages of the world. More combined the Greek words for 'no' and 'place'. The poet laureate of More's Utopia, in some preliminary verses, points out the similarity between 'utopia' (no place) and 'eutopia' (good place). This double meaning has been retained in the centuries after More invented the idea. A utopia is a nonexistent place, the description of which provides an account of an ideal place.

18. This is why Lenin was right in his well-known piece, 'Three Sources and Component Parts of Marxism' (1913), in *Collected Works*, vol. 19 (Moscow: Progress Publishers, 1968), to identify French socialism, along with British political economy and German philosophy, as one of the roots from which Marx's thought sprang.

19. See, especially, *City of God*.

20. That a philosophy of history of this sort arose in a Christian context is, on reflection, unsurprising. A world religion like Christianity that grounds its legitimacy on what it takes to be an historical event – in this case, the redemption of the human race through Christ's suffering and resurrection – calls for a sweeping historical narrative into which that event can be inserted, and from which it derives its meaning. Augustine rose to the task of concocting an appropriate story. Nearly a millennium and a half later, Hegel followed in his path.

21. See Daniel Brudney, *Marx's Attempt to Leave Philosophy* (Cambridge, Mass.: Harvard University Press, 1998). I elaborate on some of the claims made here pertaining to Young Hegelianism and Marx's relation to this philosophical tendency in *Engaging Political Philosophy: Hobbes to Rawls* (Oxford and Boston: Blackwell, 2001), ch. 6.

CHAPTER 2

1. The period in question had no clearly identifiable beginning and no decisive end. It is fair to say, though, that the idea of a New Left began to take shape in the late 1950s, and reached fruition rather quickly. By

the time C. Wright Mills wrote his famous 'open letter' to the New Left in 1960, it was already established. See C. Wright Mills, 'The New Left', *New Left Review*, no. 5 (September–October 1960), republished in *Power, Politics and People: the Collected Essays of C. Wright Mills,* Irving Louis Horowitz, ed. (Oxford: Oxford University Press, 1963). New Left politics developed rapidly and came to a head in the worldwide student uprisings of 1968. For the next few years, there were stirrings among workers too, especially younger workers. In the United States, there was even talk of transforming the student movement into a youth movement. But soon, sectarian strife and violence erupted everywhere, and the New Left began a decade-long decline. The vast majority of adherents drifted away. Others fought each other or, in desperation, turned to direct action. The Weather Underground in the United States, the Baader–Meinhoff Group in Germany, and the Italian Red Brigades are examples of this phenomenon. In Latin Europe there was also a more respectable (and respectful) electoral manifestation of New Left politics in decline, joined, briefly, with the still robust communist tradition. The so-called Eurocommunism of the middle and late 1970s was the result. Its greatest success was the victory of an electoral bloc, led by the socialists, but including the Communist Party, that, in 1981, made François Mitterand the president of France. Then, thanks to capital flight and economic recession, Mitterand was obliged to abandon nearly all efforts at 'changing life' (as the socialists' slogan of the time proclaimed). By the time, two years later, that it was clear to all that the Mitterand government had abandoned the socialist project on which it had run for office, the New Left was already well on its way towards receding into historical memory.

2. In the United States, in addition, the judiciary has de facto power to legislate indirectly by ruling on constitutional questions in a way that allows it to veto measures passed by the legislative and executive branches, and also to implement public policies of its own making. No other state vests so much authority in its judiciary, though a judiciary independent of the legislative and executive branches of government is the norm in regimes of this kind.

3. Thanks to the influence and prestige of Marx's early writings, and perhaps also to the fact that most New Leftists were themselves quite young (recall the slogan: 'Don't trust anyone over thirty!'), the reigning vision of how life should be, though fatally vague and underelaborated, nevertheless bore a strong affinity to the aspirations of Marx's own youth; in other words, to those of his writings that preceded what Althusser would call his 'epistemological break'.

4. This was the understanding advanced in the Bandung (Indonesia) Conference in 1955, where the idea of a Third World first gained currency. It was seldom taken literally, however. Traditionally neutral European countries, like Sweden and Switzerland, were never thought to be part of the Third World. Neither were close American allies like Israel, despite the absence of formal military ties with the United States. And both Vietnam and Cuba claimed membership in the Third World community, even as they were aided substantially by the Soviet bloc in

their efforts to free themselves from American domination. China's connection to the Third World was more ambiguous. By the mid-1960s it was no longer aligned militarily with the Soviet Union. It was, if anything, an enemy of the Soviet bloc. But it was also at least as much an enemy of the First World. When it served its purpose, China was happy to make common cause with the Third World, and even to identify with it, on the basis of its nonalignment. But the Chinese were never happy to accept some of the other connotations the term 'Third World' implied – especially, those that marked China off as poor or underdeveloped. These descriptions were objectively correct but politically unacceptable.

5. By common consensus, the First World consisted of the United States and Canada, the OPEC countries of Western Europe, Australasia and Japan; the Second World was the Soviet bloc, and the Third World was everything else – all of Latin America, all of Africa (except perhaps apartheid South Africa, a First World outpost), and all that remains of Asia (except Israel, another outpost of the First World). We will see presently that, for many on the New Left, oppressed racial minorities and conquered indigenous peoples living in the First World were sometimes said to belong to the Third World. It was also the case, in mainstream thinking, though usually not on the Left, that communist countries not part of the Warsaw Pact – China, Cuba, Vietnam and North Korea – belonged to the Second World, not the Third.

6. The 'political correctness' that emerged in the late1980s exaggerated this odd and even contradictory stance. 'Political correctness' is an imprecise expression – partly because, as a term of reproach, it is essentially contested, and partly because, in its most common uses, it designates a wide variety of phenomena. It is fair to say, however, that, whatever exactly 'political correctness' is, it is, at least in part, an unhappy legacy of the New Left – and later the feminist – purchase on the idea that 'the personal (including the intimately personal) is political'. Political correctness represents, at once, an extension of that conviction, and also, because it reintroduces puritanism into personal life after the New Left's brief but pronounced rejection of it, a reaction to it.

7. *The Progressive,* May 1961; quoted in Rick Perlstein, *Before the Storm: Barry Goldwater and the Unmaking of the American Consensus* (New York: Hill and Wang, 2001), p. 110.

8. Arguably, this outcome was sealed a year or so earlier in some places, as the Johnson–Goldwater electoral campaign for President raged – for example, during the Free Speech movement at Berkeley. There what began as a concerted effort by nearly all political groupings, Left and Right, soon came to be dominated unmistakably by those who had experience in the civil rights struggles in the South and who were already beginning to mobilize against the extension of U.S. military involvement in Southeast Asia. In Berkeley, by 1964, the student movement was unmistakably a movement of the Left.

9. See, for example, Herbert Marcuse, *Counter-Revolution and Revolt* (Boston: Beacon Press, 1972) and *One Dimensional Man* (Boston: Beacon Press, 1964).

10. Traditional Marxist analyses of late capitalism cohere generally with the Keynesian account, except that Marxists saw proof of capitalism's irrationality and also of its tendency to self-destruct in this permanent 'demand side' crisis, while Keynes and his followers set out to save capitalism from its effects. Left-leaning intellectuals, like Marcuse, who remained loyal to the Marxist tradition but who thought socialism unfeasible or undesirable or both, could therefore easily become Left Keynesians, advocates of public policies that, however beneficial for capitalism, nevertheless work to the advantage of traditional Left constituencies.

11. This line of criticism was well known to well-educated young people. Thus Vance Packard's *The Hidden Persuaders* (New York: McKay, 1957), an exposé of the insidious and detrimental effects of advertising, was not only a bestseller. It found its way onto many high school reading lists too.

12. In a celebrated passage from the 1843 'Introduction' to *The Critique of Hegel's Philosophy of Right,* well-known to New Left militants, Marx wrote:

> Clearly the weapon of criticism cannot replace the criticism of weapons, and material force must be overthrown by material force. But theory also becomes a material force once it has gripped the masses. Theory is capable of gripping the masses when it demonstrates *ad hominem*, and it demonstrates *ad hominem* as soon as it becomes radical. To be radical is to grasp things by the root. But for man the root is man himself...

INTRODUCTION TO PART II

1. See, for example, W.V.O. Quine, *Word and Object* (Cambridge, Mass.: M.I.T. Press, 1960).

2. See David Hume, *A Treatise of Human Nature* (Oxford: Clarendon Press, 1960), Book III, part 1, Chapter 1.

3. This is, however, only part of what the Eleventh Thesis asserts. It also expresses a view about the relation between knowing or understanding and *praxis,* activity that constitutes objects of knowledge in accordance with an ideal. The thought is that to understand the world *is* to change it or, equivalently, that to change the world, in accordance with an ideal, is what understanding the world is.

4. See, for example, Herbert Marcuse, *Reason and Revolution: Hegel and the Rise of Social Theory* (New York: Oxford University Press, 1941).

CHAPTER 3

1. See Louis Althusser (Ben Brewster, trans.), *For Marx* (London: Allen Lane, The Penguin Press, 1969), and Louis Althusser and Etienne Balibar (Ben Brewster, trans.), *Reading Capital* (London: New Left Books, 1970). However, a central essay of *For Marx*, 'Contradiction and Over-Determination', was published in *New Left Review*, no. 41 (1966). That essay attracted considerable attention at the time. Thus Althusser's views were not unknown in the English-speaking world in the late 1960s.

2. Lenin wrote: 'Aphorism: it is impossible completely to understand Marx's *Capital*, and especially its first chapter, without having thoroughly studied and understood the whole of Hegel's *Logic*. Consequently, half a century later, none of the Marxists have understood Marx!!' *Collected Works,* vol. 38, p. 180. Cited in Althusser, 'Lenin Before Hegel', in *Lenin and Philosophy and Other Essays* (London: New Left Books, 1971), p. 108.

3. Louis Althusser (Richard Veasey, trans.), *The Future Lasts Forever: A Memoir* (New York: The New Press, 1992).

4. These writings are collected in *Lenin and Philosophy* and in *Essays in Self-Criticism* (London: New Left Books, 1978). There is also Althusser's 'transitional' work *Philosophie et philosophie spontanée des savants* (Paris: Maspero, 1974), and the collection *Eléments d'auto-critique* (Paris: Hachette, 1974).

5. To cite two very conspicuous examples: Althusser used the term *historical materialism* to stand not for a substantive theory of historical development and change, but for what he called 'the Marxist science of society'. *Dialectical materialism* underwent a similar redefinition: no longer designating a substantive philosophical doctrine, Althusser used it, in his later writings, to refer to a certain 'practice of philosophy'.

6. See *Essays in Self-Criticism*. Althusser pressed this point most adamantly in his 'Reply to John Lewis' and in the 'Soutenance d'Amiens', delivered as he was awarded a Doctorat d'État by the University of Amiens.

7. The discoverer–explorer metaphor, which Althusser used repeatedly in his later writings, is set out and developed most directly in his 'Preface to *Capital*, vol. 1', in *Lenin and Philosophy*, pp. 71–3.

8. Althusser's use of 'determination' (and 'determination in the last instance') was fatally vague. Presumably, he meant something like 'causes in a decisive way'. But then this idea calls out for explication. We will see (in Chapters 5 and 6) how it was a signal contribution of the analytical Marxists to clarify Marx's understanding(s) of causality. So long as the idea remains vague or poorly analyzed, there is a risk of falling, as Althusser did, into serious error – as when he claimed (or, since the status of this claim is obscure, intimated) that philosophy's course is set *entirely* by extraphilosophical (scientific and political) conditions.

9. For an Althusserian treatment of this episode in the history of Soviet science, see Dominique Lecourt, *Lyssenko: histoire réelle d'une science prolétarienne* (Paris: Maspero, 1976). See especially Althusser's preface to this volume.

CHAPTER 4

1. *For Marx*, p. 33.

2. Ibid., p. 34.

3. 'From *Capital* to Marx's Philosophy' in *Reading Capital*, pp. 13–69.

4. *For Marx*, p. 27.

5. Among Bachelard's writings in the philosophy of science are *Le Pluralisme coherent de la chimie moderne* (Paris: Vrin, 1932), *Le Nouvel Esprit scientifique* (Paris: P.U.F., 1949), *L'Activité ratioanliste de la physique con-*

temporaine (Paris: P.U.F., 1951) and *Le Materialisme rationnel* (Paris: P.U.F., 1953). Althusser's student, Dominique Lecourt, wrote two studies of Bachelard, *L'Epistemologie historique de Gaston Bachelard* (Paris: Vrin, 1970) and *Pour une critique de l'epistemologie* (Paris: Maspero, 1972).

6. Were it not for the enormous misunderstandings his 'antihumanism' elicited in the days when Althusser's work was a subject of intense interest, it would not need to be said that the dispute between Marxist humanists and Althusser had nothing to do with their respective views about how human beings should be treated in political contexts. The debate was over the consequences for Marxist theory of the (Young Hegelian) philosophical anthropology deployed in Marx's prebreak writings.

7. Etienne Balibar, 'Sur la Dialectique historique (quelques remarques critiques à propos de *Lire le Capital*)', in *Cinq Etudes du materialisme historique* (Paris: Maspero, 1974).

8. See, especially, Althusser's essay 'Marx's Relation to Hegel', in *Politics and History* (London: New Left Books, 1972), and the 'Reply to John Lewis'.

9. 'Reification and the Consciousness of the Proletariat', in Georg Lukács, *History and Class Consciousness* (London: Merlin, 1971).

10. Perhaps the most far-reaching claim ever advanced within the Marxist camp for the ubiquity and relevance of the Hegelian dialectic was made by Engels in *The Dialectics of Nature* (New York: International Publishers, 1940).

11. 'Contradiction and Overdetermination', in *For Marx*, esp. pp. 109–16.

12. *The Critique of Hegel's 'Philosophy of Right'*, in Marx, Engels, *Collected Works*, vol. 3. (New York: International Publishers, 1975).

13. *For Marx*, p. 110.

14. That the young Marx was Feuerbachian in this respect is by no means beyond dispute. But this ostensibly historical contention was a long-standing (and invariant) feature of Althusser's elaboration of the claim for an epistemological break in Marx's thinking, evident first in those writings of 1845 (*The German Ideology* and the *Theses on Feuerbach*) in which he expressly repudiated Feuerbach.

15. *For Marx*, pp. 203–4.

16. 'Contradiction and Overdetermination', pp. 87–128.

17. See, especially, 'On the Young Marx', in *For Marx*, pp. 49–86. In that essay, Althusser maintained, in a typical turn of phrase, that from Hegel Marx received a 'formation in theory', but not a 'theoretical formation'. Presumably, the latter term designates an actual conceptual affinity; the former a sense of what the Real is like, and of strategies appropriate for producing satisfactory accounts of it.

18. 'Marx's Relation to Hegel', pp. 183–4.

19. See 'Reply to John Lewis', and 'Note sur la critique de la culte de la personalité', in the French edition of the 'Reply', *Réponse à John Lewis* (Paris: Maspero, 1973). From as early as *For Marx* and *Reading Capital*, but most perspicuously in the 'Reply to John Lewis', Althusser insisted that economism also lies at the root of Marxist humanism. Characteristically, he never quite spelled out his rationale for this claim, but perhaps it can be deduced by reflecting on Marx's own insistence, in the third of

the (1844) *Paris Manuscripts* that the condition for overcoming alienation and achieving the full richness (*Sinnlichkeit*) of human life is the development of the material-sensuous (*sinnlich*) world. It is not clear, however, whether Marx was speaking just of necessary or of necessary and sufficient conditions. If the former, his contention, though expressed in an inflated Hegelian idiom, is uncontroversial: communism, if it is feasible at all, plainly does require abundant material wealth. But this claim is insufficient for motivating an economist political strategy. To link economism and humanism, Althusser would have to show how, for Marxist humanism, the development of wealth (*Sinnlichkeit*) is both necessary and sufficient for overcoming alienation. Althusser never put forward such an argument, though he did intimate, perhaps correctly, that many Marxist humanists do implicitly suppose that something like this is the case.

20. See, especially, the contribution of Jacques Rancière in the French edition of *Reading Capital* – 'Le Concept de Critique et la Critique de l'Economie Politique des "Manuscrits" de 1844 au *Capital*', *Lire le Capital*, tome 1 (Paris: Maspero, 1967), pp. 93–210.

CHAPTER 5

1. See G.A. Cohen, *Karl Marx's Theory of History: A Defence* (Oxford and Princeton: Oxford University Press and Princeton University Press, 1978), and *If You're An Egalitarian, How Come You're So Rich?* (Cambridge, Mass.: Harvard University Press, 2000).

2. There has been to date, very little useful historical analysis of analytical Marxism. A noteworthy exception is Marcus Roberts, *Analytical Marxism: A Critique* (London: Verso, 1996). The account that follows differs in some respects from the picture Roberts presents and, more importantly, in its assessment of what the analytical Marxist legacy can be.

3. The term *Western Marxism* was introduced by Maurice Merleau-Ponty in *Adventures in the Dialectic*, Joseph Bien, trans. (Evanston, Il.: Northwestern University Press, 1973). See also Perry Anderson, *Considerations on Western Marxism* (London: New Left Books, 1976). The term denotes the work of a very wide range of thinkers – among others, Georg Lukács, Karl Korsch, Antonio Gramsci, the theorists of the Frankfurt School (Theodor Adorno, Max Horkheimer, Herbert Marcuse, etc.), existentialist Marxists (Jean-Paul Sartre, Maurice Merleau-Ponty). In these terms, Althusser was a Western Marxist. A common thread is hard to find. All Western Marxists opposed the official Marxism of the Soviet Union and the Western European Communist Parties – though, in some cases, the opposition was *very* tacit, even to the point, as in Althusser's case, of maintaining Party membership. Western Marxism drew substantially on twentieth-century 'continental' philosophy, and therefore on the work of such figures as Hegel and Husserl and others whose ideas and methods had little impact on mainstream, English-speaking academic philosophy.

4. See Chapter 2, note 12. It was these terms – 'the arm of criticism', 'the criticism of arms' – that the young Marx invoked to describe the unfolding revolutionary dynamic of Germany in the 1840s, a period of

ferment that culminated in the revolutionary upheavals of 1848. See 'A Contribution to the Critique of Hegel's *Philosophy of Right:* Introduction', in Karl Marx, *Early Political Writings*, Joseph O'Malley, ed. (Cambridge: Cambridge University Press, 1994), p. 64.

5. It also bears mention that just as the United States was already exercising cultural hegemony over much of the world in the late 1960s, the American New Left played something of a vanguard role in the emerging youth cultures of other Western countries and even in the Third World. It therefore dictated intellectual fashions, just as it did in other areas. Paradoxically, then, at the same time that a sense of intellectual inferiority helped to encourage interest in Western Marxism in the United States, the fact that this interest existed helped to reinforce Western Marxism's prominence – not just in the English-speaking world, but nearly everywhere, including Germany and France, its countries of origin.

6. For a cogent statement of this view, registered as late as the early 1960s, see Isaiah Berlin's essay, 'Does Political Theory Still Exist?' in Peter Laslett and W.G. Runcimann, eds., *Philosophy, Politics, and Society,* 2nd series. (Oxford: Blackwell, 1962).

7. John Rawls, *A Theory of Justice* (Cambridge, Mass.: The Belknap Press at Harvard University Press, 1971).

8. Among others, the journal *Philosophy and Public Affairs,* launched in 1971, opened its pages to these studies, some of which are anthologized in Marshall Cohen, Thomas Nagel, and E. Scanlon, eds., *Marx, Justice and Utopia* (Princeton: Princeton University Press, 1980). See also Alan Wood, *Karl Marx* (London: Routledge & Kegan Paul, 1981), chs. 9 and 10.

9. This literature is surveyed in Allen E. Buchanan, *Marx and Justice: The Radical Critique of Liberalism* (Totawa, N.J.: Rowman & Littlefield, 1982). See also Steven Lukes, *Marxism and Morality* (Oxford: Oxford University Press, 1985), ch. 4.

10. See, among others, Karl Popper, *The Poverty of Historicism* (London: Routledge & Kegan Paul; New York: Basic Books, 1958); *Objective Knowledge* (Oxford: Oxford University Press, 1972); and *Conjectures and Refutations* (London: Routledge & Kegan Paul, 1973).

11. One well-known place where Marx registers this insistence is in the Preface to the first German Edition of *Capital*, vol. 1.

12. Thus in the same Preface to *Capital*, vol. 1 in which Marx declared his scientificity (see note 11), he also declared his attachment to Hegelian philosophy, even crediting his scientific advances to Hegelianism.

13. See, for example, Jon Elster, *Logic and Society: Contradictions and Possible Worlds* (New York: John Wiley & Sons, 1978), esp. chs. 3–5. Elster undertook this investigation of dialectical logic (and a host of related ideas) before he expressly identified with the analytical Marxist camp, though his sympathies with Marxist theory were already evident. For a more considered view, after Elster had become a leading analytical Marxist, see *Making Sense of Marx* (Cambridge: Cambridge University Press, 1985), ch. 1.

14. See, for example, John Roemer's neoclassical reconstruction of Marx's economic theory in *Analytical Foundations of Marxian Economic Theory* (Cambridge: Cambridge University Press, 1982).

15. See Thomas S. Kuhn, *The Structure of Scientific Revolutions* (Chicago: University of Chicago Press, 1962).

16. See G.A. Cohen, 'Historical Inevitability and Revolutionary Agency', in *History, Labour and Freedom: Themes from Marx* (Oxford: Oxford University Press, 1988). On the *ceteris absentibus* understanding of historical materialism, see Erik Olin Wright, Andrew Levine and Elliott Sober, *Reconstructing Marxism* (London: Verso, 1992), ch. 5.

17. See *Analytical Foundations*.

18. For an analytical Marxist account of Marx's concept of class structure and conflict and its differences from mainstream understandings, see Erik Olin Wright, *Classes* (London: Verso, 1985).

19. See, for example, Erik Olin Wright, *Class Counts: Comparative Studies in Class Analysis* (Cambridge: Cambridge University Press,1997).

20. The more usual distinction is between *ethical* theory, which has to do with that part of normative theory that pertains to individual conduct, and *moral* theory, which is a subset of ethical theory – one that, with respect to individual conduct, proposes, where appropriate, the adoption of the moral point of view. My suggestion that we view moral theory as a subset of normative, rather than just ethical, theory is motivated by a concern to capture Marx's views not only on how individuals ought to act but also on how institutions ought to be organized.

21. In the *Groundwork of the Metaphysics of Morals,* Kant formulated the categorical imperative in several distinct ways. But the guiding idea, already implicit in the Golden Rule, is that, in appropriate contexts, one ought to act according to 'maxims', principles of volition, that one could rationally will that all other moral agents act on as well.

22. I elaborate on these claims in *Rethinking Liberal Equality*. See also Lukes, *Marxism and Morality* and Elster, *Making Sense of Marx*.

23. See John Roemer, *A Future for Socialism* (Cambridge, Mass.: Harvard University Press. 1994). Roemer is the most ardent defender of the idea that equality is what socialists really want. I discuss his position in 'Saving Socialism and/or Abandoning It', in John Roemer et al. *Equal Shares: Making Market Socialism Work* (London: Verso, 1996).

24. See esp. Elster, *Making Sense of Marx* and Roemer, *Analytical Foundations*. For a critical challenge to this tendency within the analytical Marxist current, see Wright, Levine and Sober, *Reconstructing Marxism*, ch. 6.

25. But see Wright, Levine and Sober, *Reconstructing Marxism*, ch. 6.

26. I elaborate on this claim in *The General Will: Rousseau, Marx, Communism* (New York and Cambridge: Cambridge University Press, 1993) and *Rethinking Liberal Equality*.

27. See *Making Sense of Marx*, esp. ch. 2. For Elster's views on connections between psychological phenomena and moral judgments, see especially *Sour Grapes: Studies in the Subversion of Rationality* (Cambridge: Cambridge University Press, 1983).

28. See John Roemer, *A Future for Socialism*.

29. For the most part, they have turned to the history of ideas and to political commentary (from a perspective quite removed from Marxist-Leninist orthodoxy). See, for example, the recent work of one of Althusser's favored students and the principal coauthor, along with

Althusser, of *Reading Capital*, Etienne Balibar. Some of his work is collected in *Masses, Classes, Ideas: Studies on Politics and Philosophy Before and After Marx*, James Swenson, trans. (New York and London: Routledge, 1994).

CHAPTER 6

1. To be sure, these days everyone recognizes the pertinence of the concept 'capitalism', even if not everyone subscribes precisely to Marx's understanding of it. But this fact about the intellectual culture is largely a consequence of the (often unacknowledged) influence of Marx's theorizing, not the obviousness of the concept he identified.

2. See 'Three Sources and Component Parts of Marxism'.

3. In the historical materialist view, real and juridical property relations will normally coincide, for reasons to be set forth presently. But there may be cases where the two are in discord; and when they are, what matters is what the real relations of appropriation are, not how they are represented in the law. That the two can fail to coincide explains what Maoists and others had in mind when they called the Soviet union 'state capitalist'. They would have conceded that Soviet laws pertaining to property relations were socialist. They could hardly have failed to do so, since Chinese laws were based, in large part, on the Soviet legal system. But they would then argue that this legal form masked an economic structure that was essentially capitalist in nature.

4. For Elster's views on these matters, see *Making Sense of Marx* and, among others, *Ulysses and the Sirens* (Cambridge: Cambridge University Press, 1979), ch. 1, 'Reply to Comments', *Inquiry*, vol. 23 (1980), pp. 213–32, 'Review of G.A. Cohen, *Karl Marx's Theory of History*', *Political Studies*, vol. 28 (1980), pp. 121–8, and 'Marxism, Functionalism, and Game Theory', *Theory and Society*, vol. 11 (1982), pp. 453–82.

5. See G.A. Cohen, 'Restricted and Inclusive Historical Materialism', in *History, Labour and Freedom*.

6. Max Weber, *The Protestant Ethic and the Spirit of Capitalism* (New York: Charles Scribners Sons, 1958). Originally published in 1904–05.

7. See, however, my *The End of the State* (London: Verso, 1987), *The General Will* and *Rethinking Liberal Equality*.

8. Or at least one Althusserian did. See Étienne Balibar, *Sur la dictature du prolétariat* (Paris: Maspero, 1976).

9. V.I. Lenin, *The State and Revolution*, in *Collected Works*, vol. 25 (Moscow: Progress Publishers, 1954).

10. For political philosophers in the contractarian tradition, the state is a human contrivance, constructed by individuals because, in the end, it accords with the interests of each of them that it exist. If they are right, then the consent of the governed underlies the state form of political organization. Nevertheless, even in their view, state power, once concocted, is based on force alone – even if, as democrats want, its use is in some sense determined by the will of the governed. In this sense, contractarians too hold that state power, unlike the state itself, rests ultimately on force.

11. The argument can be found in chs. 13 through 16 of the *Leviathan* (1651).
12. Franz Kafka, *Parables and Paradoxes* (New York: Schocken Books, 1946), p. 81.
13. I argue that states that incorporate liberal protections but also go *beyond* them are indeed possible in *The General Will*, chs. 8 and 9, and *Rethinking Liberal Equality*, chs. 4 and 5.
14. Rawls argued expressly that a 'basic structure', satisfying his account of what justice requires, can be either capitalist or socialist. See *A Theory of Justice*, pp. 265–74. Roemer argued for the usefulness (and perhaps even indispensability) of a form of socialist property relations in implementing generically liberal egalitarian values in *A Future for Socialism*.

CONCLUSION

1. That course is *ceteris absentibus* inevitable, for just the reasons that historical materialism's first Master Thesis makes plain. But the way forward can be needlessly protracted and painful, especially if the forces arrayed against it are sufficiently organized and intense. Progress can even be blocked for an indefinite period. Nowadays too, it is possible, for the first time in human history, for human beings themselves to halt the course of human history altogether – by an annihilating war. With weapons of mass destruction, including nuclear weapons, in so many hands, and in the unstable conditions that have emerged in the aftermath of the Soviet Union's demise, the prospect of everything ending catastrophically has become frighteningly real.
2. See 'Ideology and Ideological State Apparatuses (Notes Towards an Investigation) (January–April 1969)' in Louis Althusser, *Lenin and Philosophy*, pp. 121–76.

Select Bibliography

WORKS BY ALTHUSSER (IN ENGLISH):

Althusser, Louis. *For Marx*. Trans. Ben Brewster. London: Allen Lane, Penguin Press, 1969.

——, and Étienne Balibar. *Reading Capital*. Trans. Ben Brewster. London: New Left Books, 1970.

——. *Lenin and Philosophy and Other Essays*. Trans. Ben Brewster. London: New Left Books, 1971.

——. *Politics and History: Montesquieu, Rousseau, Hegel and Marx*. Trans. Ben Brewster. London: New Left Books, 1972.

——, and Maria Antonietta Macciocchi. *Letters from inside the Italian Communist Party to Louis Althusser*. Trans. Stephen M. Hellman. London: New Left Books, 1973.

——. *Essays in Self-Criticism*. Trans. Grahame Lock. London: New Left Books, 1976.

——. 'Afterword', in Etienne Balibar. *On the Dictatorship of the Proletariat*. Trans. Grahame Lock. London: New Left Books, 1977.

——. *The Future Lasts Forever*. Ed. Olivier Corpet and Yann Moulier Boutang. Trans. Richard Veasey. New York: The New Press, 1993.

——. *Machiavelli and Us*. Trans. Gregory Elliott. London: Verso, 1999.

BOOKS IN OR ABOUT ANALYTICAL MARXISM

Buchanan, Allen E. *Marx and Justice: The Radical Critique of Liberalism*. Totawa, N.J.: Rowman & Littlefield, 1982; and London: Methuen, 1982.

Callinicos, Alex. *Making History*. Cambridge: Polity Press, 1987.

Carling, Alan. *Social Division*. London: Verso, 1991.

Cohen, Gerald E.A. *Karl Marx's Theory of History: A Defence*. Oxford: Oxford University Press, 1978; and Princeton, N.J.: Princeton University Press, 1978.

——. *History, Labour, Freedom: Themes from Marx*. Oxford: Oxford University Press, 1989.

——. *Self-Ownership Freedom and Equality*. Cambridge: Cambridge University Press, 1995.

——. *If You're an Egalitarian, How Come You're So Rich?* Cambridge, Mass.: Harvard University Press, 2000.

Cohen, Marshall, Thomas Nagel and Thomas Scanlon. *Marx, Justice and History*. Princeton: Princeton University Press, 1980.

Elster, Jon. *Explaining Technical Change*. Cambridge: Cambridge University Press, 1983.

——. *Sour Grapes: Studies in the Subversion of Rationality*. Cambridge: Cambridge University Press, 1983.

——. *Making Sense of Marx*. Cambridge: Cambridge University Press, 1985.

——. *An Introduction to Karl Marx*. Cambridge: Cambridge University Press, 1986.

——. *The Cement of Society: A Study in Social Order*. Cambridge: Cambridge University Press, 1989.

——, and Karl.O. Moene, eds. *Alternatives to Capitalism*. Cambridge University Press, 1989.

Levine, Andrew. *Arguing for Socialism: Theoretical Considerations*. London: Routledge & Kegan Paul, 1984

——. *The End of the State*. London: Verso, 1987.

——. *The General Will: Rousseau, Marx, Communism*. New York and Cambridge: Cambridge University Press, 1993.

——. *Rethinking Liberal Equality: From a 'Utopian' Point of View*. Ithaca, N.Y.: Cornell University Press, 1998.

——. *Engaging Political Philosophy: Hobbes to Rawls*. Boston and London: Blackwell, 2001.

Lukes, Steven. *Marxism and Morality*. Oxford: Oxford University Press, 1987.

Mayer, Thomas F. *Analytical Marxism*. Thousand Oaks, Calif.: Sage Publications, 1978.

Miller, Richard, *Analyzing Marx*. Princeton: Princeton University Press, 1984.

Przeworski, Adam. *Capitalism and Social Democracy*. Cambridge: Cambridge University Press, 1985.

Roberts, Marcus. *Analytical Marxism: A Critique*. London: Verso, 1996.

Roemer, John E. *Analytical Foundations of Marxian Economic Theory*. Cambridge: Cambridge University Press, 1981.

——. *A General Theory of Exploitation and Class*. Cambridge: Cambridge University Press, 1982.

——, ed. *Analytical Marxism*. Cambridge: Cambridge University Press, 1986.

——. *Free to Lose: An Introduction to Marxist Economic Philosophy*. Cambridge, Mass.: Harvard University Press, 1988.

——. *A Future for Socialism*. London: Verso, 1994.

Van Parijs, Philippe. *Marxism Recycled*. Cambridge: Cambridge University Press, 1993.

Ware, Robert and Kai Nielsen, eds. *Analyzing Marxism: New Essays on Analytical Marxism*. Calgary: University of Calgary Press, 1989.

Wood, Allen. *Karl Marx*. London: Routledge & Kegan Paul, 1981.

Wright, Erik Olin. *Class, Crisis and the State*. London: Verso, 1978.

——. *Classes*. London: Verso, 1985.

——. *Class Counts: Comparative Studies in Class Analysis*. Cambridge: Cambridge University Press, 1997.

——, Andrew Levine and Elliott Sober, *Reconstructing Marxism*. London: Verso, 1992.

Index